Sustainable Innovation Strategy

Sustainable Innovation Strategy

Creating Value in a World of Finite Resources

Christophe Sempels
Associate Professor of Sustainable Development and Strategy, SKEMA Business School

and

Jonas Hoffmann
Associate Professor of Marketing, SKEMA Business School

palgrave
macmillan

First published 2013 by
PALGRAVE MACMILLAN

Palgrave Macmillan in the UK is an imprint of Macmillan Publishers Limited,
registered in England, company number 785998, of Houndmills, Basingstoke,
Hampshire RG21 6XS.

Palgrave Macmillan in the US is a division of St Martin's Press LLC,
175 Fifth Avenue, New York, NY 10010.

Palgrave Macmillan is the global academic imprint of the above companies
and has companies and representatives throughout the world.

Palgrave® and Macmillan® are registered trademarks in the United States,
the United Kingdom, Europe and other countries.

ISBN 978–1–137–35260–6

This book is printed on paper suitable for recycling and made from fully
managed and sustained forest sources. Logging, pulping and manufacturing
processes are expected to conform to the environmental regulations of the
country of origin.

A catalogue record for this book is available from the British Library.

A catalog record for this book is available from the Library of Congress.

Typeset by MPS Limited, Chennai, India

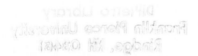

Contents

List of Figures and Tables

Figures

Tables

Acknowledgments

Christophe dedicates this book to Dominique Vian (SKEMA) and Frédéric Bielen (BSM) for their amazing discussions that help them grow and are a great source of inspiration; to Michel Bernasconi (SKEMA) for his trust, his constant support and his advices, which are an important source of improvement; to Axelle Sapy (Réseau Alliances) for her trust and the many years of close and rich collaboration; to Christian du Tertre (Université Paris VII/Atemis), for the pleasure and the richness of their collaboration; to Jocelyn Blériot (Ellen MacArthur Foundation) for his support and the pleasure associated with their collaboration; to all the colleagues of SKEMA, providing a wonderful working environment; to all the CEO's who trust him and who try to move to a more sustainable business model; and to his wife and their two boys for their constant support and the wonderful life they reinvent every day.

Jonas dedicates this book to Betina and Noah.

We warmly thank Sian Jones for her copyediting; and Eleanor Davey Corrigan, Anna Keville and the whole team at Palgrave Macmillan.

Introduction

We live exciting and challenging times. Innovation can come from any direction, and companies have never faced such a turbulent environment. Challenges are impressive: economic slowdown in mature economies confronted with many crises, impressive development of emerging markets (often mimicking mature economies' unsustainable patterns), increasing social scrutiny of companies' activities, war on talent … The list is long and shows to what extent our current development model and the related systems are under pressure.

Another key challenge significantly weighs on our future: the ability to operate in a world where Earth's resources will have to supply the needs and desires of around nine billion humans by 2050.

We have already jumped into an era of scarce resources. Its impact will crescendo in the coming decades, urging companies to rethink *business as usual* and opening several exciting opportunities for the pioneers ready to invent and experiment with new modes of production and exchanges.

We urgently need to pursue both growth and de-growth[1]: the growth of sustainable energy, of smart and decarbonated transport, the growth of healthy, environment-friendly and local food, the growth of decoupled business models and sustainable modes of production and consumption. But at the same time we need to de-grow processed food, nonrenewable energy, disposal and nonrepairable products, polluting modes of transport, toxic raw materials and modes of production, planned obsolescence, etc. In short, it is time to redefine a new development model anchored in progress *and* well-being.

These questions are not simply moral or ethical but also pragmatic and economic, as many negative environmental and social spin-offs have already begun to be internalized into the cost structure of the market's actors, either by following the rules of the market itself or due to a more pressing regulation.

Companies around the world are part of the problem *and* the solution. They are central actors to enact solutions for these challenges. There is only one path to ensure competitiveness: innovate. This book shows how sustainable innovation can be a fantastic driver of value creation and how it may reorient growth toward a desirable future.

We explore some pragmatic paths to help the leaders of today and tomorrow to become actors of these changes. Some paths are quick wins, some more ambitious and still others clearly disruptive.

Three ideas guide our exploration: eco-efficiency, circular economy and the transition from a goods-centered logic to service-oriented one. Above all, it is a matter of increasing the productivity of resources to meet our various and varied needs and, consequently, to offer new venues of competitiveness for companies. Figure I.1 illustrates how these three ideas lead progressively to the construction of radically new strategies. Circularity encourages eco-efficiency. The transition toward service – to grasp its full potential – calls for the implementation of eco-efficiency and circularity, consequently making planned

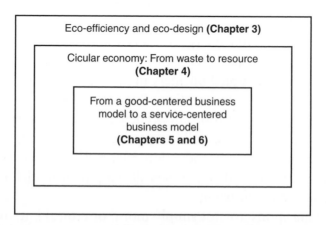

Figure I.1 *Developing a sustainable innovation strategy*

obsolescence economically obsolete. This integrated approach is essential to enter the enriched value-creation process at the core of this book. This is presented in Chapters 3 to 6.

In terms of structure, we first introduce how strategy is the appropriate lens to think and act on these evolutions (Chapter 1). It is indeed at the strategic level that sustainable development can fully uncover its value-creation potential for a company. Ignoring it may come at the price of facing serious competitiveness issues in the medium and even short term. It is advisable to prepare one's company for the challenges to come so that it may create the future and its related markets.

We mainly approach a company strategy through its business model. As a matter of fact, the process of value creation, distribution and capture are under pressure in a world of finite resources. We introduce a tool to operationalize the business model, the sustainable business model canvas, enabling the strategic evolution of a company to be controlled toward eco-efficiency, circularity and the transition to use, and result-based services (Chapter 2).

We aim to be concrete and operational. The concepts presented are illustrated by a large number of examples systematically showing how these propositions have been already experimented and implemented by some innovative companies.

Obviously, we do not have the ambition to provide solutions to all the challenges. These new paths fit well in certain contexts, but are less relevant in others. They are not an end in itself, but rather steps enacting the emergence of a new economic model, integrating the strain on natural resources and potentially more respectful of the planet and its inhabitants.

We wish you an enjoyable read and hope modestly that this work will be able to provide you the insights and the willingness to sustainably innovate!

1
Tackling Sustainable Development at the Corporate Strategic Level to Create Value

Sustainable development is often presented, almost ritually, as a tremendous source of development, opportunity and value creation for companies. Titles of books, articles or conferences on the subject leave little room for doubt: sustainable development appears to be inseparable from innovation, corporate performance, or with the opening up of new, buoyant markets for a passionate cohort of consumers. Some do not hesitate to qualify it as a true goldmine; others associate it with a rich source of jobs for all skill levels. Based on these promises, it would not be unreasonable to expect that sustainable development would be naturally and rapidly integrated into companies.

In reality, however, this is rarely the case. Often, this line of argument fails to convince companies and their leaders. Skepticism prevails, especially among small- and medium-sized companies. Sustainable development tends to be perceived more as a constraint, or even a threat or a risk, pushed by regulations that are deemed to be developed too hastily. It may also be seen as a source of sometimes-considerable expenditure with only a dubious return. Those who do wish to engage in sustainable development generally feel unsupported or ill equipped, believing that they lack resources and expertise to tackle this multidimensional, complex field.

If we look at the scientific evidence supporting sustainable development, a number of studies have sought to understand the relationship between a company's "sustainable performance" and its financial performance.[1] A large majority has identified a positive relationship between these constructs, suggesting that sustainability "pays." Others, however, have highlighted an absence of relationship, and even, for a very small number, a negative relationship.

What conclusions can we draw from these contradictory results? Is it possible to analyze the relationship between the sustainable and the financial performance of a company without considering how sustainability is integrated in the company? Given the complexity of modeling both the financial and the sustainable performance of a company, would it not be more effective to study the conditions that foster a positive synergy between these two constructs? This is the question we will attempt to answer.

A company's capacity to create and capture value is largely dependent on the quality of its strategy, its business model and its value propositions for its target markets. In the search for contributions to the process of value creation, how then can we separate sustainable development from strategy?

This chapter will briefly clarify what we mean by the notion of strategy – by describing its main pillars. It will then position sustainable development at the corporate level of strategy, showing why this is the most appropriate gateway for the successful integration of sustainable development in the pursuit of value creation. The impact of sustainable development on the pillars of strategy will then be analyzed, demonstrating that a manager can simply no longer afford to ignore consequences of sustainable development on the company without running the risk of threatening its competitiveness and possible survival.

WHAT IS STRATEGY?

Corporate strategy is a vast field of knowledge built around many schools and currents of thought. Describing these is neither the intention nor the goal of this book, but the interested reader can find many good sources to further his or her understanding.[2] It is commonly agreed, nevertheless, that strategy aims to enable a company to create value for customers and build a unique position on its market(s) taking into account a constantly changing environment. More specifically, corporate strategy involves (a) configuring the company's scope of activities, (b) effectively and distinctively allocating its resources and skills in order to (c) be able to develop a sustainable competitive advantage, (d) allowing it to reach a higher level of performance than its competitors, and thereby (e) satisfy its stakeholders.[3]

Strategic decisions are thus based on four main pillars:

1. The definition of the long-term direction of the organization and its scope of activities

2. The organization of the processes of value creation, distribution and capture

3. The management and allocation of resources and competences within the company

4. The steering of necessary adaptations to a constantly changing environment

Companies in direct competition evolve in similar environments. Ford, Volkswagen and Renault are active on the worldwide car market facing a comparable competitive environment with all its legal, political, socio-economic and technological issues. The performance of these companies, however, differs because of their respective strategic capabilities. A company thus builds its competitive advantage, its competitiveness and its capacity to create value by constructing and developing its strategic capabilities, and its capacity to make strategic decisions more effective and more difficult to imitate by its competitors. Moreover, because the environment in its multiple components is constantly changing, the capacity of a company to perform above average in its sector is largely determined by its "ability to integrate, build, and reconfigure internal and external competences to address rapidly changing environments," in other words, by being faster than its competitors.[4]

SUSTAINABLE DEVELOPMENT AND STRATEGY

Given the numerous challenges raised by sustainable development, we can conclude that strategy is indeed the appropriate
corporate level for the integration of sustainable development
into the business agenda. The reasons for this are listed here and
developed in more detail later in this book:

- Strategic decisions hinge on four main pillars. Sustainable
  development impacts these four pillars, sometimes significantly.
  The following section describes these impacts, illustrated with
  many supporting examples. A failure to recognize the impact
  of sustainable development on the strategic pillars of the
  company can be seen as strategic myopia, with potentially det-
  rimental consequences in the short, medium and long term.

- Climate challenges, scarcity of resources in terms of quantity
  and quality and the associated pressure on prices; loss of biodiversity; financial, economic and social crises; extreme poverty;
  impoverishment of the middle classes and the rise of unemployment in developed economies; ageing societies; public health
  issues; and so on are only some of the issues related to sustainable development. Potentially, they can have a considerable
  impact on a company's competitiveness. Or, if they are properly
  understood, and if they encourage the company to innovate,
  they can be a rich source of differentiation and profitability.

- Through the definition of the company business model(s)
  (explained in Chapter 2) and the configuration of resources
  and competences, corporate strategy structures and creates
  the conditions for the successful implementation of the processes of value creation, distribution and capture. In short,
  and without minimizing the importance of other corporate
  functions, corporate strategy is primarily responsible for
  value creation and management. Therefore, how can sustainable development contribute to value creation if it is not
  closely linked to the function intrinsically in charge of the creation and the management of value?

- Sustainable development promotes the concept of responsibility and openness to stakeholders, both internal and external to the organization. While the ultimate goal of corporate strategy is to satisfy stakeholders, how can we exclude sustainable development from its scope?

As of 2012, a growing number of companies are becoming aware of this necessary connection between strategy and sustainable development. Veolia Environment is a global company providing a full range of service in the fields of water, waste management, energy and transportation. Its sustainable development division started four years ago with the hiring of Geneviève Férone and now has more than 30 full-time staff.[5] IBM started to work on its Smarter Cities initiative five years ago and this now forms a central component of its strategy.[6] And the Global Reporting Initiative provides an array of examples of how sustainable development is considered at a strategic level. Nevertheless, medium-sized companies, and even more so small businesses, are finding it more difficult to integrate sustainable development into their strategy.

IMPACT OF SUSTAINABLE DEVELOPMENT ON THE PILLARS OF STRATEGY

Sustainable development calls into question the conception and execution of strategy by impacting its pillars, in all contexts but at varying degrees.

Pillar 1: The definition of the long-term direction of the company and its scope of activities

Strategic choices are made at several levels. At the strategic business unit level, it is a question of defining and adopting a certain strategy to build and maintain competitive advantage. At the corporate level, it is a matter of formalizing the scope of activities, which markets to enter and the associated value propositions. These major decisions require long-term commitment from the company and affect the strategic positioning of the organization.

Sustainable development, in its multiple dimensions and challenges, is likely to impact these long-term strategic decisions. It may, for example, call into question a dominant design in a particular industry, generating strategic uncertainty over the future of the industry as a whole, as well as over the prevailing technological design. In the car industry, thermal engine propulsion has been the dominant design for several decades. Its environmental record, however, raises severe questions about its survival as a dominant design in the long run. And even if thermal engine propulsion continues to be the principal technology for years to come, all manufacturers are exploring alternatives, even though they have little idea at this stage what the next dominant design could be. Will the car propulsion of tomorrow be fueled by hybrid energies, electricity, compressed air, hydrogen, combustible battery or even water? Will it be solar? Will it be made of ultra-light composite materials?

Carmakers bet differently on the new dominant design for car propulsion

Private light vehicles represent 12 percent of the total European CO_2 emissions. Reducing these emissions is at the heart of Europe's commitment to fight global warming.[7] A European directive recommends that manufacturers will have to reach an average rate of 130 g/km of CO_2 emissions for new vehicles by 2015, and 95 g/km of CO_2 emissions by 2020 (for comparison, the European average was 160 g/km of CO_2 emissions in 2006).

To meet these targets, manufacturers have been investing massively in the development of technologies to reduce carbon emissions, while at the same time betting on alternative technological solutions. French constructor Renault, for example, is focusing on a 100 percent electric car; other

European carmakers such as Audi and Peugeot are focusing more on hybrid diesel technologies.

The debate is particularly heated regarding electric vehicles because of the huge infrastructure changes their use will entail. Until early 2011, one variable that could be taken for granted was the reliance on (cheap) nuclear energy to power electric vehicles. And then came Fukushima. Japan announced its intention to shut down all its nuclear plants by 2042, a decision already made by Germany. And in countries like the US and France, existing plants will have to comply with new (and expensive) standards. All this casts a shadow on the future of 100 percent electric cars, and Toyota and Honda, pioneers in hybrid cars (electric-thermal propulsion,) could be reassured by their choice.

Local constraints also have a part to play. Electric cars in India would hardly be an option in the foreseeable future given the country's poor electric infrastructure. Brazil has championed sugarcane ethanol as an alternative to petrol. Italian Fiat and German Volkswagen are two manufacturers with extensive experience in Brazil of developing flex engines alternating ethanol and petrol use.

In North America, the United States has championed shale gas extraction leading to what has been called a "gas bonanza"[8] that will last for decades to come. This will certainly impact carmakers' considerations, at least for the US market.

Who has made the best bet? Only the future will tell. But environmental regulations will just add uncertainty to an industry that is already facing turmoil and will give a clear competitive advantage to those manufacturers that have made the right choice.

The car industry is not the only sector to face such uncertainty; the energy sector is likewise in turmoil. The International Energy Agency "World Energy Outlook 2010"[9] report describes a world of energy facing an unprecedented level of uncertainty, and one whose future will be largely determined by the response of governments to the twin challenge of climate change and energy safety. Areva, world leader in nuclear power technology, is repositioning itself as a champion of energy solutions with a low carbon footprint. It intends to be one of the three world leaders in the renewable energies sector by the end of 2012, by betting on wind energy, bioenergy, solar energy and hydrogen.[10] The scope of the company is therefore evolving through organic growth and a policy of acquisitions. And one of the drivers of this evolution is, without doubt, sustainable development.

Many industrial sectors will see their strategies and dominant technologies challenged by sustainable development. While this would seem logical for high carbon-emitting sectors (like energy), the same goes for sectors requiring access to rare resources (rare earths, for example) like electronics. This is also true for pharmaceutical, cosmetics or chemical industries, where the erosion of the biodiversity and new regulations aimed at limiting the "privatization" of the common natural property are imminent. Countless other sectors can be listed.

In addition, sustainable development can generate a shift in the structure and competing dynamics of a large number of sectors. The dematerialization of media, presented by some as a promising path[11] for satisfying certain needs at a lower environmental cost, has already shaken up the music industry, and is now challenging the press and publishing industry. The balance of power is changing, with the appearance of actors who had previously played only a minor role, or who were not even present in the sector. Amazon is not just a simple distribution network of physical books and e-books, but it now offers self-publishing services,[12] giving each author the opportunity to self-edit while taking advantage of a worldwide distribution network. Apple has close to 70 percent market share in the United States in the sector of digital cultural goods, and 90 percent for digital music.[13] This is impressive for a company that only entered the music industry in 2001. And the reconfiguration of the music industry is certainly not over.[14] A failure by existing market players to understand these changes can be fatal. Kodak, which has just filed for bankruptcy after decades at the top of the photography industry, is a dramatic proof of this.

Aside from the digital sectors, changing requirements in the purchasing policy and public procurement requirements can open the way for unexpected competitors. When the City of Paris published a call for tender in December 2009 for the development of Autolib' – an electric car-sharing service – bids were submitted from all the traditional mobility operators. It therefore came as a surprise to Veolia Transport, Ada and the SNCF-RATP-Avis-Vinci consortium when the contract was awarded not to a mobility operator, but to Bolloré Group, a conglomerate that, among other things, produces electric batteries. Its partnership with Italian car design company Pininfarina resulted in the creation of the Bluecar.

Examples of this sort abound and highlight a major impact of sustainable development on company strategy: it is likely to fundamentally change the structure and the competition dynamics of a large number of industrial sectors. By extension, the strategic positioning of a large number of existing companies is likely to be affected, while, at the same time, new entrants are likely to penetrate these markets unexpectedly. This is the revolution that Apple introduced in a number of sectors by elevating user experience to the pinnacle. The same logic applies here, but with the key value being (intelligent) sustainability. That is promising for start-ups, often the locus for disruptive innovation, and for existing companies capable of expanding their horizons and experiment with new business models.

Pillar 2: The organization of the processes of value creation, distribution and capture

Any Chief Executive Officer or company founder must be able to formalize the processes of value creation, distribution and capture in an original and effective way. Creating value for a client, and ultimately to society, is the goal of strategy. Among the various tools available to achieve this are the business model (presented in detail in the following chapter) and the value chain.

Here we will show how sustainable development can boost the value chain or the business model, while the tools and answers to these questions will be provided in the rest of the book.

Value chain and sustainable development

In 1985, Michael Porter, professor of strategy at Harvard, introduced the concept of the value chain. It is a simple tool that allows an organization to develop a sustainable competitive advantage by describing the various stages and activities to generate value for its customers.[15] It breaks down the overall activity of a company into its basic activities, which are structured around primary activities (inbound logistics, operations, outbound logistics, marketing, and sales and service) and support activities (firm infrastructure, human resource management, technology and procurement). The interested reader can find many references to learn more about this concept.[16]

Sustainable development in the broadest sense is likely to question each elementary activity of the value chain. By doing so, it questions the content and the configuration of the competitive advantage, and leads to a consideration of the role it plays in creating or reinforcing this competitive advantage.

Two examples of activities in the value chain will be highlighted here – a primary and a support activity – which are probed by the principles, the challenges or the consequences of sustainable development.[17]

Finance and management system. Finance is generally considered to be far removed from issues of sustainable development. How wrong can one be! A recent report by PricewaterhouseCoopers[18] underlines the impact of sustainable development on the investment strategies and portfolio performance of financial assets. Sustainable development is also becoming a concern for investors, and not just Social Responsible Investment (SRI). A coalition of investors led by Aviva Investors recently required United Nations countries to force companies to include information about the social and environmental impact of their activities as part of their financial reporting, or to explain its absence.[19] There is indeed an international trend to including a report on sustainability efforts in the annual report, and to change management systems to allow integrated data to be published. Finance is also involved in the assessment and management of financial risks related to environmental or social risks. In M&A (mergers and acquisitions) operations, environmental risk assessment is taken into account in the valuing of the target company through the process of environmental due diligence. New financial instruments and new markets related to sustainable development are also appearing, creating opportunities, for those who are able to, either to cover a particular risk (e.g. via climate derivatives), or to obtain new financial resources (via energy savings schemes for reselling energy saving certificates). Those who think they can ignore sustainable development issues may find that they are missing out on value creation opportunities or a better management of financial risks.

How Sadia finances environmental improvements through the sale of carbon credit certificates[20]

Sadia is a Brazilian food company founded in 1944. It has more than 650 products in its portfolio, distributed in more than 300,000 points of sales in Brazil and exported to more than 100 countries. It employs 55,000 and has partnerships with around 10,000 poultry and swine integrated farms. It has recently partnered with Perdigão to create BRF Company, a Brazilian champion and one of the largest food companies in the world by market capitalization, with a 9 percent trade share in the sector and the largest world exporter of poultry meat. In 2010, it sold 5.7 million tons of goods corresponding to net sales of US$ 22.7 billion (~US$ 11 billion).

Sadia's Program for Sustainable Swine Production (3S) has received many awards for its innovative mechanism for reducing greenhouse gas (GHG) emissions from their farm operations. It has been developed in four steps: enrollment of producers, installation of biodigesters, installation of equipment to burn and measure methane and CO_2, and energy generation.

As it can be imagined, the environmental consequences of swine production are colossal. At the start of the program, it was not uncommon for small producers to dispose excrement directly into soil and water sources, resulting in pollution and unpleasant odors. Studies have shown that a farm with 300 pigs generated the equivalent waste of a town of 75,000 people. Given Brazil's annual production of more than 2.4 million pigs, the environmental challenge is huge.

Whereas the implantation of biodigesters to collect methane gas and generate energy is not in itself new, the financial mechanism of this project was. Swine waste was fermented by bacteria in the biodigesters' closed tanks that prevented methane emission. Methane gas was converted into CO_2 in the process, "which is 21 times less intensive in terms of GHG effects. Such sequestration of GHGs generates carbon credits under the Kyoto Protocol Clean Development Mechanism (CDM) that can be traded with other companies in need of carbon offsets."[21] The negotiation of such carbon credits is performed by Sadia, which takes a fee to cover its expenses related to the activity. These revenues helped cover part of the cost of the biodigesters. What's more, the gas was used as an alternative source of energy, and the result of the fermentation process as a fertilizer or food for fish breeding.

As a whole, the 3S project reduced the environmental impact of swine production, improved working conditions and generated a new revenue stream for its swine producers' partners.

Similar schemes have been mushrooming around the world. For instance, in the United States, operators like ESCO (Energy Saving Economy)[22] are creating schemes in which they engaging in renovation works to enable energy efficiency projects to be implemented with no initial capital requirement, and are remunerated through the energy bill savings that are generated.

Marketing. Putting marketing and sustainable development in the same basket may seem contradictory, to say the least, in the eyes of public opinions in many developed economies. Marketing is more often thought of as a manipulator and the driver of a hyper-consumption society.[23] However, marketing in its role of enabling market exchanges by distributing and communicating a certain value proposition, exerts a central function as an interface between the company and its markets. In this respect, it acts in association with the strategy, primarily at the level of the business unit, to build the competitive advantage and differentiation toward competitors, and to facilitate access to markets. This said, the nature of sustainable development modifies, sometimes radically, access to certain markets. Sustainability-oriented action plans around the world like the Climate Act in the United Kingdom, China's 12th Five-Year Plan actions on Sustainability or France's Environmental "Grenelle 1 and 2" are reshaping public procurement. For example, the French Government action plan for sustainable public procurement and the laws issued from the "Grenelle 1 and 2" have considerably changed criteria for issuing calls for tenders by integrating environmental and/or social considerations. An increasingly significant number of local government agencies are developing their Agenda 21[24] by modifying their purchasing policy for a greater sustainability. The European Parliament and the European Commission are currently working on "The Single Market Act"[25] with the objective of establishing a directive at the end of 2012 aimed at simplifying access to European public contracts for small and medium enterprises (SMEs) and directing them toward greater sustainability. When it is known that public procurement spending represents approximately 16 percent of the European GDP, around €2,000 billion annually, the implications are massive, as is the potential development of markets for sustainable products and services. But this presupposes that companies are ready to seize these opportunities and anticipate them in the development of their offer. Marketing is primarily concerned with these measures in its role of identifying market opportunities.[26] Over and above these market considerations, marketing must also build, in close collaboration with strategy, the differentiation of the company's value propositions. In saturated markets, with increasingly marketing-savvy consumers, the building of distinctive points is complex. Sustainable development offers the space to build distinctive value propositions based on traditional benefits to which environmental or social benefits can be added.[27] In addition to the added value that is classically used in differentiation, marketing can build a value proposition with positive environmental or social benefits. The life of the product before and after its "consumption life" can be taken into consideration by integrating environmental and social considerations upstream and downstream from the time the product is actually used. This has far more potential than certain "green washing" initiatives taken here and there that quickly come back and hit the company as soon as they are uncovered by vigilant clients or consumer associations.

Centifolia 2011: In search of the perfect cosmetic product

Every 18 months in Grasse, France – perfume capital of the world – Centifolia, the international congress, is held, bringing together international actors of the beauty industry.[28] Avant-gardist by essence, Centifolia is known in the industry for its vision, innovation and commitment. The 2011 event was no exception to the rule, with its topic of the "The Perfect Product: Beautiful, Good and True." Yet, for two days, participants discussed not products, but the world vision associated with their creation and manufacturing. By tracing the natural ingredients that go into the composition of the products, by observing the relationships with the local communities holders of an ancestral and invaluable knowledge about these noble materials, by addressing the intelligence of nature as a source of renewed inspiration to develop biocompatible products, or by tapping into the creative inspiration of a perfume creator, the participants were shown a renewed vision of the concept of a perfect product, by exploring the wealth of the upstream chain of development. Empowered by this collective intelligence, the congress invited the industry professionals to cocreate their own vision of the perfect product around the concepts of beautiful, good and true:

- Beautiful, for a product guided by the creative impulse to be found in each one of us, full of artistic, stylistic and cultural expression, and based on noble materials from a cultural and ancestral tradition.

- Good for each participant in the long production line, from the raw material to the final customer, but also good for the planet.

- True, in terms of an approach based on transparency, moved by the will to say what one does and to do what one says.

We could continue to demonstrate all the primary and support value-chain functions, but this is not the objective. Intuitively, the reader can picture the impact of sustainable development on logistics and the management of the supply chain, on the production, the research and development, without speaking of the strategy – at the heart of this book – and of the governance, for which "the process of construction and implementation of the decision becomes as important as the decision itself."[29]

QUESTIONING THE BUSINESS MODEL

After the value chain, it is generally the business model itself that in many cases is unsuitable for the integration of sustainability in order to create value. For instance, how can an energy supplier, whose income relies on a volume of sales of kWh or m^3 of gas, encourage the overall reduction of energy consumption without sawing the branch on which it sits? How can a car manufacturer drastically reduce its steel consumption, for example, while generating its turnover by the volume of cars sold? How can a chemical company operating on the pesticides market actively aim for a drop in the consumption of products spread by farmers when its growth and its economic performance are based on the sale of these products?

In all these situations, the business model does not allow financial and environmental performance to converge naturally and synergistically. Similarly, how can a lively industrial fabric be maintained in developed economies while it is possible to produce at a much lower cost in developing economies? How can companies be encouraged to favor noble ingredients or sustainable raw materials when, in these times of crisis, cost reduction is on everyone's lips?

There are relatively few answers to all these questions. If the business model cannot align economic, environmental and social issues, the only credible solution is to change it. To express this in a more positive way, the business model should be innovated by integrating sustainability in order to build or keep a competitive advantage in an ever-changing economy. This is obviously the goal of this book, and the following chapters will provide answers to all these questions.

Patagonia on the sustainable economy[30]

Patagonia is a California-based clothing company founded in 1972 by Yvon Chouinard that produces mainly high-end outdoor clothing and has a distinctive environmental record. Co-founder of "1% for the Planet", the company commits 1 percent of its total sales or 10 percent of its profit, whichever is more, to environmental causes and strives to be transparent about its supply chain: "The Footprint Chronicles®." It is also taking part in initiatives to protect regions like the Alberta Sands in Canada or Patagonia in Argentina, concerns that are clearly reflected in its mission statement: "Build the best product, cause no unnecessary harm, use business to inspire and implement solutions to the environmental crisis."[31]

One of the main claims of the company is that business should integrate all the externalities in its pricing structure. Therefore, outsourcing to a developing economy to "reduce" labor costs whereas increasing environmental products should be an aberration and the "true" cost should be paid by the client. This calls for a renewed accountancy to include inputs that are traditionally uncosted. This is not an easy endeavor because many impacts are hard to evaluate with any precision, or to assign fairly to a company.

As Yvon Chouinard, Jib Ellison and Rick Ridgeway stated in a recent Harvard Business Article,[32] sustainability evolved from an operational stance aiming to reduce costs to a driver for innovation, focusing on whole value chains. The next step is for sustainability to pervade all decision-making processes. Three driving forces sustain this process: correct calculation of "uncosted" inputs, capital flowing into companies able to manage these "hidden" costs, the establishment of indices to correctly compare sustainability efforts all along the value chain.

The latter is particularly challenging with regards to the business model. What Chouinard and colleagues call a value-chain index would enable the assessment of a final product's associated costs related to categories such as land use, water, energy, carbon, toxics and social welfare. The authors cite the example in the United States of the Sustainable Apparel Coalition that was endorsed by Walmart. In only 18 months, this coalition has expanded to include 40 companies representing 30 percent of the global market share for apparel and footwear.

For a company like Patagonia, this is great news given its consistent focus in tracking its entire value chain. This will moreover enable decision-makers to be fully aware of the sustainability consequences of their choices and could eventually lead to what the authors call Sustainability 3.0: (a) valuations of ecosystem services integrated into the value-chain index, (b) investors learning to rely on value-chain indices, (c) banks taking notice and lending to compliant companies, and (d) comprehensive product ratings guiding consumer choices. Business model consequences are tremendous and we hope this initiative will serve as a benchmark for other economic sectors by acting as a catalyst for disruptive innovation attracting investors and the animal spirits required to keep this revolution for the planet going.

Beside these apparent contradictions between sustainable development objectives and the current business model, new competitive forces are likely to challenge the competitive advantages of many companies built on hard-to-evolve business models. For instance, companies as diverse as Veolia and IBM see each other more and more as competitors. They both manage flows in a town – physical (e.g. water) or data flows. Given that IBM is positioning as an integrated manager of flows for *smarter cities*, Veolia could risk losing its direct connection with municipalities and thus be reduced to a simple provider of outsourced services to IBM. It goes without saying that this activity leaves a lot less room for value capture.

This is knowledge economy entering one of the economic sectors that need it most and seriously challenging established volume-based business models. Many companies that have positioned themselves in the "energy efficiency" market could face a similar situation.

Otherwise, in a context of market globalization, if companies in developed economies take too long to reconfigure themselves, they are likely to be threatened by the appearance of innovative businesses models from emerging economies. This is already taking place and several Western companies have been facing new competition on their home markets.

Innovative business models from the "bottom of the pyramid" economies

Despite the impressive record of China, India and Brazil in helping people out of extreme poverty, many people continue to struggle for basic needs. In the face of State failure (or difficulty) to tackle these issues, a number of entrepreneurs have decided to act on this precariousness by setting up companies aimed at satisfying some basic needs of this group at "the bottom of the pyramid." The example of the Grameen Bank is well-known, and its creator, Muhammad Yunus, was awarded the Nobel Peace Prize in 2006. But he is far from being alone in his entrepreneurial efforts, and the number of exemplary companies to have developed a business model adapted to these consumers in precarious conditions is growing ceaselessly.

For instance, Aravind Eye Care System became the first ophthalmologic institution in the world, carrying out more than 2.5 million consultations and 300,000 cataract operations between April 2010 and March 2011.[33] The distinctive characteristic of Aravind is to be able to perform 52 percent of its consultations and 49 percent of its operations for free, while presenting a perfectly profitable business model. And this is not done by applying premium pricing to some clients in order to finance the poorest patients. The price of an operation varies between US$50 and US$300, at a cost of US$25, with a service quality meeting the most exigent international requirements. These figures provide food for thought when it is known that the same operation would cost between US$2,500 and US$8,000 in America, for example. To reach such a cost structure, Aravind obviously had to innovate. Cataract surgery requires, for example, intraocular lenses, whose average cost around the world is around US$200. It was impossible for the Indian company to use such expensive lenses. They therefore developed their own lenses at a cost of US$5. Approved by international health agencies, these lenses are nowadays exported to more than 85 countries in the world. This particularly innovating and powerful business model has spawned others. It has already been reproduced in more than 270 care institutions throughout the world. In 2007, Aravind negotiated with the UK National Health Service to treat patients at a much lower cost than would be possible in UK hospitals.

This is not an isolated case. Grameen Bank has just opened its first branches in the United States to offer banking solutions adapted to people without access to the formal banking system. Success was immediate. Jaipur Foot develops orthopedic prostheses at US$70, whereas the price of the Western prostheses is at least US$6,000. Which prostheses will be favored in this context of world competition? At a time when developed economies are facing a gloomy economic outlook, it is time to re-examine innovation transfers and analyze the development of promising and accessible technologies and business models in emerging economies more seriously to identify a possible Emerging–Developed economy (or South–North) transfer. These reversed innovation transfers[34] are attracting the attention today from centers of studies and are the subject of particularly promising research projects.

Pillar 3: management and allocation of resources and competences within the company

Sustainable development is a complex, protean field requiring numerous and varied competences that many companies and more industrial sectors in general simply do not have. For example, reconfiguring the building sector to respect the new regulations with regards to sustainable architecture will take time. Sustainable development also has a strong impact on the competitiveness of companies that will see their resources, their expertise and their strategic capabilities called in question by new requirements.

Although large companies can mobilize the necessary human and financial means, and create partnerships up to the task, this is much less the case for small companies that feel particularly ill equipped. This said, as we saw in the introduction, the capacity to reconfigure internal and external competences in order to respond to a changing environment is a key factor of competitiveness and the perpetuation of a competitive advantage. A leader who fails to integrate these changes and adapt the company's resources and skills accordingly, would simply endanger his or her company in the short or the long term.

While the reconfiguration of competences is obviously essential, the basic access to purely material resources is also challenged by sustainable development. Numerous reports prepared for the Rio + 20 United Nations Conference on Sustainable Development held in Brazil in June 2012 came to the same conclusion – that the current scarcity of resources and constraints on access to raw materials will reach a crescendo in the 21st century.[35] The European Commission, in a July 2010 report,[36] measured the level of criticality of access to 41 raw materials essential to the competitiveness of European companies in two areas: economic importance and risk of supply disruption. Fourteen of the 41 raw materials were found to have both a high risk of supply disruption and strong economic importance. Among these resources, we find, for example, cobalt, gallium, graphite or rare earths – materials that are essential for today's production, and also for the development of tomorrow's economy (cobalt, for example, is used in the composition of the lithium-ion batteries and synthetic fuel, and gallium in photovoltaic panels). For companies dependent on these raw materials, the access to the resource and the guarantee of its supply have become major strategic issues.

Managing the supply of rare earths

Rare earth elements are a set of 17 chemical elements in the periodic table which, despite their name, are pretty abundant on the earth surface, but due to "insufficient" profits, the world's production moved in the second half of the 20th century from the United States to China, where 90 percent of the world production is now concentrated.[37]

Given their use in industries as varied as aerospace (e.g. scandium to make light aluminum–scandium alloy), optic (e.g. cadmium for camera lenses) or medical (e.g. thulium for portable X-ray machines), demand has been growing exponentially with some sources stating that it has been exceeding supply.[38] To add to the tension, since 2009, China has announced restrictions on its exports. This is of less concern for companies producing in China, but for others this is a serious issue that is driving up costs. Geopolitical reasons are fueling this problem, particularly the Japan–China islands dispute, but consequences for companies are real.

This major risk has been highlighted by the European Union report cited previously, as well as by industrial reports like that of the French Federation of Electric, Electronic and Communication Industries (FIEEC)[39] that brings together 27 trade unions representing 2,300 companies, including 86 percent of SMEs, which employ a workforce of more than 400,000. This vast economic fabric turns over €96 billion per year, including 46 percent export.

In May 2011, the FIEEC rang the alarm bell: the industry as a whole is largely dependent on strategic raw materials and this constitutes a serious threat to the companies' competitiveness. To tackle this, the FIEEC has presented the French government with a list of 16 proposals aimed at building an effective strategy on raw materials. The main points of this proposal include identifying key strategic resources, creating industrial ecosystems to promote better access to these materials, re-exploring possible French underground deposits and seabed, recycling and following up agreed policies relating to international trade.

In addition to these proposals, the FIEEC recommends that its members invest in the following aspects:

- Security of the supply chain and development of partnerships regarding strategic raw materials

- Eco-conception of equipment to reduce the consumption of resources at equal performance level

- Search for substitute materials

- Development of recycling and circular material flows

Pillar 4: Steering of necessary adaptations to a constantly changing environment

This fourth pillar is a consequence of the previous three pillars. The decision to change a company's scope of activity or its strategic positioning, reconfigure its value chain, radically modify or innovate its business model, obtain new resources and competences involve major strategic changes. Such changes rarely occur spontaneously and naturally, however, and any adaptations must be driven by strategy.

Strategy must tackle issues of change on several levels. To start with, at an organizational configuration level, the leader must be able to transform its organization into an agile company.[40] This means not only developing an organizational model able to react more quickly, but also to be flexible, and what's more, to anticipate and innovate constantly, in particular through an exceptional understanding among all the company's actors, both internal and external.[41] This agility is not dictated; it must be organized; and for this, knowledge and its management play a particularly important role. The ability to identify and amplify weak signals and to use them to reconfigure a competitive advantage becomes an essential strategic asset.[42]

However, this ability depends largely on the organizational configuration and the interaction among the different members of the organization, coupled with the necessary intelligence related to the outside environment. This calls for new managerial practices based on cooperation, collective intelligence, open innovation or co-creation. These new practices find support particularly in the pillars of sustainable development. As an illustration, the principle of participation presented at the 1992 Rio Earth Summit is closely related to sustainable development and bases its dynamics on collaboration and the widespread participation in decision-making.

Without advocating the introduction of a democratic approach to the running of the company, and without calling in question the traditional role of decision-makers, it is nevertheless important to question the leaders about the conditions in which employees (and stakeholders), can take part in decision-making, enabling new knowledge creation, and facilitating its dissemination and sharing. This takes us back to the governance issue and more largely of the managerial practices encouraged in the organization.

In this respect, the first steps of a convergence seem on the way. For purely competitive and economic reasons, the company must be reinvented to be able to keep pace with the constant changes. On the one hand, lean principles are a powerful vector to push for sustainability. In a time of crisis, cost chasing is no longer a management trend but a matter of survival. As a columnist in *The Economist* recently put it, sustainability "fits nicely with lean production and tight supply-chain management."[43]

On the other hand, the company posture must change. The model of a company folded up on itself, hermetically sealed and seeking only to produce knowledge useful to its competitiveness seems outdated. Instead, it must open up, federate stakeholders, generate cooperation. The involvement of stakeholders helps here. By integrating internal and external stakeholders into the decision-making process, the scope of knowledge flowing into the company widens, bringing with it a greater awareness of the interdependence of the company's actions and their impact on its various ecosystems.

The management of these impacts then becomes more than a moral or ethical question; it becomes a managerial question converging with the company's own rationality, or more exactly, with the individuals in their expected professional roles. The wider the circle of stakeholders becomes the more the "awareness level of the company" is enriched. Being in constant contact with the environment in which it evolves, the company is better able to identify weak signals that would have passed by unnoticed had it been isolated. New opportunities emerge in parallel with an increased capacity to anticipate threats. And – the highest reward – the company's credibility and legitimacy are strengthened.

The successful reconversion of a Bosch factory in Vénissieux, France[44]

In a morose economic climate, with successive announcements of layoffs and closures, the case of the Bosch de Vénissieux factory (in the French Rhone department) represents a success story and is an excellent example of the need to adapt to a constantly changing environment. In January 2012, this factory, after decades of manufacturing diesel pumps, started producing photovoltaic solar panels, intending to become the leading photovoltaic production site for Southern Europe and North African countries.

Vénissieux has a solid history of adaptation. In 2004, employees already agreed to reject the 35-hour working week and accepted a three-year pay freeze in exchange for a €15 million investment to strengthen the competitiveness of the site and to protect jobs. But in 2009, a new bombshell hit the factory. The main diesel pump manufactured by Vénissieux was no longer up to standard, and Bosch France announced its decision to close the site. What would probably have been met with anger or fatalism at other French companies gave trade union leader, Marc Soubitez, an opportunity to show his tenacity and a welcome example of dialogue and goodwill among stakeholders. Discussions with the Bosch management and stakeholders turned the announced nightmare for 850 employees into a successful adventure of reindustrialization.

To save the site, there were not many solutions. A new production line had to be found and everyone involved was up for the challenge. For one year, discussions were led among an impressive array of concerned parties: the French (CFDT/CGT) and German (IG Metall) trade unions, the factory management, as well as Bosch France, the board of Bosch Germany, the factory workers, external experts, the Economic Development agency of the Region of Lyon, the government, the French Commission of Re-industrialization and others – all worked together to build a credible and sustainable alternative.

By spring 2010, one thing was clear: the solution did not lie with the automobile industry. What's more, if a solution were found, any changes would be more radical than so far expected. All the while these discussions were going on, workers never lost hope and not a single day of strike was called.

Finally, the combined effort, the discussions, the collective intelligence, the control of any negative energies within the factory paid off, and a solution was found. The head of the solar energy division of the group agreed to locate the production of photovoltaic panels for Southern Europe and North Africa in Vénissieux, thus giving the site an ambitious industrial project. The cost of reconverting the site reached €25 million but 450 jobs were saved. A lot of money, but far less than the cost of closing down the factory, which would have cost Bosch four times as much more, not to mention the disastrous social impact on the region.

CONCLUSION

To get the right answer, it is important to ask the right question. Rather than waste time wondering whether sustainable development creates value, it is undoubtedly more relevant and effective to ask what conditions are required to successfully integrate sustainable development into the company in order to enhance the value creation process.

The first condition – and a fundamental condition – consists in linking sustainable development, in all its multiple components and challenges, with the strategy of the company. While acting as a force for change in the environment, sustainability questions the structure of an industry, its dominant design and its competing dynamics. It is also likely to question the business model of a company, its strategic positioning and its scope of activities. It questions the configuration of the value chain, and consequently the configuration of the competitive advantage. More basically, it reminds us, if needed, of the need to break with paradigms of the past based on a stable and predictable environment. The instability and the uncertainty that characterize the current economic environment demand new organizational configurations and new practices aligned with sustainable development.

A second more fundamental condition is also necessary: the courage of the leader to stand above the crowd and take his or her company out of its comfort zone, with a proven business model and traditional methods of management. Innovation today is primarily incremental, but sustainable development calls for disruptive innovation. It has different requirements, requests other forms of rationality, and is a fertile ground for experimentation. The leaders who first have the courage to make this shift will prepare their company to be permanently ready to face the challenges of the future.

2
The Business Model – A Powerful Tool to Drive a Strategic Shift

Sustainable development is a powerful driver of change. It can have an immense impact on a company strategy, and strategists would be advised to take an in-depth look at its consequences and opportunities if they want to keep or create tomorrow's competitive advantage.

But although willingness to change and convictions are necessary, they are not enough to drive the integration of sustainable development into the business strategy. It is necessary to have the appropriate conceptual tools to think this integration through. And it is the business model and the related tools that are really powerful to pilot the strategic reconfiguration.

The concept of the business model is not new; its origins date back to the late 1940s,[1] but it is only in the last decade that it has become widely diffused, particularly since the burst of the Internet bubble and the need to better understand value-capture mechanisms for Internet-based companies.

Another role of the business model, and the one that interests us here, is that it opens new perspectives for innovation. Although innovation is often seen through its technological dimension, one must not lose sight of the fact that it can also be organizational, social, managerial or business-model based. Low-cost aviation, free press, social business,[2] car-sharing, collaborative platforms and so on are just a few examples of business-model innovations that have resulted in long-lasting competitive advantages for their creators, even in highly saturated markets.

Companies may be motivated to innovate their business model for many reasons. One reason could be the catalytic effect of a new technology outdating current value-capture methods and imposing the development of a new business model. When Skype developed a peer-to-peer technology that resulted in a new mode of telecommunication, it certainly innovated on a technological level, but it had also to invent a new value-capture model (something that free Skype-to-Skype communication definitely is not). By contrast, when Southwest Airlines created the low-cost model in the United States – a model that was strongly criticized at its launch and made more than one CEO of traditional companies at the time laugh – no technological invention was involved. This successful business model resulted from a major redefinition of the air transport passengers' value curve.

Sometimes the business model has to be reinvented following the redefinition of an organization mission. When French company Danone collaborated with the Grameen Bank to create Danone Grameen Food in Bangladesh, the goal was to reduce poverty, bringing health via food, and support local economic development. In order to set up a production unit, sales and proximity distribution of dairy products at a very low price, adapted to the nutritional needs of disadvantaged populations, a new business model had to be built, one that created employment and respected the environment.

Among all possible triggers of business model reconfiguration, sustainable development plays a prominent role. As discussed in Chapter 1, sustainable development calls into question may businesses models that prevent a convergence of economic, social and environmental performance. This is still the norm in most industrial sectors, where companies are locked in to the scope of the existing business model that is, by definition, difficult or impossible to sustain. But, if the company is courageous enough, or if environmental changes impose a rethink of its scope, a potentially large field of innovation may emerge. The main objective of this book is to explore this field.

This chapter will first explain what exactly a business model is and what it is composed of. It will then propose the *sustainable business model canvas* (SBMC), a frame of analysis and action based on existing and validated tools empowered by sustainable development. A running example will be used to illustrate the different components and the dynamics involved in the construction of a business model.

WHAT IS A BUSINESS MODEL?

The business model describes the principles according to which an organization creates, distributes and captures value.[3] It is generally structured around three building blocks[4]:

- The value proposition, which is the center of the business model and answers the core question: "What do our clients want? What can we offer that is a source of value for them?"

- The value architecture, which is how the company is organized to create and distribute the value proposition to the targeted customers. It refers not only to the value chain of the company, but also to its value constellation: the external actors that contribute to the creation and distribution of the value proposition to customers (partners, suppliers, distributors, institutions and so on).

- The economic equation, which enables an analysis of the revenue streams generated by the value proposition and the costs incurred by its value architecture.

A company eager to adapt its business model can choose to act at the value-proposition level (new product, new service, new customer experience, reconfiguration of the value curve and so on), at the value-architecture level (optimization of the value chain, reconfiguration of activities or key resources, innovative partnership approach, etc.), or on the economic equation (new income sources, dynamic mechanisms of price fixation, better control of the costs, transformation of fixed costs into variable costs, etc.), or indeed on a combination of these approaches.

Quirky: An original collaborative development platform[5]

Have you ever woken up one morning with a promising idea for a new product, but without the means to make it happen? Developing an idea into a product requires skills and resources that most of us lack. It is as a result of this observation that the collaborative community platform, Quirky, appeared. Quirky's value proposition is to transform good ideas into products ready to be marketed. Concretely, the platform lets you submit your idea to the website in exchange for a US$10 fee. The only requirement is that the idea must relate to the development of a physical product with a retail price of less than US$150. If your idea has real potential, you may find yourself on the brink of a wonderful new adventure. Once submitted, the idea is evaluated by the Quirky community that gives feedback on its innovativeness, identifies existing market alternatives, specifies the product characteristics, suggests improvements and votes for or against the development of the idea. Quirky's community is its main asset given its reliance on the principles of collective intelligence and crowd sourcing. It favors virtual bridges with online social networks (Facebook and the like) and develops incentives to encourage participation. During a one-month period, the ideator is able to edit and improve the idea, at any moment based on the community feedback. Strongly supported ideas will then face a tougher evaluation by a team of experts, based on three criteria: design, marketing and economic viability. After this stage, the idea is either rejected (and its initiator then receives feedback from the expert and community), or is validated to pass onto the development phase. This is when Quirky in-house teams get involved.

A team of designers and developers will prototype the product in constant interaction with the community. For its members, each interaction is an opportunity to score points on the influence brought to the project. These points will eventually determine the remuneration of each contributor to the global project. Once the prototype finished, its marketing strategy is defined and the product is put on sale at the Quirky e-shop. Each order is recorded, but it is necessary to reach a minimum number of orders for the product to be finally sent for production. Obviously, the Quirky community facilitates the launch of the product and its communication through viral tools inside and outside the community via the connection with online social networks. And once the product is sent for production, a marketing team takes charge of the online communication and also contacts potential distributors (Quirky has a network of partners in several hundred stores in the United States).

Quirky has, unquestionably, been able to develop a particularly innovative value proposition and value architecture. Still, it is necessary to be able to attract and motivate members of the community to take part. This is possible given the platform's smart economic model. First of all, each posted idea generates US$10 to Quirky. Each contributor to the project, in any phase of development, will be credited with a score calculated on the basis of her contribution to the final result. A vote for a promising project, a suggestion selected to improve the specification of the invention, a sponsorship of the prototype in the e-shop, etc. are likely to increase the number of points.

Once sales start, Quirky receives the revenues and remunerates the various actors of the chain as follows: 30 percent of the online sales revenues and 10 percent of the indirect sales (via distributors, for example) are redistributed to the community: 35 percent of this sum goes to the ideator and the remaining 65 percent is distributed among the contributors according to their score. The more a member of the community contributes to the project the more money he or she earns. And these royalties are distributed throughout the commercial lifetime of the product.

Does it work? Quirky receives an average of 10,000 ideas per week and federates more than 100,000 members within its community. At the end of this very selective process, one or two ideas are eventually developed. For example, the 2011 best seller was a pivotable power strip, sold in tens of thousands of units. An idea that earned its inventor US$150,000 in 2011 and the forecast for 2012 exceeds a million dollars! No fewer than 700 members of the community took part in this development, and will share several hundreds of thousands of dollars according to their contribution.

This resolutely innovative business model enabled Quirky to achieve a turnover of US$10 million in 2011. This success attracted investors and Quirky recently raised US$68 million from venture capital to continue the adventure.[6]

THE SUSTAINABLE BUSINESS MODEL CANVAS AND ITS COMPONENTS

This section presents the SBMC. This tool builds on and expands the Business Model Canvas proposed by Alexander Osterwalder and Yves Pigneur. The add-ons explicitly address costs and benefits for society and environment.

The SBMC is structured around 13 building blocks, completing the traditional approach of the bottom line (financial profits) by the triple bottom line (planet, people, profit).[7]

A central tenet underlies the comprehension and use of the SBMC: its systemic and interdependent character. Since the 13 blocks are eminently related to each other, any modification in one block induces effects on others. In fact, it is impossible to determine the value proposition without understanding the customer segments. Any modification of the value proposition potentially requires new activities to be deployed and new resources to be controlled. That will impact the cost structure and the company revenue model.

Table 2.1 *Sustainable business model canvas*

Costs for Society and the Environment	Key Partners	Key Activities	Sustainable Value Proposition	Customer Relationship Management	Customer Segments	Benefits for Society and the Environment
		Key Resources		Distribution Channels		
Shared Costs	Cost Structure		Revenue Streams			Shared Benefits

Source: Adapted from the 'Business Model Canvas' published in A. Osterwalder and Y. Pigneur (2010), *Business Model Generation: A Handbook for Visionaries, Game Changers and Challengers*, Hoboken: John Wiley & Sons)[8]

We present these components next, using our running example of Skype's business model and comparing it to that of a traditional telecom operator.

The value proposition

At the core of any organization business model sits the value proposition made to a market. It is the reason why a customer chooses one company over another to solve a problem or satisfy a need. An offer has no value per se, it only acquires value when it convinces a customer to buy and use it in a certain context.[9] Before that, it only constitutes a proposition in the market. Consequently, a photovoltaic solar panel, in spite of its power, acquires value only when it is bought and used.

So the question of the meaning of the value proposition is central. Beyond the functional characteristics of an offer, which are the benefits obtained in comparison with the consented sacrifices (monetary and non-monetary)?[10] Taking the example of the solar panel, arbitrations of a financial (cost of the installation and return on investment), ecological (contributing to the development of renewable energies, energy decentralization), aesthetic (adequacy with the habitation aesthetics) and symbolic (energy autonomy, responsible citizen act) nature could take place. The capacity of the company to frame its communication to stimulate a favorable evaluation is central, especially when a change of consumer behavior is demanded (such as, for example, giving up the use of one's individual car in favor of a carpooling solution).[11]

Value drivers are many and varied. Design, performance, innovativeness, service, accessibility, low cost and so on are only some of the possible attributes to position an offer to target customers. Certain studies have identified up to 250 customer advantages constitutive of a differentiating advantage.[12]

As the client's perception of value is at the core of the value-proposition construction, it is impossible to separate it from the markets to which it is addressed. Its development thus supposes a dynamic interaction with its target markets.

Skype, the "troublemaker" of the telecom industry

Skype, acquired in 2011 by Microsoft, is nowadays a well-established actor in the international telecommunications landscape. This was not the case in the last decade of the 20th century. Skype's central technology, VoIP (Voice over Internet Protocol), sparked a revolution and thoroughly transformed a sector that was resistant to innovate on its core (and profitable) activity of voice communication.

Not that long ago, making phone calls was not cheap. Monthly subscription plus communications billed according to the length, the moment of the call and the number called could generate pretty expensive invoices. This value proposition, generating juicy profits, lasted until the arrival of a radically new value proposition made possible by a new technology (VoIP): free telephony. Since voice took the same channels as data on the Internet, its cost of transmission became negligible. Admittedly, flexibility and quality were not the same and it was necessary to have an Internet connection. But by downloading Skype, the whole world became instantly reachable for free with Skype to Skype Communication. Very quickly, this value proposition gained in sophistication, with the possibility of coupling video to an audio call. The teleconference became possible for any web user, without spending a dime. Thanks to this innovative value proposition, Skype experienced an exponential growth.

Target market

The dyad, "value proposition–customers," is inseparable, a value proposition being strictly related to the customers whom it must be able to seduce. In the strategic configuration of a business model, several cases are possible concerning the target market. At this stage, it is not a matter of defining the target market in its marketing sense. Although this may be the case later on, the business model takes a broader view to understand the sources of value creation, distribution and capture, and thus does not demand a fine-tuned specification of the target customers.

- Mass market: In a business model directed at the mass market, a single value proposition is likely to interest a vast heterogeneous public. When Henry Ford launched the Ford T in 1908, he addressed the mass market. One model, one color, a proposition of a highly standardized value, new means of production, a wage increase to create the market and a price able to interest a broad mass market – these are the secrets of the Ford T.

- A segmented market: Contrary to a business model directed to the mass market, the market can be structured in various segments that vary in their needs, their expectations or their behaviors. The market segmentation invites the company consequently to develop a unique value proposition for one or more segments or niches having specific needs or problems to be solved. The Ford T soon left room for a vast range of vehicles adapted to the specific needs of various customers. And it is easy to understand that a three-child family living in a rural neighborhood will undoubtedly have different needs than a single person living in a big city like London with only occasional use of a car. Most markets today are segmented, even hyper-segmented, and empowered by technological solutions able to customize solutions. The capacity to adapt the value proposition to the unique requirements of these segments becomes a key lever of competitiveness and the creation of profitable niche activities.

- Multiple markets: The emergence of the free press critically illustrates the concept of a double-sided market. A free newspaper must certainly be able to seduce a broad readership, but it is advertisement that generates revenue flows. These two markets are closely related – the size of the readership making it possible to attract more advertisers and to invoice them for more expensive inserts. A large number of companies work on multiple markets. The real estate broker must at the same time convince the seller to entrust their goods to him, but also to seduce candidates to an acquisition; eBay must be able to attract both sellers of goods and clients for these goods; a workforce agency must at the same time attract qualified candidates and companies to hire them.

When an activity is created, it is generally structured around these possible configurations. During its development, it can be decided to diversify and consequently to target markets not meeting the same basic needs. Diversification can be concentric – in which case it meets different, but interrelated needs – or pure – that is, aiming to address completely disconnected markets.[13] When Solomon decides to produce skis, then shoes and then ski clothing in addition to ski fixings, it diversifies in a concentric way. When Yamaha decides to pass from the musical instruments to the motorbikes and jet skis, it practices pure diversification. In general, this kind of diversification will call on a specific business model for each sphere of strategic activities.

The market of Skype

Skype is a typical example of a mass-market solution. All that is needed to use Skype is a computer (or more recently a cell phone) and Internet access, which means that a very broad range of web users is likely to be interested. This is, once again, revolutionary. Traditional operators like Vodafone, Orange or Telefonica may have global operations, but their revenue streams are divided by country and consolidated at the group level. Even if some economies of scale are possible (e.g. in terms of procurement and infrastructure deployment), when it comes to responding to customer needs and customer relationship management, activities must be developed for each specific market needs. Therefore, a traditional operator must first and foremost address a national market that it must segment. Vodafone UK market operations are limited to the population old enough to have a phone subscription, and the various companies and organizations operating in this geographical territory. Admittedly, the market is substantial, but it is complex, expensive to segment and without any common measurement with the 2.2 billion[14] people connected to the Web in the world, representing de facto the potential market size of Skype.

The exact number of Skype users remains unclear with the company saying in 2011 that it had 170 million active users.[15] Whatever the real figures, they are in any case far superior to the potential market size of a traditional telecom operator.

Moreover, internationalizing operations for traditional telecom operators implies large capital investments to enter a market, be it through an acquisition, a merger, direct implantation or some other form. Besides procurement, there are no economies of scale when it comes to deploying physical infrastructure. Distribution channels must also be localized and teams must be hired. As a whole, costs increase proportionally to the number of markets served.

This is a completely different picture from internationalization at Skype. Even if costs are incurred to comply with local regulation (e.g. customer service requirements), a considerable degree of standardization to adapt the web interface and communication (content translation and so on), and to provide adequate infrastructure, is possible given that the software is exactly the same.

Distribution channels and customer relationship management

Every company must be able to reach its target market via distribution and communication channels. These channels can be direct or indirect, as the distribution system can be internalized or include external distributors, with whom a trade and partnership relation is tied. The choice depends on the size and the level of atomicity of the market to be served, of the control that the company wishes to exert, and its financial means and strategic resources. A direct distribution network will generally generate higher margins per product sold, but will be potentially expensive to deploy, especially if the target market is broad and geographically dispersed.

The configuration of the distribution channel is thus eminently strategic, since it enables the value distribution to a customer and its capture. It can thus be a central element of the competitive advantage or differentiation. For instance, one of the main assets of Coca-Cola, besides its powerful trademark, is its very broad distribution to the four corners of the world. This product is known for being available even in the most improbable places. In the computer industry, Dell had once innovated distribution by direct selling at a time when it was considered foolish; it was then able to build a competitive advantage that eventually led it to become the market leader, before being displaced by Hewlett-Packard and lately by Lenovo.

Distribution channels will concern all the touchpoints in a client's "life cycle" with a company: awareness, evaluation, purchase, delivery and after sales. The Internet has been the game changer in that respect and there is much more to come. For instance, compared to Amazon.com, why would a consumer make the effort to go to a physical store, during certain opening hours, spending time and money with the risk of not finding the item he or she was looking for?

The future of retailing is, in fact, being called into question.[16] Stores are likely to become showrooms more than sales points, like the Audi car dealer in London;[17] and to fully integrate online and offline, like the Burberry flagship in London's Regent Street.[18]

In parallel to channel configuration, and often in close relation, the company must define the kind of connection it wishes to establish with its customers. Possibilities are many and conditioned by the choice of distribution channel:

- Personal assistance is based on the human interaction between the company's staff and customers. Strongly present in the labor-intensive service sector, personal service can powerfully shape the customer experience and become a key differentiation criterion. Singapore Airlines, famous for its service excellence, built its reputation on the "Singapore Girl" icon representing the company's stewardesses in their capacity to provide customers with an exceptionally high utility of service. When an interlocutor is assigned to a customer in an identified way, it characterizes a dedicated personal assistance. Thus a large number of banks propose personal assistance by assigning an identified account manager to each of its customers who is then responsible for managing the relationship with a portfolio of clients.

- In self-service relations, it is the customer who manages the interface, either completely or partially, while the company provides the means and tools for self-servicing. Internet banking, for example, offers customers the possibility to carry out the banking operations they wish to undertake.

- Automated relations are generally situated in a more thorough self-service setting. When the Amazon.com web site proposes its customers reading suggestions according to their profile and their past purchases, it is an automated relation giving the impression of a personalized relation, but founded on the exploitation and analysis of patterns of customer data.

- Community relations support exchange within a community of users. Quirky, as described previously, shows to what extent a community relation can bring value to all its members. In a more developed form, it is possible to talk about value co-creation with a company's customers or stakeholders. When Boeing developed its new 787 Dreamliner, no fewer than 120,000 frequent flyers took part by providing their insights throughout the development process through a co-creation platform, the World Design Team.[19] More and more organizations are inviting their customers to co-create new solutions by supporting the interaction and exchange of ideas, in the image of Starbucks, Procter & Gamble, Nokia, Sumerset and Lego, among others.[20]

- Here, the Internet has a disruptive force: those companies better able to add intelligence to customer data have been able to forge a distinctive advantage, as the IBM and Amazon testimonies. No surprise that addressing "Big Data" appears on the top of marketeers' priorities for the current decade.[21]

Skype, automation for rule

In the late 1990s, distribution channels and customer relationship management in a traditional telecom operator were particularly diversified. Self-owned shops, distribution partners, call centers, sales representatives, dedicated sales force and the Internet constituted the pillars of the multichannel strategy of existing actors. They offered a broad coverage of the market, but one that weighed heavily on the cost structure. Similarly, client relationships mirrored the distribution by being multiple and varied: from personal assistance for certain segments to automated self-service relations enabled by the Internet for others.

Skype took the opposite view of this multichannel model: a single distribution via the Internet by a simple download of an application, then a largely automated management of the relation. Admittedly, the market is limited to Internet users. But this is the essence of the Skype model, and the connected population keeps growing. The coverage capacity is thus large, for an infinitesimal fraction of the cost supported by the traditional operators.

Key resources and activities

Developing a value proposition and being able to distribute it to a customer presupposes a value chain based on multiple activities and resources. Configuring this value chain and allocating resources and competences are at the core of the strategy activity. Chapter 1 has already presented how sustainable development questioned this strategy pillar, and the following chapters will present how value chain and resource reconfiguration empower the company to create value through sustainable development.

The resources of a company are vital in building its competitive advantage, *a fortiori* if it is able to assemble proprietary resources or to reach them in a more advantageous way than its competitors. A central resource for an airline company is fuel (e.g. kerosene), representing up to 25 percent of its cost structure. However, not all companies face the same challenges. For instance, whereas Western airline companies like United, British Airways or Lufthansa have to put up with oil price fluctuations and the corresponding impact on the cost structure and competitiveness, companies from the United Arab Emirates, such as the Emirates or Etihad, do not face the same constraints. Sometimes, strategic decisions at the resource level have a significant impact on a company's competitiveness, as Brussels Airlines found on its cost when it signed a fuel hedge contract to cover against fuel price variations at an unfortunate moment and was obliged to pay higher prices in spite of a drop in oil prices.[22]

The key strategic resources of a company can be categorized as follows.

- Human resources are obviously at the center of any company. The term 'human resources' is, incidentally, an unfortunate name in a knowledge economy, and we could imagine a time when HR no longer stands for human resources but for human *richness*. No company can exist without people; however, their importance in the building of the competitive advantage differs. As already evoked, a labor-intensive service firm depends largely on human interaction to build the customer experience. A hospital is, for example, seldom a pleasant place to visit. Nevertheless, the relational quality or its absence will weigh heavily in the appreciation by a patient of its medical and nonmedical care. Medical care institutions have understood this and have started to think about how its services can be improved to better serve its patients/clients. And it is undoubtedly useful to recall here that satisfied patients depend first and foremost on satisfied employees. An innovative management of human resource – or we should say of human talents – can thus exert a strong impact on the competitiveness of a company, as illustrated by the following case study.

And if diversity was a source for company development?[23]

In 2010, the French consulting company Goodwill Management revealed the results of a study evaluating human resource diversity on economic performance. The results challenge some preconceived ideas.

Managing diversity is a thorny problem in the business world. Staff diversity is defined as

> the opening of the human capital of the company to an individual, whatever the age, gender, nationality or origins (real or supposed), possible handicap, religion, sexual orientation, political convictions, and so on.[24]

Even though many countries around the world seek to promote diversity within organizations, in particular with policies of positive discrimination, the results are not very eloquent. Thus a French law, for example, states that for companies with more than 20 employees, disabled workers should make up at least 6 percent of the workforce. Similar regulations exist in Germany, Austria, Italy, Luxembourg and Greece, and companies can be fined heavily for failing to comply. Despite this, some companies prefer to pay the fines rather than comply.[25] Even political parties in most countries do not set a good example, given the disproportion between male and female representatives.

The study of Goodwill Management was carried out in partnership with four big French companies: Axa (insurance), L'Oréal (cosmetics), Orange (telecommunications) and Vinci (construction and infrastructure operator).

The conclusion is particularly striking: if diversity is well managed, it creates value and wealth for the company, with increases in the profitability of a company possible between 5 and 15 percent, according to the type of activity. The main conclusions are as follows:

- Senior employees perform 4 percent better than juniors, as long as adapted methods of management are in place. And at equivalent job positions, they do not cost more to the company.

- The difference in aptitude between a disabled and non-disabled employee is negligible or nonexistent if his or her workstation is adapted. And only 10 percent of disabled workers need an adaptation of their workstation.

- With the exception of maternity leave, women are not more absent from work than men. Maternity leave represents 2.8 percent of the remunerated time on the whole of a career.

- Diversity of origins results in a reduction of absenteeism and staff turnover, and, if it is well managed, contributes directly to economic performance.

- The study shows that the most diversified teams are also the most efficient.

All these results encourage companies to develop a management policy favoring professional diversity. The interest is obvious: in the absence of social indicators relating to diversity, the company would be unable to identify its contribution to the company profitability. By developing an integral dashboard related to diversity, it is possible to connect social and economic performance, control it and in effect create social and economic value.

- Intangible resources constitute a second and particularly important pool of resources for a company's competitiveness. Among them, intellectual resources are closely related to the human resources mentioned before. Knowledge indeed plays such a core role in today's economy that we do not hesitate to describe it as a knowledge economy. Knowledge management is thus a central strategic issue, particularly in the innovation process, and the interested reader will find excellent books on the matter.[26] More broadly, the intangible resources relate to the power of the brand in its capacity to encapsulate the whole of client perceptions, copyrights and intellectual properties, and customer databases that become source of intelligence thanks to increasingly sophisticated capacities for data processing (Amazon being a case in point), among others.

- Physical resources are all the physical assets and the materials needed for a company to function. Raw materials, machines, production facilities, offices, computer equipment are only some examples. As we saw in Chapter 1, the access to physical resources – in particular certain raw materials – becomes an increasingly strategic challenge in this period of resource scarcity. Undoubtedly, it forces the companies to be much more efficient in the use of these materials in their production process. A recent trend has been the reversal of outsourcing, mainly in the UK and US: companies started to figure out that because some activities have been outsourced, (1) they were losing sight of their customer base, thus being less reactive to market evolutions and (2) they were giving birth to future competitors, in the image of Samsung, once an outsourcer for Japanese companies.[27]

- Financial resources enable the company to deploy its value chain and to obtain the means of its ambitions. Certain business models are particularly dependent on the capacity to mobilize important financial resources. For example, leverage buyouts or LBOs have been largely used for company's acquisitions in the last decade, and there, too, innovation can transform apparent constraints into opportunities, as the example of Sun Edison described next shows.

When Sun Edison reinvented the business model of the solar energy

Sun Edison, an American company, was able to reinvent the solar energy business model creating a major rupture in an industry characterized by high capital requirements.

In the beginning, the company had a business-as-usual approach trying to sell photovoltaic solar panels to medium-sized companies (logistic centers, hypermarkets, production plants, etc.). They had the same problem of other market actors: it was necessary to convince the customers to support substantial up-front investment costs, with a return on investment that was certainly measurable, but with a payback spread out over several years. Not an easy solution to commercialize.

The company changed its bracket: it no longer sought to sell solar equipment but to propose Solar "Power Purchase Agreement" (PPA), that is, an energy supply agreement at a predefined price and concluded over a given period with no up-front cost. In substance, Sun Edison stopped selling photovoltaic material, but instead sold solar energy at a given price. This was a strong argument in a very volatile energy market. And the contracts guaranteed to Sun Edison a certain and foreseeable cash flow, which, thought the company, would allow it to convince bankers to lend capital to finance the power stations. Alas, the banks did not agree to play the game.

Far from giving up, the chairman of the company then created, by an intelligent process of securitization, a vehicle of investment at low risk made up of the PPA and sold it to institutional and private investors. Admittedly, the result of this vehicle is not fabulous, but it has low risk. And, especially, it is associated with tax incentives specific to the solar sector that enables investors to profit from tax exemption. It was the recipe for success. Sun Edison passed from a single market to a multiple market, where companies were approached to buy PPA, and investors were approached to buy the financial vehicle. With such a value proposition, the company is no longer a seller of solar panels, but in fact a trader of energy contracts and an installer and operator of solar power stations held by investors.

This particularly innovative business model required the configuration of a very different value chain, the acquisition of resources and new competences, in particular in financial engineering and regulation. Selling became even more a central activity, with the PPA being the strategic resource to compose the investment vehicle. But, in the end, this disruptive business model innovation paid off: Sun Edison is now one of the leaders in the solar energy industry in the United States, and it has expanded abroad, being present nowadays in France, Italy, Spain, Greece, and also in India, Malaysia and Korea.

In 2012, the company launched a pioneering initiative to provide solar power to the bottom of the pyramid with its "Eradication of Darkness" electrification program in rural India.[28] It will provide off-grid a solar energy plant to remote villages with no electricity, creating a micro-grid to supply houses directly. According to the WWF-UK,

> operational costs will be paid by revenues collected from houses supplied with the energy. To cover capital costs, the Indian government has awarded the program a 90 percent subsidy and the firm is seeking partnerships with other organizations that would benefit from the rural areas having access to electricity.[29]

The company eventually aims to find a commercial and sustainable model for rural electrification that moves away from dependence on subsidies and grants, not a minor achievement with regard to Bottom of Pyramid (BoP) initiatives.

Besides possessing and configuring these key resources to support the company operations and build its competitive advantage, it is necessary to deploy the value chain that organizes and structures the various company activities. Far from exhaustively enumerating these activities in the SBMC, it is a matter of identifying those that most contribute to the company competitiveness, that is, those the company must uniquely control and master. These activities will obviously depend on the nature of the company. For a low-cost operator, excellence in operations management and the associated efficiency of operational processes are eminently strategic activities, because it is decisive in the capacity to maintain the lowest possible costs. Marketing is certainly necessary, but does not deserve a substantial budget. This explains, for example, why low-cost actors often use provocation to generate the maximum possible noise without having to put in the associated budget. By contrast, for companies possessing premium brands like Procter & Gamble, Danone or Unilever, marketing is a key activity because it builds the brand – a fundamental intangible resource – and frames the consumers' perceptions.

Skype, a software model versus an operator model

With a VoIP technological solution based on peer-to-peer, Skype entered the telecommunications market not with an operator model, but with a software model. And unlike traditional operators, Skype's value chain is far from cost savvy.

Offering a voice telephone service for a traditional operator involves a considerable infrastructure – lines, relay antennas, fiber network, servers, etc. – to create the value proposition. Therefore, all the activities of installation, management, maintenance and repair of the network are essential for the existence of the service, the network constituting a major physical resource. These activities mobilize a large staff and require significant financial resources to be deployed and managed. Similarly, in the highly competitive telecom market, the capacity to acquire and generate customer loyalty is essential.

Consequently, the already evoked distribution, marketing, sales force and communication are key activities, the brand becoming an intangible resource demanding constant investment. All these labor and capital-intensive activities weigh heavily on the cost structure of the traditional telecom operator.

The activities and key resources of Skype are quite different. They relate initially and above all to web and data-processing skills, the human resources (richness) and knowledge becoming crucial. The capacity to attract talented developers is thus central to perform cutting-edge R&D activities, the only lasting source of competitive advantage for the company. It is also necessary to have IT resources to ensure the service. These resources and activities obviously have a cost, which should not be underestimated. They are nevertheless far lower than the cost structure of a traditional operator.

If we look at Skype marketing and sales needs, they are almost inexistent, at least regarding the basic offer. The Skype model is in fact an example of a network model with positive externalities. The service as such has little value if you are the only one to use it. It gains in value as your friends, families and contacts join you on Skype. The viral effect is thus played to the full and, like Facebook, the development of the brand and its diffusion are carried out through buzz marketing. In comparison to the high investments in infrastructure, staff, marketing, sales force, communication and distribution of the traditional model, Skype has a lean value chain that is much less demanding in financial resources.

Key partnerships

A company is never alone in a market. On the contrary, it evolves within a business ecosystem nurturing relations and establishing strategic links to varying degrees. Managing these links and the interactions with different actors in an ecosystem is central to enable the company to advance toward its objectives.

Partnerships are potentially many and varied. Some fit naturally in the value chain of the company and are generally common to all the competitors in the same sector (mass-market retailers with fast-moving consumer goods companies, for example); others are more original and specific to certain companies. Sustainable development offers a particularly favorable ground for the amplification of this second type of partnerships, as we will see in the following chapters.

The motivation behind the decision to enter into a partnership is variable. In certain cases, the partnership falls under a traditional customer–supplier relation. Danone, for example, implements a partnership approach with its milk suppliers through the program "Danone and You," as does Sadia in Brazil[30] and other food production companies. These relations traditionally exist but can be leveraged and contributed to the innovation capacity, through co-development processes or installation of communities of practice for knowledge access and sharing.

The partnership can also find its origin in the will to access or develop new resources or activities. When Nestlé decided to launch Nestea, it partnered with Coca-Cola and they jointly created Beverage Partners Worldwide. In this win–win partnership, Nestlé brings its expertise and its value chain in the world of tea, whereas Coca-Cola places at the disposal its powerful world distribution network to make this brand a planetary success.

As we will see later on, this kind of partnership is particularly promising with regard to sustainable development, given its demand for skills and expertise. This is particularly true for SMEs or local governments that do not often have access to needed resources due to a lack of financial capacities. For instance, the partnership of DONG Energy and Novo Nordisk in Denmark enabled the latter to reduce its total global energy consumption by 21 percent between 2007 and 2011, while its sales grew 59 percent over the same period. Novo Nordisk then used these savings to purchase renewable energy certificates from DONG Energy, which were used to invest in the renewable wind farm project Horns Rev 2 that has a production capacity of 209 MW.[31]

In other cases, the motivation for the partnership may lie in the desire to pool expensive infrastructures, obtain economies of scale or reduce risks. Thus, Renault-Nissan, PSA Peugeot Citroën, Mitsubishi and various partners such as Schneider Electric have decided to form an alliance to develop a common technical reference of charging stations for electric vehicles: launched in 2010, the EV Ready® aims to become the recognized reference in the field of electric vehicle charging solutions. So far more than 60 European companies – ranging from energy providers, network operators, energy products manufacturers, installers of charging stations – are working together to facilitate the development and the diffusion of EV Ready®.[32]

Natura's Priprioca line development[33]

Natura is the Brazilian cosmetics market leader. Founded in 1969 by Antonio Luiz da Cunha Seabra, the company earned net revenues of US$5.59 billion (approximately US$3 billion) in 2011, with an EBITDA of US$1.42 billion (25.5 percent).[34] The company is now present in several Latin American markets and in France, with more than 90 percent of its turnover coming from Brazil.

The company adopted early in its life direct sales as its sales approach and at the end of 2011 had a sales force of nearly 250,000 consultants in its international operations and an impressive 1.175 million in Brazil.[35] This means that wherever you go in Brazil, it is likely that you will find a Natura sales rep to offer you their products.

Another distinctive trait of the company is its commitment to sustainable development as stated in the company policy: "Natura believes that a company's values and longevity can be measured by its ability to promote sustainable development of society."[36] The company has carefully studied the Brazilian biodiversity to create unique product lines in its Ekos line.

A textbook case[37] is the development of the Open Value Chain for the development of the Priprioca product line. Priprioca is a common Brazilian plant from the Amazon region with a bulb that releases a perfume when it is cut or pressed.

The value chain included the Priprioca producing local communities in the northern state of Para in Brazil, Beraca Brasmazon for processing the plant and producing the oil, Givaudan for carrying out the secondary processing, and then Natura for buying the refined essences from Givaudan. Natura had to structure all this value chain from scratch and work with stakeholders like local and regional government, the national environmental agency IBAMA and the agricultural supporting agency EMATER to make this project come true.

One business model choice should be highlighted in building its success: transparency. The assurance that "All partners knew the costs throughout the product development stages, and fair payment for work"[38] was given and this was true along the process:

> Communities incur costs, such as labor, raw materials and natural fertilizers. When the weight of each cost component was clear, it was possible to recalculate the total cost and renegotiate a new value distribution among the parties.[39]

Natura has indeed an active policy for sharing benefits issued from the Sustainable Use of Biodiversity and

Traditional Knowledge and this constitutes the first section of its Sustainable Development Policy. Besides Priprioca it had launched several other products based on the Brazilian biodiversity such as mate, pitanga, cocoa, buriti, cupuaçu, andiroba, breu branco and Amazon nuts.[40]

Recognition and awards for this innovative approach are legion: it has been elected for the last decade as the most admired Brazilian company, the best place to work and among the world's most innovative companies.[41]

Being at the core of the value-creation and value-distribution processes and affecting value capture, partnerships must be integrated into the business model.

The cost structure and revenue streams

The value architecture, and more specifically the value-chain organization and gathering the required resources, will lead to a certain cost structure that has to be at least offset by revenue streams. The dynamic character of the business model canvas shows its full reach here, because the choice of key activities, key resources, distribution channels, ways of managing customer relationships and partnership management will directly affect the cost structure depending on their scale and configuration. Moreover, cost-structure assessment can be an innovation source, for example, by transforming a fixed cost into a variable one for the customers, making the offer more attractive commercially. Thus, when Michelin decided to develop the Michelin Fleet Solutions offer for Fleet Operators,[42] it is no longer selling pneumatic tires, but an outsourced service of pneumatic management invoiced by distance travelled. In fact, this offer allows operators to convert a fixed cost (the purchase of pneumatic tires) in a variable cost dependent on the volume of activities. This is a strong asset in a trade negotiation.

If it is possible innovating the cost structure, it is even more possible to innovate revenue streams. Over and above the simple sale of an asset in exchange of a payment, there exist many other mechanisms to build revenue streams. For example[43]:

- Usage fee: while this kind of pricing is widely used in some industry sectors, like telephony for example, it can be a real change for others. The example of Michelin is representative of "pay as you drive insurance" that was first launched in the US, UK and Australia;

- Subscription fee;

- Lending/renting/leasing: as we will see in Chapter 5, offer alternatives for new businesses models in particular with regards to sustainable development;

- Licensing: aiming to monetize the use of intellectual property (like a patent) or the use of a trademark;

- Brokerage fees: to remunerate an intermediation activity. New collaborative consumption platforms like AirBnB,[44] a community marketplace for unique event or meeting spaces, generally function on this model;

- Success fees: remunerate the provider on its capacity to reach an agreed service level. Chapter 6 will present offers based on a contractually stipulated environmental service level. The capacity to reach this level will define the income generated. Failure to reach the level will generate penalties, while any level beyond is rewarded;

- Advertising is largely present on the Internet, as much as it is the main source of revenue for the free press, for example.

It is certainly possible to combine several approaches in the same value proposition. Spotify, for example, is a legal music platform offering three levels of sophistication in its value proposition. A basic version offers free music listening from a catalog of several million titles for a limited amount of time. The associated revenue model is the advertising model, since the listener can avoid payment for the service in exchange for listening to some adverts. Part of the revenue is used to compensate copyright holders (i.e. the major record labels), the remainder going to the company. Two types of paid subscriptions are offered, both advertising-free, with varying levels of service offered to music lovers.

How does Skype earn money?

As already described, Skype innovated in a sector dominated by the telecom operator model. By proposing free voice communication, Skype made an appealing offer for millions of users to download and use its service. But how does it earn money in a free model? By proposing other paid offers, like Spotify, and by building a business model substantially different from traditional operators.

For instance, this traditional model is based on a high-cost structure, dependent on the value-architecture configuration: an expensive multichannel distribution network, varied methods of management of the client relationship (for some labor-intensive), high capital-demanding key activities and key resources – just consider network installation, management and maintenance. This fixed cost must be absorbed by a large client base, but one that is inferior to that of Skype. The guiding pricing mechanism is the maximization of earnings per customer. This often resulted in high communication fees and high marketing expenditures.

The structuring principle of Skype revenue streams is at odds with this. Having a customer base of a hundred million users,[45] a lean value architecture and consequently a reduced cost structure, the company is able to capture value from a small base of users seeking enhanced services. This is made through certain premium offers. For individual users, Skype sells credit for telephone calls to landline or mobile numbers at competitive prices compared to those charged by traditional operators (offers such as Pay As You Go, Subscriptions and Premium). Skype Premium offers an array of services like group video calling, group screen sharing, live chat customer support and unlimited calls to some countries. These features are increasingly being targeted at workers at home (Home Office), small and medium businesses responding to needs of telecommunications cost reduction, easier collaboration and global reach.

Thus, the company announced a turnover of US$800 million in 2010.[46] This success must, however, be put into perspective, as, in the same year, the company posted a net loss of US$7 million. But the repurchase in May 2011 of Skype by Microsoft, for a record amount of US$8.5 billion, is expected to make the model profitable, due to the many synergies with the Office Suite or Xbox LIVE. Premium offers have indeed been boosted since the Microsoft acquisition and synergies seem to be working with 2011 first quarter revenues of US$406 million, up by 24 percent.[47]

From the bottom line to the triple bottom line

In its traditional version, the business model canvas focuses exclusively on the company's bottom line, that is, the last line of the income statement, a sort of Holy Grail supposed to resume in a single number the total performance of a company. It is, however, desirable (and will soon be mandatory) to widen the frame of value creation by looking beyond just the financial value, to integrate the environmental and social value. In so doing, and remembering the dynamic principle of construction and interdependence that characterizes the business model components, it would be possible to identify powerful synergies among the environmental, social and financial performances. This interdependence that we strive to highlight in the business model simply mirrors the natural interdependence of our human and environmental systems; the economic activity cannot be separated from the natural environment and the social fabric in which it is grounded. An economic crisis results in a social crisis that amplifies economic impacts. An economic development generates an environmental cost that generally has economic or social impacts (e.g. the generalization of pesticides and insecticides used to increase the productivity of the crops increases the mortality of bees in some agricultural areas. This reduction of bees impacts the natural pollination that in turn calls for either the need to pollinate manually (very expensive) or to pay a beekeeper to install temporarily hives near the crops). This elementary principle of system interdependence has not yet been translated in corporate accountancy, the environmental and social costs still being largely considered as externalities and thus taken into account in the construction of the income statement. In its defense, it should be admitted that these externalities are complex to understand, measure and evaluate, and that a company decision can have macro consequences that far exceed its scope and do not affect it directly.[48]

For instance, when Amazon.com enters a market and, due to its economies of scale, offers free shipping for several of its products, it creates value for its clients. Its impact on traditional retailing is, however, substantial, resulting in job losses in certain sectors. We could hope this would be balanced by job creation in logistics and at Amazon itself. Even if this is the case, the consequences for many communities who are slowly seeing their retail activities fade are real but cannot be taken into account by Amazon.

We therefore propose a sustainability check that incorporates four building blocks: cost for society and environment; shared costs/sustainable cost killing; benefits for society and environment; and core shared value-creation opportunity/shared benefits.

These four additional blocks may be related to positive and negative social and environmental externalities any business activities may generate. These externalities refer to situations when the effect of production or consumption of goods and services imposes costs or benefits on others that are not reflected in the prices charged for the goods and services being provided (OECD dictionary).

Externalities may be positive or negative and may concern both environmental and social aspects. Pollution is an example of negative environmental externality that may generate a negative one on health (social). Contributing to a biodiversity restoration (positive environmental externality) may help medicine to find new molecules in, for example, cancer treatment (positive social one).

The two last blocks of the SBMC aim to integrate these externalities on the business model but are expanded to the notion of benefits and costs for society and the environment.

Cost for society and environment

Among the negative impacts that may be generated by business activities, some will generate costs that are not supported by the company while others may impact the cost structure of a company. This business block refers to the former and any relevant negative impact toward its stakeholders and the environment will be reported, for instance:

- Biodiversity damages

- GHG emissions

- Perturbations to its neighboring communities

- Negative impact on health

Shared costs

Some of the social and environmental negative impacts can also represent a financial burden for the company. In this case, the company is actually destroying value creation for itself (affecting its balance sheet) and its stakeholders. Therefore, the interest to face those impacts is sizeable. Shared cost could possibly be

- Energy consumption

- Lack of projects' social acceptance causing delays (opportunity costs)

- Expensive raw material made up of finite resources (e.g. rare earth materials)

Benefits for society and environment

Business activities may also generate socially and/or environmentally positive impacts. By providing the society with social and environmental benefits through its operations, the company increases its social legitimacy and enhances its clout. A lower footprint than the sector's standards can be understood as a social or environmental benefit. Benefits for society and the environment could be

- The contribution to the restoration of the biodiversity

- Positive impact on health of local population

- Stimulation of local employment

Shared benefits

A fully sustainable organization pursues its economic interests and aligns them with stakeholders' expectations and future generations' needs by taking into account social and environmental issues.

Therefore, the share benefits block presents elements characterizing this alignment between the company and society/environment. For instance, the shared benefits could be

- Saving costs by reducing the amount of raw materials used in the operation

- Relying on free ecological services as an activity contributing to the delivery of the value proposition

- Increasing the spaces of differentiation and contributing to enhance a positive image

The innovative social business model of Danone Grameen Food Ltd exemplifies these four building blocks. The company is a

Table 2.2 *Sustainable business model canvas of Danone Grameen Food Ltd*

Costs for Society and the Environment	Key Partners	Key Activities	Sustainable Value Proposition	Customer Relationship Management	Customers Segments	Benefits for Society and the Environment
• Downstream; upstream environmental externalities of the economic activities (like cattle breeding, milk production, distribution and transport, store/ shop facilities, etc. • Environmental negative externalities related to the operations Even if a true effort is achieved on eco-efficiency, the operations generate environmental impacts leaving room for improvement	**Financial partners** • Grameen Bank • Danone Communities **Expertise partners/ resources sharing** • Danone communities • Grameen Bank (micro-lending and distribution) • GAIN NGO (Global Alliances for Global Nutrition) – support for the development of a relevant product for the BoP (e.g. in terms of nutritional properties) • Care NGO (assistance to develop the local ecosystem of partners)	**R&D** • Simplifying the formula without losing quality **Sourcing** • Supply at the local cost among 500 local producers supported by the Grameen Bank • Training of farmers and services from veterinary to improve milk quality • Quality control, traceability verification and negotiation of the milk price **Production** • Simple production processes to avoid skilled labor (cost of the microfactory: €700,000, 50 to 100 times smaller than a conventional plant) • Production and storage **Distribution** • One of the most challenging issue in countries with poor or no infrastructure **Market education** • Proximity marketing (communication during social and religious events, opinion leaders in the villages, etc.) • Development of educational material for illiterate people • Training of Grameen Ladies	Daily intake of essential nutrients (30% – vitamin A, iron, zinc and iodine) primary for growing children with a yogurt at very low price (5 takas = 6 euro cents)	A multidimensional customer relationship management related to the channel used: • (Dedicated) personal assistance • Community relationships • Self-service in stores	The bottom of the pyramid: • Very poor and rural population • Very poor people of small urban cities • Very poor people of big cities First geographical scope: Bangladesh; Bogra District Type of customers: • Primary audience: malnourished children and old people • Secondary audience: other children, adolescents, adults	• Improved nutrition for poor people (with indirect impact such as concentration of children for education) • Development of local activities generating employment with direct benefits, like an improved revenue, and indirect impacts, like a better access to consumption, potential improvement of infrastructure and so on • Eco-friendly factory • Biodegradable packaging allowing to avoid solving a problem (food provision) by generating a new one (waste generation)

Key Resources

Physical resources
- Eco-friendly micro-factory with a low operating cost
  - Lines of production simplified at a maximum level
  - Biodegradable packaging
  - Rationalization of energy (renewable) and recovery of rain water (monsoon)
  - Transport using few fossil fuels (rickshaw vans)
- Points of sales (8,000 in 2010)
- Communication supports on nutritional benefits of the yogurt

Intangibles
- Combined expertise of Danone, Grameen Bank, GAIN and CARE

Human (coming mainly from Bogra district)
- Milk and molasses dates suppliers (supported financially through the Grameen Bank micro-credit)
- Managers and employees of the micro-factory
- Rickshaw van sellers, supplying retail outlets located within 5 km of the plant
- Distribution center managers, supplying Grameen ladies
- Grameen ladies, door-to-door sellers of yogurt (supported financially through the Grameen Bank micro-credit)

Financial
- Equity from initial shareholders (Danone and Grameen Bank)
- The Danone communities fund – Danone communities is a "social businesses network." Its mission is to fund and develop local businesses with a sustainable economic model, oriented toward social goals: reducing poverty and malnutrition. Alongside social entrepreneurs, this support goes through both investments via a SICAV general public but also by a technical support through a network of committed experts who convey their experiences.

Distribution Channels

A complex supply chain based on
- Door to door selling (rural)
- Partner stores (cities)
- Shops (cities)

(see Figure 2.1 for the supply chain)

(continued)

Table 2.2 *Continued*

Shared Costs	Cost Structure	Revenue Streams	Shared Benefits
Costs associated with the impacts related to the operations (energy consumption, raw materials consumption, etc.)	In 2013 – Break-even will be reached • Variable costs = 636,803 Tk • Fixed costs = 206,913 Tk Profit: 40,130 Tk	2013 Revenue = 883,846 Tk (= 9,600 tons of yogurt)	• Development of local activities (a reliable local supply chain and quality control) • Provision of local employment, resulting in improved purchasing power with a potential for range extension toward more valuable products • Production of new knowledge and fostering of innovation: simplification of formula, simplification of production processes, eco-friendly factory, biodegradable packaging are clear outputs of this societal innovation that may potentially benefit the whole group in case of reverse innovation

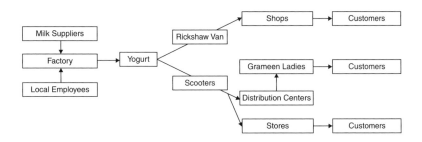

Figure 2.1 *The supply chain of Danone Grameen Food*

joint venture between the Grameen Group and Danone created in March 2006 with a mission to reduce poverty by providing health through nutritive food (dairy products) and develop an economic model of proximity to create jobs while being environment friendly. Its goal is to develop an affordable yogurt to the poorest people by generating financial and nonfinancial value. Key performance indicators (KPI) include: number of direct and indirect jobs created (producers of milk, small wholesalers, door-to-door sellers), improving the health of the children and protecting the environment, among others.

Detailed information on this project can be found in the Danone corporate web site and on the Web.[49] We focus here on the four building blocks consisting the sustainability check of the business model.

CONCLUSION

This chapter has described a powerful concept and strategic tool: the business model and the sustainable business model canvas. This tool is certainly useful for a better understanding of the processes of value creation, distribution and capture for a company, but it is pivotal to empower the innovation process. In this respect, sustainable development appears to be a particularly suitable framework to reconsider the business model and to align environmental, social and economic performances. In the hyper competitive market of the coming years, innovation is a necessary, if not the only driver of sustained competitive advantage.

We are obviously conscious that decisions about the business model are highly strategic, and two situations need to be distinguished. The entrepreneur has the advantage of starting from scratch, and we invite them to seize this tool and the advice given in the following chapters to configure a unique business model to generate real holistic performance. The other case is that of an established company with secured incomes from its traditional business model. Change here is more delicate. Nevertheless, worldwide competition and evolving regulations constantly challenge this position. In this case, we advise company leaders to experiment with new business models in parallel with their existing business model, in a business unit or by creating spin-offs, as BASF or Philips have done (see Chapter 6). More and more organizations support intrapreneurial behaviors and projects. Business model innovation shall be encouraged and implemented in such projects.

The remaining chapters of this book will make substantial use of the SBMC to identify innovations enabled by embracing sustainable development, be they minor business model modifications or truly radical innovations.

3

Eco-Efficiency and Eco-Design – A First Step toward Sustainable Performance

Do you know how many liters of water are necessary to produce 1 kg of beefsteak? And a 250 ml glass of wine? And half a kilogram of bread? And a pack of 500 sheets of paper?

The water footprint of a 1 kg beefsteak is approximately 15,000 liters; a glass of wine, 120 liters; the bread, 800 liters; while the pack of paper uses 5,000 liters of "blue gold."[1] You are probably skeptical.

To produce a 1 kg beefsteak, a cow eats more than one ton of cereal and seven tons of grass, which will have needed irrigation and rainwater, for around three years; similarly, the cow will have drunk more than 24 m^3 of water, not counting the water needed for the maintenance and cleaning of the cattle shed and equipment. The same reasoning is used to calculate the water footprint of the bread, the wine or paper. These simple examples show the extraordinary quantity of resources hidden in each product or service that we use in our daily life.

In the first chapter we highlighted the growing importance for a company to manage its resources more efficiently, particularly in terms of energy and raw materials, in order to safeguard its competitiveness and to reinforce its innovation capability. When hidden resources are integrated into the reasoning, the challenge becomes greater.

There are several ways to use resources more efficiently, as we will show hereafter. Eco-efficiency is the first step to a broader change. This chapter will first of all explain what is meant by eco-efficiency and eco-design, what are their guiding principles and the best ways to deploy them. It will then highlight the impact of eco-design on the company business model, based on the *sustainable business model canvas* presented in the previous chapter. We do not intend to present the operational steps of eco-design implementation, but rather understand its strategic reach.

WHAT ARE ECO-EFFICIENCY AND ECO-DESIGN?

Broadly speaking, for companies, eco-efficiency means doing better with fewer resources. Taking the previous example of water consumption, eco-efficiency invites companies to reconsider their modes of production in order to drastically reduce the resources needed to achieve the same result. For the wine producer, for example, this would mean rationalizing the use of water in the vineyard by replacing a sprinkler irrigation system (40 to 50 percent efficiency) with a system of drip irrigation (90 to 95 percent efficiency) supplied with circuits for rainwater recovery and wastewater treatment. An industrial example, concerning the manufacture of Levi's jeans, is presented later in this chapter.

Obviously, resource use efficiency is not limited to the use of water. For the World Business Council for Sustainable Development,[2] eco-efficiency refers to the effectiveness with which natural resources (mineral, energy and biological) are used by the industrial systems of production and consumption to meet human beings' needs, at competitive prices, while reducing environmental consequences. It aims to gradually reduce the environmental impact and the quantity of the natural resources used throughout the life cycle of products and services, in order to reach a level in harmony with the earth's capacity for self-renewal.

The Water<Less program of Levi's[3]

Levi's jeans is a major textile brand with its iconic 501 model. The company was created in 1853 by Levi Strauss and has been consistently responsible and recognized as such, both in the United States and abroad. Sustainable development is a core value of the company's strategy, and product and services development. The company also seeks to encourage better practices among its consumers.

The Water<Less program is one of its achievements. The textile industry is known for its heavy water footprint, from the cotton production through to the manufacture of the final article. Levi Strauss Co. was the first company in the sector to address this issue, establishing in 1992 guidelines for the good use of water, for both itself and for its suppliers, in particular by controlling the amount of effluents in wastewater produced during the manufacturing process. In 2007, the company ordered a study on the resource consumption of the whole lifecycle of the Levi's 501 jeans, from the cotton plantation to the end-of-life of the product. This study showed that 55 percent of the water consumption was connected to the Levi supply chain with the remaining 45 percent linked to the laundry of the jeans after purchase. During the complete lifecycle of a pair of jeans, more than 3,000 liters of water are used. Taking as their motto that what is not measured cannot be improved, Levi Strauss and Co. has been systematically tracking the water consumption of its own operations since 2008, extending this to its suppliers in 2009.

The results of this water monitoring encouraged the company to reduce its water footprint in two areas: in its supply chain, particularly by participating actively in the Better Cotton Initiative, and among consumers, by creating initiatives for more efficient water use. Efforts made in R&D and in reviewing the manufacturing processes and upstream cotton production paid off. By 2011, the company had achieved average water savings of 28 percent compared to the initial benchmark, with up to 96 percent water savings on certain models. This represented a saving of more than 16 million liters of water during spring 2011 alone, with even more ambitious savings forecast as new water recovery and recycling extensions are being explored. All these savings were achieved without affecting the aesthetic and functional qualities of the jeans.

In parallel with its own efforts during the manufacturing stage, Levi's launched a vast program of incentives to encourage more eco-efficient behaviors on the part of its consumers in partnership with Goodwill International Industries – a network of 165 independent community-based agencies offering job training, employment placement and other services to people who have disabilities, lack education or job experience, or face relocation difficulties. This program invites consumers to use only cold water when washing their jeans, to limit washing to once per week rather than the usual twice per week, and to donate the jeans to Goodwill for recycling at the end of their life. Combined with Levi's internal efforts, this would result in annual savings of 858.4 million liters of water. This double approach, both internal and external, gives the Water<Less program a powerful reach, allowing substantial savings of such a valuable resource as water.

The eco-efficiency principle naturally applies to both products and services. It can also apply to the process and the whole of a company's activities. Dior, for example, was able to reduce its energy consumption by almost 48 percent per ton of perfume produced between 2000 and 2003 by reengineering its production processes.[4] Osklen, a Brazilian fashion company labeled by WWF-UK as a future maker,[5] revised its full supply chain to assess its carbon footprint and is currently able to measure emissions for several items of its product line. It has also become carbon neutral for its retailing and headquarters operations; and its assessment methods are currently being benchmarked by Italian fashion companies.[6] The French postal services group La Poste has deployed an ambitious eco-driving training program for the 60,000 workers driving its fleet of 42,000 vehicles.[7] This training enabled a first-year saving of five million liters of fuel, 10,000 tons of CO_2 (a 15 percent reduction) and a 10 percent decrease in car accidents.

Applying eco-efficiency thus encourages a reconsideration of the design of a product, a service or a process in order to decrease its environmental impact. This application is better known as eco-design.

ECO-DESIGN SPECIFICATIONS

For "hardliners" or the "orthodox", eco-design should begin upstream to the product conception with a question about the raison d'être of the project and its intrinsic legitimacy. This question is far from being anecdotal in the search for value creation, given the possibilities for differentiation discussed in Chapter 1. A company or a brand seeking to increase its uniqueness with an eco-design approach must seriously analyze its perceived credibility and legitimacy to adopt such an approach. If not, it risks being labeled as yet another company trying to "greenwash" its operations, with regretful consequences for the brand image.

Beyond this initial questioning, the eco-design approach is based on a number of specifications. An eco-designed product must[8]:

- Be adapted to its use, form following function: The design should be at the service of the function of the object in order to improve usability and use efficiency. For example, in 2011 Unilever introduced a new design for the Vaseline Petroleum Jelly jar that reduced the amount of plastic by three percent, saving about 113 tons of resin a year. By using polypropylene, the pack has become more recyclable, needing less energy to be produced, saving 13,000 MW a year. Consumers also appreciated the change: the packs are more visually appealing and easier to open.[9]

- Reduce the material intensity and minimize the use of non-renewable resources (raw materials and energy): When the cognac brand Hennessy, part of the LVMH group, redesigned its bottle to make it more environment friendly, it reduced its glass content by 23 percent (making annual savings of 715 tons of glass), replaced the stopper, formerly made of tin, with one made of beech from a sustainably managed forest (Forest Stewardship Council label) thus saving 30 tons of tin, labeled the glass using enamels without ink or glue or paper and used FSC certified packaging, bleached without chlorine.[10]

Another interesting business case is that of the cosmetics company Lush with its solid shampoo bar, as described next.

Lush beautiful environmental commitment

Lush is a niche player in the cosmetic industry when compared with the likes of L'Oreal, Procter & Gamble, Shiseido or Amore Pacific. But the quality of its products, its great customer service, original communication and interactions with clients, and consistency in respecting its core values has allowed it to build a unique market position for the company. Among the core values is a firm commitment to a policy against testing products and ingredients on animals that prevents the company from operating in (huge) markets like China.

Environmental concerns are central to the company and have led to the creation of the first-ever solid shampoo bar. Lush's environmental policy is applied to:[11]

– Packaging: Half of the company's products can be taken home with no packaging, saving six million plastic bottles, just from selling shampoo bars; 90 percent by weight of the packaging material is recycled; Lush encourages clients to return the "black pots" in exchange for a free product (five pots for a face mask). The company has also pioneered disclosing its plastic usage under the Plastic Disclosure Project.[12]

- Waste and recycling: "All organic waste at the UK factory is sent for composting, plastic gets recycled in the UK and our wood waste gets burned in our biomass boiler. We also donate any products which are fit for use, but not for sale to charities."[13] The company has an aggressive policy to reduce waste at the shops. Cribbs Causeway shop, for example, was accredited by the SKA standard assessment method in 2012 for the store's refit and environmental impact.[14]

- Transport: With its operations in 46 countries, Lush acknowledges that transport is its biggest contribution to climate change.[15] To tackle this, the company "has reduced the amount of air-freighted raw material to less than five percent in weight of everything [they] bring into the UK and will keep that as [their] target;" they also work with the partners on this issue. Moreover, the company localizes its production with several manufacturing plants around the world, and tries to minimize air travelling as much as it can.

- Raw materials: The company has stopped using palm oil in their soaps, all the products are biodegradable and compost easily; over 70 percent of Lush's product range is totally preservative free and the company aims to improve this.

- Water: Solid shampoo bars save 450,000 liters of water per year in their production.

Other developments are being pushed regarding energy and reporting. Recognition for this environmental commitment abounds for Lush, one of the most recent being the "National Recycling Awards 2012" for its joint venture with Remploy.[16]

The company turnover in the 2010/2011 fiscal year was nearly £215 million with profits of almost £14 million.[17]

- Reduce the energy intensity: Philips LED lamps for instance consume less electricity, at equivalent luminosity, a much longer lifespan and lifetime.[18] At Legrand group, specialists in electrical and digital building infrastructures, intrusion alarms, fire alarms and the autonomous safety lighting have all been redesigned. Thanks to a life cycle analysis (LCA), the company was able to identify that the main impact of these products was their energy consumption. By applying eco-design principles to R&D, this consumption was divided by two for safety lighting with the lifecycle of tubes multiplied by 20, while for alarms, energy consumption was divided by four, and the lifecycle of accumulators increased fourfold. Efforts to reduce the quantity of materials used per product resulted in savings of between 10 and 60 percent of total product mass, bringing a total reduction of the environmental impact from 35 to 50 percent across the whole of the indicators.

- Minimize the toxic components or replace them whenever possible: The European Ecolabel certifies, for example, that labeled paint limits air pollution by solvents, reduces the sulfur emissions during its production, reduces dangerous wastes resulting from the production of titanium dioxide, and is deprived of heavy metals and hazardous substances for the environment and human health. The ZDHC[19] initiative, championed by apparel and footwear giants Adidas Group, C&A, H&M, Li Ning, NIKE Inc. and Puma, aims to lead the apparel and footwear industry toward zero discharge of hazardous chemicals[20] for all products across all pathways in their supply chains by 2020.

- Be reliable and useful, and designed to last: Eco-design breaks with the logic of planned obsolescence, a planned and controlled process which limits the useful life of a product, making it obsolete before the end of its possible technological lifetime. Widely used in a large number of industrial sectors, planned obsolescence is exemplified by a printer that is set up at manufacturing to print a maximum number of copies by an internal counter system. Once this limit it reached, the printer will display an error message and block the machine.[21] Given the prices of new printers and reparation costs, the "logical" choice for most end users is to purchase a new printer and discard the "old" one. Moving from planned obsolescence logic requires a major change for economic models based on volumes of goods sold. By lengthening the lifetime of a product, the company is likely to be deprived of or to delay revenue streams from the replacement market, thus being penalized economically. Chapters 5 and 6 present alternative economic models to the concept of planned obsolescence and allow the full expression of eco-design, like Michelin that has multiplied by 2.5 the lifetime of its tires by adopting an alternative business model.

- Be easy to maintain, repair and support recyclability: In the continuity of the preceding principle, an eco-designed product must be able to be repaired easily, in particular by allowing the replacement of the single flawed piece. Apple's iPod, for instance, was overtly criticized for its sealed battery in its first, second and third product generations. Due to the impossibility of battery replacement, the product lifetime was 18 months maximum. Consequently, the iconic Californian firm was condemned and forced to allow its replacement by redesigning the product and to provide an extended warranty of two years. This exemplifies the legal risk of such practices.[22]

- Minimize its environmental impact on the whole life cycle: Eco-design imposes an analysis of the environmental impact of the product over its whole life cycle, from the extraction of raw materials to the end of its useful life, through all the stages of the supply chain, manufacturing, distribution and use of the product. The objective is to prevent a transfer of pollution between various phases of the life cycle. For example, let's take the example of paint A which is evaluated without taking the principles of LCA into account and compare it with paint B. Let's assume paint A presents half the amount of consumption and a rejection of toxic inputs compared to that of paint B.[23] Intuitively, we would be led to believe that paint A offers better environmental standards. Imagine now that paint A covers only half the surface area compared to paint B, so to paint one m², it is necessary to apply twice as much of paint A than paint B. Let's also suppose that the lifetime of paint A is half as long as that of paint B. Consequently, paint A would be half as efficient as paint B in terms of consumption and toxic substance rejection. This example illustrates the transfer of pollution between the phase of design of the product and its phase of use. Similarly, the redesign of paints could make it possible to use half as much water, but if lower quality means that the wall has to be washed three times more often, the gain is transformed into a loss. This is why any comparison of eco-design with a traditional alternative is based on the functional unit, which does not refer to a quantity of goods given but rather to the rendered service. Thus, in our paint example, the functional unit, the standard of the evaluation for a measurement of the real environmental gains, would, for example, be defined as the capacity to cover one m² with an opacity rate of 98 percent for a ten-year period.

For these specifications to be respected, any eco design project must comply with the codified and normalized ISO or European Ecolabel processes.

Ben & Jerry's and the sweet flavor of sustainability[24]

Besides making delicious ice creams and delighting its owners, Ben & Jerry's ice cream-making company has a strong engagement to environmental and social issues. Its social mission states three major goals: use the company to create equal and sustainable economic opportunities, make ice cream with minimum negative impact on the environment, and take the lead in promoting global and sustainable dairy practices.

Under the first goal, the company is moving to buy all its commodities from Fair Trade initiatives to have a positive impact on farmer livelihoods. This is already the case in Europe and it is being currently implemented in the United States. Other actions on this path are help for Fair Trade Universities and towns, Peace partnerships and the Scoop Shop Community Action.

Of more interest in this chapter are the actions related to the second goal. In Europe, the company has been using certified cage-free eggs for its cream-base since 2005. This now the case for 99 percent of the eggs used in the US and Asia. The company has made significant eco-design efforts in sustainable packaging. Since 2009, all US pint containers have used certified paperboards by the Forest Stewardship Council (FSC).[25] Moreover, boxes used for ice creams bars in the US are made from 100 percent post-consumer recycled paperboard. In their Vermont manufacturing plants, the company has invested "in energy-efficient technology from cooling systems to lighting, to water and waste management systems. With an eye toward closing loops in their supply chain, they now send dairy waste from the Vermont plants back to two of the farms that supply the company with fresh dairy ingredients. Their waste is put into methane digesters with other farm waste – where it generates energy to power the farm"[26] (more on that in the coming chapter). The company has also achieved "Climate Neutral" status in Europe according to the standards of HIER.[27] Another move is the use of hydrocarbon freezers that are more energy efficient and use gases with lower global warming potential than standard freezers, which use hydro fluorocarbons (HFC).

The third goal stands for sustainable dairy practices to help push farmers and suppliers in this direction under the Caring Dairy™ program. Two-thirds of the milk in the US, and up to 90 percent of that in Europe comes from certified farmers. In the United States, the company also stands against the use of recombinant bovine growth hormone (rBGH), a genetically engineered hormone given to cows to increase their milk production.

Ben & Jerry's thus represents a remarkable company in an agro-industry sector with an impressive footprint as our starting examples in this chapter showed.

IMPACT OF ECO-EFFICIENCY ON THE SUSTAINABLE BUSINESS MODEL CANVAS[28]

Even if it does not fundamentally challenge a company business model or the nature of its economic model, eco-design principles have a considerable impact on the SBMC. We examine hereafter the impact of the redesign of an existing product on the canvas components (knowing that these impacts are similar in the case of an eco-design project related to a new product, service, process or activity of a company).

We will present, step-by-step, the implementation method of an eco-design project as well as the impacts on the various components of the SBMC. The main effects of the canvas will be summarized at the end of the chapter.

First question: Who pilots the project?

A project without a pilot is like a boat without a captain. It risks drifting or being running aground. It is thus advisable to assemble a team in charge of the eco-design project within the company (demanding new human, financial and intangible resources in the SBMC).

In such a project, it is worth bringing together multiple skills, even in a small company. Ideally, a minimum of four profiles should be part of the team: R&D/product innovation, operations/manufacture, marketing/sales and environmental management (if that profile exists).

Marketing is particularly important because it represents the interface between the product and its markets, and tries to understand how value can be created from the beginning of the project. At certain stages, finance people will have to be associated with the team. It is important to bring together open-minded, curious people who are *problem-solvers*. Moreover, full support from the top management is essential because the project will reassess the company value proposition and will demand financial investments. The project group must thus be entitled to take decisions that will engage the company. This is the case for any innovation project, but is even more central here.[29]

Often competences and expertise necessary to an eco-design project are not fully available in-house, especially on technical dimensions (e.g. carrying out an LCA). It is therefore advisable to call on external experts (new partnerships). Several financial or technical aids are available to help companies bring together the necessary competences. The United Nations D4S (Design for Sustainability) program provides tools and materials in several languages. Several countries have their local environmental agency: the Environmental Protection Agency[30] in the USA, the Environment Agency[31] in the UK, ADEME (Agency of the Environment and Energy Control) in France, the Environmental and Industry Governmental Ministries in Brazil, and so on.

An overview of the possible aids should be carried out (new activity). Thus, a company with limited financial and human means can innovate by establishing new partnership and creative value-creation approaches without inevitably mobilizing important means.

Second question: Where to carry the eco-design effort?

We focus here in the eco-design of an existing product. The resulting question is which product should be chosen.

The selection of the product is based primarily on the expected objectives of the eco-design project. The pursued goals can concern internal and/or external factors:

- Internal factors: Reasons include seeking cost reduction by better efficiency in energy and material use, a reduction in dependence on a critical raw material by reduced use or substitution, a facilitation of the re-localization of part of the production by the development of an added-value (see the example of Sullair next), abandoning a toxic component generating health risks for staff or concerned by new regulatory measurements.

- External factors: Reasons are potentially numerous, such as the search for marketing enhancement aimed at increasing differentiation or the perceived value by the customer, filling requirements for a market demanding certain environmental criteria (e.g. more and more public procurement contracts integrate environmental and/or social clauses in their call for tenders with minimal thresholds to respect), answering new regulations or anticipating future measurements, responding to competitive pressure or movement at the industry level.

It is obviously important to connect these objectives to the main strategic orientations of the company, the eco-design project taking a much richer course if it is directly attached to the strategy of the company or one of its brands.

Sullair, a successful relocation thanks to the eco-design[32]

Sullair Europe is a company specialized in the production of air compressors and pneumatic tools for the building and infrastructure industry. Based in France, it made the unusual decision in 2005 to relocate in France part of its production of compressors previously outsourced in China.

Given that the cost of labor in France was 17 times higher than that of China, there was no question of assembling the same compressors. On the contrary, the company had to evaluate the product in depth to simplify it and enhance its added-value. That was done by an eco-design process. The first goal was to reduce the production costs through a more intelligent design. To do this, the management of the machine throughout its lifetime was studied. Five goals guided the process: to reduce toxic raw materials and components, to facilitate manufacturing processes, to improve the use of the machine, to facilitate its maintenance, and to improve the product recyclability once at the end of the lifetime.

The choice of materials was completely re-examined, to support the integration of recycled or recyclable components, and to minimize or remove potentially dangerous components. Thus the engine block and oil filters no longer contain mercury; screws and bolts are covered with a chromium-free coating; plastic substances contain neither mercury nor polybrominated biphenyls (PBBs) or polybrominated diphenyl ethers (PBDEs). Paints used contain no CMR chemicals (carcinogenic, mutagenic and reprotoxic). Insulating foams are now recyclable and are encased in the doors via a new time-saving process without using glue. As a whole, assembly was simplified, facilitating not only assembly but also maintenance through easier access to the critical components. The machines are now made with up to 20 to 30 percent of recycled materials, up to 94 percent of which can be recycled in turn. Their electricity consumption was reduced by 20 percent for the first generations of machines (savings increasing to 36 percent for the following generations). Thanks to a more astute assembly, the noise, the vibrations and the pollutant emissions of the machines were halved, and thus made more comfortable to use. A system of tank oil recovery makes it possible to avoid any contamination of the grounds, even in the case of leakage. The design of the machine is such that it no longer needs to be packaged, resulting in economic and environmental savings.

Thanks to all these efforts, the machine is currently assembled in seven days, compared to the 32 days needed in China. Quality processes are completely controlled and manufacturing costs of the compressor dropped by 10 percent, in spite of the higher labor overheads. The machine is qualitatively better and has unique characteristics in terms of performance, increasing the product differentiation and its added-value for the customers. The delivery period was reduced from five months to six weeks, generating a better customer satisfaction and a faster rotation of stocks, with a consequent reduction in working capital require-ments. This success naturally led the company to consider all new projects through the lens of eco-design.

Beyond the specific project objectives, other considerations can help to select the product to be redesigned:

- Product improvement potential: Certain products have intrin-sically greater possibilities for improvement than others because of their composition or the raw materials used. The greater the potential, the more the return on investment of the redesign effort can be important.

- The relative simplicity or complexity of the redesign: All things being equal, a company will prefer to begin in a simpler rede-sign project, especially if it is the first ever eco-design project, that will serve as a pilot project for the company.

- Capacity to reach a higher number of goals: The more a project is able to meet several goals the more it gains in inter-est. Thus, all things being equal, a product simultaneously enabling the achievement of internal and external goals will be preferred to a project generating only internal results. Moreover, communication potential and increase in the perceived value for the customer will be particularly valued.

PUMA Environmental Profit & Loss Assessment[33]

PUMA has long been a pioneer for sustainability in the apparel industry. It has been a listed member of both the Dow Jones Sustainability Index (since 2006) and the FTSE4Good (since 2005).

In 2011, PUMA established the first ever Environmental Profit and Loss Account, which puts a monetary value on the impacts that sourcing, production, marketing and distribution of PUMA products have on the environment.

It aimed to answer "the seemingly simple question: How much would our planet ask to be paid for the services it provides to PUMA if it was a business? And how much would it charge to clean up the 'footprint' through pollution and damage that PUMA leaves behind?" It represents simultaneously a strategic tool, a risk management tool and a transparency tool.

The company identified its most significant environmental impacts throughout the different tiers of its supply chain as GHG emissions, water use, land use, air pollution and waste:

- Tier 4 – Raw Materials: Cattle rearing, rubber plantations, cotton farming, petroleum production, other production. Example of environmental impacts (EI): Methane from cattle ranching and nitrous oxides in agriculture, irrigation water use in agriculture, conversions of ecosystems for agricultural land

- Tier 3 – Processing: Leather tanning, petroleum refining, cotton weaving and dyeing. Examples of EI: Water use in leather tanning and industry, GHGs from energy use and transport of materials, nitrous and sulfur oxides from energy use and transport of materials

- Tier 2 – Outsourcing: Outsole production, insole production, textile embroidery and cutting, adhesive and paint production. Examples of EI: Waste from material cutting, GHGs from energy use and transport of components, nitrous and sulfur oxides from energy use and transport of components

- Tier 1 – Manufacturing: Shoe manufacturing, apparel manufacturing, accessory manufacturing. Examples of EI: Waste from material cutting, GHGs from energy use and transport of products, nitrous and sulfur oxides from energy use and transport of products

- PUMA operations: Offices, shops, warehouses, business travel, logistics, IT. Examples of EI: GHGs from energy use, product distribution and travel, nitrous and sulfur oxides from energy use, product distribution and travel

The company estimated its total Environmental Profit and Loss at €145 million for 2010, that is, according to Jochen Zeitz, Former Executive Chairman of PUMA SE,

> if we treated our planet as we treat any other service provider, PUMA would have to pay €8M to nature for services rendered to our core operations such as PUMA offices, warehouses and stores in 2010, alone. An additional EUR 137 million would be owed to nature from PUMA's supply chain of external partners that we share with numerous other companies, and where we have less influence. So if PUMA is to successfully reduce its environmental impact, we have to address the activities of our

supply chain partners that generate 94 percent of our total environmental impact.[34]

This is detailed in the table next.

Table 3.1 *PUMA's 2010 Environmental Profit and Loss*

EUR million	Water use	GHGs	Land use	Other air pollution	Waste	Total
Tier 4	25	17	37	4	<1	83
Tier 3	17	7	<1	3	<1	27
Tier 2	4	7	<1	2	1	14
Tier 1	1	9	<1	1	2	13
PUMA Operations	<1	7	<1	1	<1	8
Total	47	47	37	11	3	145

Source: Adapted from the PUMA's 2010 Environmental Profit and Loss report, p. 8.

The detailed methodology and results are found in the report but is noteworthy that PUMA had the courage and energy to conduct this assessment.

The company has also set ambitious goals for 2015. It targets 25 percent savings on water and energy, and a 25 percent waste reduction globally on the operational side compared to a 2010 baseline. It also plans to offer 50 percent of its products made from sustainable materials according to the company's Sustainability Index. The company has also committed to eliminate the discharges of all hazardous chemicals from the whole life cycle and all production procedures by 2020.

One example of eco-design that received great interest in 2011 was the introduction of the PUMA Re-Suede snickers developed

using the latest materials and processes through eco-friendly product innovation. The Re-Suede

material is composed of 100 percent recycled polyester fibers, produced by a chemical recycling process
that reduces both the energy consumption and the
CO_2 emissions compared to production using new
materials. The recycled polyester is scrap waste from
manufacturing processes that is repurposed to create
the synthetic material.[35]

Obviously, PUMA did not fail to take the opportunity
to communicate extensively on its sustainability actions,
therefore consolidating its pioneering image as a sustainable
footwear and apparel brand.

An eco-design project will more naturally focus on a product
with high sales volume, because the total benefit will be ampli-
fied by the volume effect of the incremental improvements.
However, customer acceptability of these improvements must
still be validated, in particular by offering, at least, the same
functional and esthetic benefits. The impact of these improvements on price must also be considered seriously, the customer
being seldom ready to pay more without a clear explanation of
the new added-value.

Once the product has been identified, the effort to redesign
must be undertaken: As already stated, what is not measured
cannot be improved. It is thus essential to assess the environmental impact of the product throughout its life cycle (new resource
allocation and new activity). This is possible by carrying out an
LCA, a process that is strictly codified by the ISO 14040 and
associated standards. The LCA study will allow identification
and assessment of any impact from the complete product lifecycle phases, starting with the extraction of the raw materials
up to the product end-of-life. In particular, LCA will recommend
opportunities for improvement.

The technical dimensions of the LCA will not be detailed here,
but it is worth mentioning at this stage the close association of

LCA with marketing. In the event of a significant change in the value proposition, a usage-oriented voice-of-customer study is essential.[36] Any innovation occurs in a particular context: the user has a particular know-how, particular practices, with a particular personal/professional identity and in a particular environment. On these four levels, the user will build his usage significations that will determine the degree of acceptability of the innovation. This study will clarify user needs and expectations throughout the product redesign, making the resulting offer more meaningful for the clients. This requires marketing and sales involvement to access customer information and evaluate market opportunities for the redesigned offer, especially if new benefits are developed.

An LCA also allows the field of marketing promotion to be extended both upstream and downstream from the use of the product (see Figure 3.1) or to connect these dimensions together by conferring a new meaning to them. In other words, over and above a marketing positioning based primarily on traditional characteristics expressed in the consumption/use stage, additional

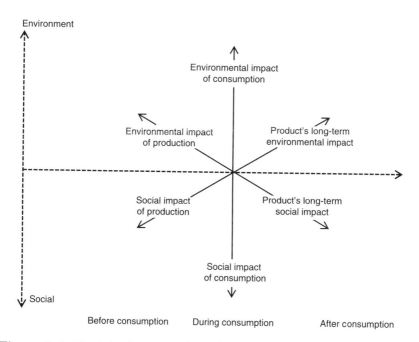

Figure 3.1 *Enriched space of marketing differentiation*[37]

environmental or social benefits can be identified and communicated up or downstream. We will speak then about a combined positioning that associates traditional and sustainable criteria.

Consumers are generally more sensitive to egocentric benefits (what do these new characteristics bring to me personally or to my relatives?) than with environmental or pro-social benefits.[38] The capacity to connect environmental or social benefits to personal benefits is thus a real asset, as we will see in the example of Guayaki next.

Guayaki places positive economy to the service of health[39]

Guayaki is an American company which sells drinks containing yerba mate, a South American plant cultivated in Paraguay, Argentina, Uruguay and the south of Brazil. Using a technique based on an ancestral knowledge of the Guarani Amerindians, the yerba leaves are dried then infused. The resulting drink presents the same stimulating virtues as coffee or tea, while offering better health benefits: it is rich in vitamins, antioxidant and anticancer phenolic components, it boosts physical energy, helps stimulate focus and clarity, aids elimination and diet.

These health benefits are attested by scientific studies, but are dependent on the harvesting processes of the mate. Traditionally, mate trees grow in the shade of the canopy of the Atlantic Forest.[40] The industrialized process of harvesting the yerba mate, however, means that the plants are now grown in the open air. The flip side to this is that, in addition to contributing to deforestation, open-air plantations produce smaller leaves due to the loss of an important part of their nutritional quality.

Based on this diagnosis, Guayaki wished to develop an innovative business model by setting a core mission to take part in the restoration of the Atlantic Forest and offering local populations a decent income compatible with the protection of the forest. A cut tree generally has a higher economic value than a standing tree, thus providing incentives to the local populations to participate in the deforestation undertaken by large wood or intensive farming companies. A model was needed that gave the forest an economic value at the very least equivalent to that of the cut tree. This was achieved by the local Guarani population reintroducing ancestral modes of mate cultivation. More specifically, Guayaki decided to develop a premium quality product, practicing an ancestral agriculture in the shade of the Atlantic forest, and producing a yerba mate rich in nutritional qualities. In parallel to the plantation of mate under the canopy, the company engaged in a reforestation program of hardwood species for future generations. It thus intends to restore not less than 200,000 acres[41] of Atlantic Forest while creating more than 1,000 long-term jobs by 2020. In terms of employment, the company developed an equitable model that offered the local populations a mate repurchase price three to four times higher than the traditional price.

This program of reforestation enabled the development of a positive economy model, that is, a model of regeneration of ecological capital. An LCA of a Guayaki pack of yerba mate infusion shows that the choice of these cultivation methods and the related reforestation programs reduces atmospheric CO_2 by 875g per pack. The supply and production chain production emit up to 302g of CO_2, so the total emission assessment is negative: each pound of yerba mate helps reduces atmospheric CO_2 by 573g. This is therefore a model that is positive for the environment.

The environmental and social benefits related to the production choices of Guayaki abound: positive model, certifications of fair trade and organic farming, payment of a fraction of the turnover to the descendants of the Guaranis for the promotion of the ancestral knowledge and the use of their war name as a brand and so on. Nevertheless, to convince the American consumers, it seemed more judicious to develop a positioning centered on the health benefits. It was thus decided as a marketing approach to present the cultivation methods as a way to maximize the nutritional benefits of the product. The choice seems appropriate, since 90 percent of Guayaki consumers buy the product for health purposes, the remaining 10 percent being sensitive to the environmental and social arguments. And taking into account the exceptional quality of the product, a price premium could be practiced, making the company profitable despite the overheads associated with the agricultural and social choices. The economic model is thus perfectly profitable and the company presents a growth rate of 30 percent each year, for a turnover of US$12 million in 2010: not that bad in a mature US market.

As already mentioned, the carrying out an LCA is generally entrusted to an expert company, able to guarantee the quality of the implementation of the approach, or to new partnerships. The improvement recommendations resulting from the LCA will generally relate to the following issues:

- Selection of lower impact raw materials (e.g. cleaner, renewable, less energy consuming, recyclable or recycled matter, material presenting a particular social benefit and so on).

- Reduction of the material intensity (e.g. reduce weight or volume, or to reduce empty spaces).

- Optimization of production techniques (e.g. by the simplification of the process, a reduction of its energy intensity, by the removal of toxic products, improving work environment, by a better management or valorization of waste and so on).

- Optimization of logistic flows and delivery systems (e.g. shorter circuits, reduction of packaging, use of soft modes of transport, relocation of some activities or recourse to local suppliers and so on).

- Optimization of the use and reduction of the impact during the use/consumption phase (e.g. reduction of energy consumption, reduction of the nuisances, reduction of consumables (accessories) needs, offering a healthier product and so on).

- Improvement of the product lifetime (lengthened lifetime, disassembly and reparability of the components, local maintenance operations and so on).

- Optimization of the management of the product at the end of the lifetime (to envisage the recycling of the components and its possible reuse – see Chapter 4 – consideration of local infrastructure and waste collection systems, facilitation of toxic substance recovery and so on).

The choice of engagements will depend again on several factors:

- A financial analysis of the project will have to evaluate the amount of investments necessary to redesign the product and the associated return on investment.

- A technical analysis dependent on the feasibility of the recommendations and their relative simplicity or complexity of implementation. This analysis will also integrate the time of development of the project in order to estimate the time-to-market of the redesigned product.

- A marketing analysis on the potential valorization of the choices at the marketing and sales level.

At the conclusion of this project, the team will have to write a report specifying the actions taken and its improvement results compared with the initially set objectives.

Third question: The implementation

The implementation stage is by nature a technical one and will not be developed here. Initially, a concept is developed and the environmental, social, economic, functional and esthetic improvements are evaluated and validated before moving to the development stage.

The evaluation procedure will depend on internal considerations (impact on the supply chain, production modes, financial assessment, amount of training and coaching to accompany the change, traditional tests of intrinsic quality of the product and so on) and also external (acceptability test, concept test with target customers and analysis of market opportunities).

If marketing opportunities are identified, a new marketing plan is developed in parallel to the launching plan of the redesigned product. The collaborators must be trained to the new processes at the production, operations, logistics and sales levels, and must be able to grasp the whole of the project benefits to correctly market them to customers. Internal communication must be developed to make employees aware of the benefits of eco-design.

At the end of the process, a follow-up score card must be set up to measure and validate the attainment of the objectives set initially, and to facilitate the communication or implementation of a sustainable development report, if necessary.

Finally, is an eco-design project profitable?

An 18-month study was conducted in Canada and France to evaluate the economic profitability of eco-design processes.[42] Based on a literature review and analysis of 30 case studies of companies implementing eco-design (half Canadian/half French), the study concluded that there is supportive evidence of the economic benefits of eco-design. In a large majority of the cases (26 out of 30), eco-design resulted in an increase in product sales or services incomes with a positive margin. Profitability thus evolved positively in absolute terms. For a small group (four cases), no rise of income was noted. No company degraded its profitability at the end of the project. For half of the companies that had not improved their incomes (two companies), a reduction in the costs generated a positive impact on profitability. The last two cases experienced neither an income rise nor a cost reduction, thus with a zero impact on profitability but an increased environmental benefit.

Of the 30 companies analyzed, 27 released a unit margin per product at least equivalent to the previous non eco-designed product. For 11 companies, the margin even improved. Only three cases of eco-design resulted in lower margins, while having, however, a positive impact on the overall company profitability due to new revenue streams.

For the sake of completeness, it shall be noted that of the 26 cases showing a general increase in income, 17 related to the development of a new product generating an additional income that had not existed beforehand; seven were conducted by new ventures; one case related to the redesign of an existing product with an increase in the sales by an improvement of the perceived value of the product; and another case also related to an existing product, but whose sales increased due to price decreases enabled by cost reduction.

On a methodological level, the sample of companies analyzed respects diversity in terms of industry sectors and size of workforce. Half the companies undertook an eco-design project over the last five years, but all were selected in a way that the product has been available in the market for at least 12 months. For 13 of them, it was their first ever eco-design project.

Beside these tangible and financial results, several studies[43] also highlight intangible benefits related to eco-design projects. Among these benefits, we can quote:

- An improvement of customer satisfaction by the provision of an enriched added-value.

- A catalyst in terms of creativity and innovation, and an enriched vision for the design of new products or the redesign of existing products.

- A positive impact on employee motivation and a reinforcement of the membership feeling and commitment to the company.

- A reduction in the rate of turnover of young employees and an increased capacity to attract interesting profiles.

- An improvement of the intangible capital related to the new knowledge absorbed by the company.

- A positive impact on the notoriety of the company and an improvement of its image, fed in particular but not exclusively by the free press or media coverage generating a greater exposure of the company.

- Improved relations with stakeholders such as government institutions, media, NGO or the local community.

As a summary, the following table shows the impact of the eco-design of an existing product on the sustainable business model canvas.

A PROMISING NEW FIELD: BIOMIMICRY OR LEARNING WITH NATURE

Numerous developments can be expected in the years to come especially due to technology development. We present one that seems particular relevant with regards to improving eco-efficiency: biomimicry.

According to The Biomimicry 3.8 Institute,[44] biomimicry (from bios, meaning life, and mimesis, meaning to imitate)

> is a design discipline that seeks sustainable solutions by emulating nature's time-tested patterns and strategies [...
> The] core idea is that Nature, imaginative by necessity, has already solved many of the problems we are grappling with.

Applications can be seen in numerous fields: agriculture, architecture, climate change, energy, energy efficiency, human safety, industrial design, medicine, natural cleaning and transportation.[45]

For example, the front end of the Shinkansen Bullet Train of the West Japan Railway Company, the fastest train in the world traveling 200 miles per hour, was modeled "after the beak of kingfishers, which dive from the air into bodies of water with very little splash to catch fish, resulted not only in a quieter train, but 15 percent less electricity use even when the train travels 10 percent faster."[46]

Michael Pawlyn details its application in architecture, making the case for buildings addressing issues like water purification, energy needs and heating in a complete close loop model (see Chapter 4) with no waste.[47] Arup Associates is one of the leading companies in this sector having designed, with architect Mick Pearce Eastgate, a building that uses 90 percent less energy for ventilation than conventional buildings of the same size, and has already saved the building owners over US$3.5 million in air conditioning costs.[48]

Another promising application is the dye-sensitized solar cell developed by Dyesol in Australia. The technology works like

"artificial photosynthesis" using an electrolyte, a layer of titanium (a pigment used in white paint and tooth paste) and ruthenium dye sandwiched between glass. Light striking the dye excites electrons which are absorbed by the titanium to become an electric current many times stronger than that found in natural photosynthesis in plants.[49]

These solar cells could replace existing glass windows or be integrated into areas from building facades to tents. According to the WWF-UK, this kind of innovation has "the potential to provide affordable solar power generation while dramatically increasing the surface area we can use for solar technology."[50] Dyesol is currently collaborating with Tata aiming to supply a third of the UK's renewable energy needs by 2020.[51]

Table 3.2 *Impact of eco-design of an existing product on the sustainable business model canvas*

Costs for Society and the Environment	Key Partners	Key Activities	Sustainable Value Proposition	Customer Relationship Management	Customers Segments	Benefits for Society and the Environment
• Downstream and upstream environmental externalities of the economic activities (e.g. water use for Levi's; raw materials for PUMA) • Environmental negative externalities related to the operations (e.g. transport for PUMA, Lush and Ben & Jerry's)	• Technical Partners • Local or national partners (e.g. Environmental Agency, Chamber of Commerce, etc.). Motivation to partner may range from financial reasons to the access of valuable resources such as expertise.	• Business Intelligence (regulations, subsidies, competition) • New partnerships identification, negotiation and management • Portfolio analysis for the selection of the product to be redesigned • Life cycle analysis (technical, marketing, R&D and financial dimensions) • Development and test of the concept • Adaptation of the supply chain and manufacturing equipment/training of the employees to the new processes • Marketing launch of the redesigned product (if relevant) **Key Resources** • Project Team • Financial Resources • Dedicated technical expertise • Associated marketing expertise	An enriched value proposition with improved environmental benefits and at least equivalent functional and aesthetic benefits (these benefits should be translated into customers benefits as the value proposition is always expressed from the customers' point of view)	Potentially impacted if the distribution systems are re-examined. In certain cases, new automated and dematerialized flows can replace current physical flows **Distribution Channels** Optimized or reconfigured distribution system	Potential access to new markets with certain environmental standards (e.g. public contracts) + possibility of targeting additional customer segments who are sensitive to the environmental benefits of a product	• Development of local activities (e.g. Guayaki; Ben & Jerry's)/relocalization of business activities (e.g. Sullair) • Preservation of ancestral knowledge (e.g. Guayaki) • Preservation/enhancement of ecosystems and biodiversity (e.g. Atlantic forest restoration for Guayaki) • Eco-friendly factory with limited impact on the environment (e.g. Lush and Ben & Jerry's) • Use of recycled material preventing fabrication of new materials (preservation of raw materials) and reducing waste (e.g. PUMA Re-Suede snickers) • Recyclability of packaging (e.g. Lush) Reduction of toxic substance (environmental and social/health benefits) Enhancement of the use value of a product (that may generate social benefits)

Shared Costs	Cost Structure	Revenue Streams	Shared Benefits
• Energy costs and entrants (raw materials) • Transportation costs • Associated waste due to a volume strategy	• Associated costs with the mobilization of the project team + costs of partnerships + R&D and technical costs + costs of adaptation and building up manufacturing capacity + possible marketing costs of product launch	• Cost reduction/better margin + potential extra revenues related to the opening of new markets, extension of the target market or the development of a distinctive advantage for the customer	• Positive financial returns (in a vast majority of observed case) • Increased added-value of the value proposition and new spaces of differentiation/positive impact on the image • Better control of the quality/the supply chain/an improved time to market (e.g. Sullair) • Costs saving through an improved efficiency (in terms of raw materials and energy). Cost reduction in terms of waste management (e.g. Lush) • Reduction in transportation needed due to solid format (e.g. Lush) with associated financial savings • Production of new knowledge and fostering of innovation

These are just a few examples of biomimicry application that show its great potential to help on some of the most pressing environmental challenges.

CONCLUSION

The application of the eco-efficiency principle through the eco-design approach is not in itself a revolution to the company business model. Indeed, even if the value proposition is enriched, new resources and new activities must be mobilized and deployed, and this eventually impacts all the components of the business model, its center of gravity does not change. The company continues to sell a product or to deliver an opti-mized service. In contrast, Chapters 5 and 6 dislocate the busi-ness model in a more radical way by modifying its center of gravity (the true nature of the value proposition and the driver of revenue).

Eco-design nevertheless presents a large number of benefits. The profitability of such a project is generally granted. It is an interesting first step to integrate sustainable development in the company strategy, certainly engaging and mobilizing, but not demanding a cultural, managerial and behavioral revolution. It does present some challenges, especially technical difficulties or obtaining useful information from suppliers, but as a whole, the tangible and intangible benefits are generally numerous, and can encourage the company to continue forward its sustainable development path based on this first success.

4

Circular Economy: Transforming a "Waste" into a Productive Resource

On a macroeconomic level, economic activity can be relatively inefficient in terms of use of resources and energy; it is, on the other hand, extremely efficient in terms of waste generation. The industrial revolution can be characterized by a linear model of production and consumption, following a "take-make-dispose" pattern, in contrast to the circular operations of the natural world that recycles all its by-products giving them a productive value.[1] We extract great quantities of raw materials[2] that are directly or indirectly encapsulated in the products and services we consume, and which are then converted into nonproductive waste. To give an idea of the scale of this waste, 93 percent of the exploited natural resources in the United States are not integrated into an end product, 80 percent of these products are only used once, and 99 percent of the materials contained in sold goods become waste after only six weeks.[3] Worse, the proportion of products that go directly from production to waste reaches 30 percent in some industries, like agriculture.[4] The figures speak for themselves. While it is difficult to know exactly how much waste is discarded annually in the world, it has been estimated to range between 2,500 and 4,000 billion kg.[5] In the UK, total waste generation was estimated at 288.6 million tons (mt) in 2008, coming from the following sources: construction (101 mt), mining and quarrying (86 mt), commercial and industrial activities (67.3 mt), household sources (31.5 mt) and the remaining waste (including health-care waste, batteries and accumulators,

and waste containing polychlorinated biphenyls (PCB) combined (2.7 mt).[6] The United States alone consumes 210 billion
plastic bottles per year, which truly represents a huge mountain
of plastic; 720 million cell phones are thrown away each year
around the world. Endless other examples could be given.

But what if these millions of tons of waste were really con-
cealing a source of unexploited treasure? Umicore,[7] the world's
number one recycling company, seems to be convinced. Near
Antwerp, in Belgium, is situated a gigantic factory, the largest of
the world nowadays in its scopes of application, which aims to
recover precious metals from electronic waste. It has capacity to
treat more than 350,000 tons of waste a year, including 40,000
tons from electronic rejects. The results are impressive. With
50,000 old cell phones, the company is able to extract a 1 kg bar
of pure gold (that is to say a commercial value of US$54,700 at
December 2012 prices), 350 kg of copper, not to mention silver,
platinum, rhodium or germanium, whose rates are currently
escalating in this period of tension on resources price. Through
its "urban mining," the company intends to recover per year
no less than 25 tons of 24-carat gold reaching a purity of 99.99
percent and a multiplicity of other precious metals.

The A7 company has similar clout in Brazil where it currently
recycles 9.9 percent of the approximately 600,000 tons of electronics discarded annually,[8] contributing to Brazil's good recycling record: approximately 95 percent of aluminum cans and 55
percent of all polyethylene bottles are recycled, half of all paper
and glass is recovered, generating a value of more than US$ 2
billion and avoiding 10 million tons of GHG emissions.[9]

You may think that this is all about recycling, and not very
innovative. But is it not possible to go much further in the valorization of by-products and waste than is currently done?

The objective of this chapter is to reconsider the concept of
waste and to imagine new ways of valorization of end-life products or unvalorized resources to make them productive and
creators of richness. Based on circular economy principles, the
cradle-to-cradle[TM10] philosophy and the cyclic behaviors of
nature, it is foremost a question of replacing the very idea of

waste with that of a by-product to be valorized. Several examples will be presented, providing cues to innovate at product, process and industrial operations levels.

FROM LINEAR ECONOMY TO CIRCULAR ECONOMY

The great majority of our economic models are structured around linear flows of materials, as schematically represented in Figure 4.1.

In times of resource abundance and strong capacity for waste treatment, the first model can be considered, even if it fails to be effective. But when resources become rare, and thus expensive, when the price of energy increases so does the degradation of the biosphere and when the generation of waste results in increasingly intolerable environmental and social issues,[11] the model is unacceptable in all its dimensions, even on the traditional economic plan. Moreover, this model brings us many aberrations, some of which we are barely becoming aware. For instance, let's consider the energy efficiency of a common situation in most companies: the computer server room is expensively cooled by air-conditioning, while the next door office is heated by energy-voracious installations. On one side, calories produced by the servers are quickly eliminated by refrigeration consuming energy. On the other, calories are necessary and are produced

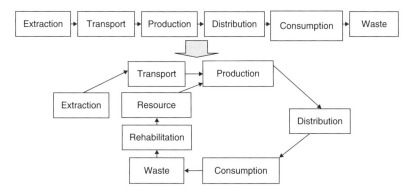

Figure 4.1 *Going from a linear economy to a circular economy*

again using energy at high cost to heat the building. Would it not be possible to recover the calories emanating from the server room to heat the next-door office? This may appear ridiculous or utopian. However, the following examples show how realistic this intuitively simple principle is.

Toward a new consideration of neglected calories

The "Palais de la Méditerranée"[12] is a landmark of Nice, on the French Riviera. A luxury hotel located on the "Promenade des Anglais," it is easily identifiable thanks to its large white Art déco façade that made this hotel a legend. Its current director, Christophe Aldunate, the youngest CEO of a luxury hotel in Europe, is a man of strong convictions, where the environment occupies an important place. Helped by an engineering team directed by a truly "Gyro Gearloose," they carry out innovations in several domains. One of the more astute was to recover lost calories and give them a new value. By a system of heat exchangers, the calories emitted from the servers and inverters room of the hotel are used to heat the swimming pool, helped by a serpentine circulating along the conduit of the boiler chimney of the hotel to recover the residual heat. This double system makes it possible to heat the swimming pool without any additional energy.

Another example is the Stockholm train station[13] where 250,000 people commute daily. Imagine the calories released by the simple movement of these "walking sources of energy" at a constant (body) temperature of 37 °C. An engineer had the clever idea to conceive a system to recover these calories naturally emitted by commuters to heat the building located in front of the station. By an innovative technical system, no less than 25 percent of the heating needs of this building are now being recovered by the body heat of train commuters, for investment costs of only

€21,000. As a comparison, approximately 500,000 passengers commute daily at Paris "Gare du Nord" train station while 4.78 million daily use the Shanghai tube.

Similarly, at L'Oreal Canada, the residual energy from the effluents, the boilers and the compressors is now reused to preheat the plant's washing waters, the heat generated by the compressors is used to heat the warehouses, and the recovery of the heat from effluents reduced the boilers operation by 15 percent and the emission of GHG by the same proportion. The same goes for the UK's largest single glasshouse that uses recovered carbon dioxide and heat from the neighboring Wissington Sugar factory.[14]

To enable this kind of project, new solutions have been designed by existing and new companies like Triogen, a Dutch supplier of ORC (Organic Rankine Cycle[15]) that converts waste heat from business processes (landfill sites, digesters, diesel engines, wood burners, furnaces and so on) into electricity.[16] It provides solutions for the utilization of waste heat flows between 500 kWth and 5 MWth and their efficient conversion into electricity. It has so far developed solutions for clients in Germany, France, Czech Republic, the Netherlands, Portugal, Italy and Belgium.

By switching from a linear model to a circular model (see Figure 4.1), a new relation with waste or the output of activities can be developed. And this principle does not apply to calories alone, but potentially to everything that surrounds us. Thus each product at the end of its lifetime or each waste is likely to become a resource for a new cycle of production.[17]

The "circular economy" – this is its official name – is a new industrial system that replaces the "end-of-life" concept by restoration and regeneration by intention and design.[18] It shifts toward the use of renewable sources of energy, drastically reduces or eliminates the use of toxic materials. By redesigning products, services or processes, it transforms a waste or previously unvalorized resource into a productive one that may be reused in closed-loop systems.

The circular economy was initially based on the 3R principle – Reduction, Reuse and Recycling – a principle originally created in the context of waste management. The first stage calls for the maximum reduction in the use of resources and energy in the development of products, services or processes, and this for an equivalent output. We find here the idea of eco-efficiency described in the previous chapter, which is a precondition to any circular approach. The reuse principle calls for the maximization of the use period of products either by a prolongation of their lifetime, or by a judicious replacement of certain components, so that maximum material can be preserved for the longest possible time. In addition, it is a question of being able to give a new life to the products and their components by reintegrating them in new cycles of production and consumption. Finally, recycling at the end of the lifetime seeks to revalorize maximum materials contained in products, in order to recondition raw materials to be reintroduced in new productive cycles. But as we will see later, circular economy is much more than recycling as we consider it traditionally. The concept of waste is indeed eliminated, products being designed and optimized for a cycle of disassembly and reuse.

THE CRADLE-TO-CRADLE™ PHILOSOPHY[19]

The philosophy of cradle-to-cradle (as opposed to cradle to grave), introduced by Walter R. Stahel and developed by William McDonough and Michael Braungart in the book Cradle-to-Cradle: Remaking the Way We Make Things is based on the principle of the circular economy, and classifies all materials entering productive processes around two metabolic logics – the biological metabolism and the technical metabolism.

Application of the biological metabolic principle

The biological metabolism is based on the "biological nutrient", where a material or a product is designed from the beginning to reintegrate the biological cycle, by being 100 percent biodegradable. A natural cotton tee shirt could thus be manufactured in a logic of biological metabolism, so that once it reaches the end of its lifetime, it can be composted "to return to the ground" by nourishing it (natural cycle). A large number of applications can be built around this logic. For example, Motorola[20] conceived, in partnership with a research team of the University of Warwick, a biodegradable cell phone case. In order to "tangibilize" this benefit, a sunflower seed was built into the case, so at the end of its lifetime, all that is needed is to plant this case and see a sunflower springing up after a few weeks. Another example is the Climatex® Lifecycle biodegradable fabric originally developed by the Swiss company Rohner. It is a compostable material used extensively in the office furniture manufacturing business, having among its main clients Steelcase.[21]

gDiapers, the only diaper brand with a C2C certification

It is rare to talk about disposable diapers in positive terms regarding the environment. As a disposable product, it consists of a little more than 40 percent of wood paste generally bleached with chlorine, the remainder being made of plastics polymers – of which the famous superabsorbent polymer is able to absorb up to a hundred times its weight in liquid – of adhesive, bands and rubber bands.[22] To date, disposable diapers are the third most present household waste in garbage dumps, representing no less than 4 percent of the planet's solid waste,[23] and requiring more than 500 years to break up, releasing a considerable amount of chemical residues.

Given these figures, an American couple, Jason and Kim Graham-Nye, decided to launch gDiapers, a range of ecological diapers. More specifically, there's a reusable diaper cover and a disposable diaper insert that is 100 percent biodegradable and can be flushed, composted or tossed.

Thus the model of disposable diaper insert gRefill is today the only diaper in the world to profit from a cradle-to-cradle[TM24] certification. Concretely, it is conceived in such a way that once soiled, it can simply be put in the family compost and, in approximately 45 days it will be completely biodegraded and will produce a quality humus that can be used completely safely in a garden, and thus help provide ground biomass which is beneficial and completely free of any chemical residues.

Analogical application: The industrial metabolic principle

Not all products have the same potential to be developed following a biological nutrient logic. In fact, for a great many, the concept makes no sense. How can we imagine that a car, a refrigerator or an office chair can simply go back into the earth? It is possible, on the other hand, to apply this same principle in logic of industrial metabolism based on the idea of a technical nutrient. This concerns materials that are not biodegradable and are consequently designed in such a manner to be recovered and reintroduced in a closed productive cycle, without any loss of quality.

How does this differ from recycling? Recycling is in practice *downcycling*: the properties of a product are degraded during the process of recycling that prevents the recycled material from being reintegrated into the same industrial cycle, but into an industrial cycle requiring lower quality material. Thus the body of a car, being an alloy of more than 40 types of metals, cannot generally be recycled to be used in the production of a new car, but can be used, for example, in the production of gardening tools, which, once recycled, will become components of a cell phone, which in turn will finish at the dump. A PET (polyethylene terephthalate) mineral water bottle will never be able to become again a 100 percent new PET bottle. Obviously, the plastic that comes into contact with the mineral water must be free from any toxic substance that could migrate in the water. And the process of recycling cannot guarantee the absence of such substances, given that a consumer could have stored petrol in a bottle before throwing it away, which would have modified the physicochemical properties of the plastic. For this reason, multilayer technologies have been developed so that any layer in direct contact with the liquid is made from new plastic, rather than from recycled material, which could only be used for the external layers.

The principle of industrial metabolism on the other hand seeks to maintain both the qualitative and functional properties of the material so that a component can be "recycled" in the same industrial cycle indefinitely, with no degradation of quality, and thus being turned into waste. This a great leap forward! Developing such a prowess demands a whole new product design upstream that supports downstream disassembly and recuperation of materials for their rehabilitation and further reuse. It also has to guard against any contamination or any mixture of substances that would be irreversible.

Steelcase presents its Think Chair[25]

Steelcase was recently integrated in the *Fortune* magazine ranking of the world's most admired companies,[26] an additional award for a company that seems to be accumulating them. Steelcase is a global company proposing a portfolio of workplace products, furnishings and services, including tables, seats, storage units, accessories and lighting, among others. It is one of the companies holding the highest number of certified cradle-to-cradle™ models by MBDC (McDonough Braungart Design Chemistry).

Among several certified products, the office chair, Think Chair, enjoys an international reputation. It was entirely developed on the basis of the C2C specifications, on the following grounds[27]:

- All the materials used in the product must be listed and evaluated if they represent more than 100 ppm (particles per million), that is to say 0.01 percent of the product. Their chemical composition as well as levels of concentration must be specified for their recycling.

- Each component must be categorized as a biological nutrient or a technical nutrient. If a component integrates both categories of nutrients, those must be separable. The unit must be able to be completely disassembled in order to reach any single component in a simple way. The Think Chair can thus be entirely dismantled in less than five minutes, 99 percent of the chair being completely recoverable and recyclable, according to the previously defined metabolic principles. This possibility of disassembly makes the chair completely modular – the seat can be adjusted to the required comfort. Also, a vast choice of cushions, fabrics, balustrades, headrests, lumbar support and so on means that the chair can be fully customized. The design of the product and the possibility for it to be completely disassembled (environmental benefits) thus support and reinforce customers' egocentric benefits, and provides several opportunities for marketing and sales differentiation (see the discussion in Chapter 3). Moreover, if a single component is degraded, it can be individually replaced.

- Each identified component must be assessed for its impact on the environment and on the health of the future users, according to strictly defined criteria. The objective is obviously to reduce this impact. Moreover, the conditions of production and transformation are also evaluated, and their social and environmental benefits identified. Thus Steelcase chose to assembly its products close to its final markets with factories located in Europe, the USA and Asia. The upstream social benefits of the manufacture of chairs can thus benefit each of the markets served by the company.

- For all the components presenting an environmental or health risk, the company must set up a strategy of progressive elimination. The C2C certification distinguishes several levels: the gold and platinum levels require an integral substitution of the components or substances classified in red, which present a health hazard to the environment or public health. Steelcase has in particular set up an ambitious R&D program to replace PVC, and has found a quality substitute that brings a differentiating competitive advantage to the company.

This development philosophy is at the core of the company strategy and results in substantial environmental and financial benefits. Thus, between 2001 and 2008, the water consumption of the European operations was reduced by 64 percent, along with a fall in GHG emissions of 49 percent. Waste has been reduced by 71 percent, and with it the cost of its treatment. Lastly, the company reduced its emissions of volatile organic components in the air by 95 percent.

Compared to the linear system, this circular organization of flows allows four clear-cut sources of value creation, based on increased material and energy productivity[28]:

- The "power of the inner circle" refers to minimizing material use compared to the linear production system. The tighter the circle (i.e. the less a product has to be changed in reuse, refurbishment and remanufacturing) and the faster a product returns to use, the higher the potential savings on material, labor, energy and capital embedded in the product and on the associated externalities (such as GHG emissions, water, toxicity). Tighter circles are also generally associated with a higher virgin material substitution effect, generating another source of value.

- The "power of circling longer" refers to maximizing the number of consecutive cycles (be it reuse, remanufacturing or recycling) and/or the time in each cycle. By keeping products, components and materials in use longer in closed loop systems (either by going through more consecutive cycles or by spending more time within a cycle), the revenue generated by unit of mobilized resources is drastically increased, as is the generated value.

- The "power of cascaded use" implies that if it's impossible to maintain the materials/components in the same economic cycle, an assessment should be made to cascade the resources across different product categories, by diversifying reuse across the value chain. As an example, cotton clothing may be reused first as second-hand apparel, then cross to the furniture industry as fiber-fill in upholstery, the fiber-fill being later reused in stone wool insulation for construction. In each case, this cascading approach substitutes for an inflow of virgin materials into the economy before the cotton fibers are safely returned to the biosphere (based on the biological nutrient approach).

- The "power of pure circles," finally, lies in the fact that uncontaminated material streams increase collection and redistribution efficiency while maintaining quality, particularly of technical materials, which, in turn, extends product longevity and thus increases material productivity. This calls for a new approach of designing goods and services in a way that allows the quality of components across the same economic cycles to be maintained, which facilitates the disassembly processes.

CIRCULAR ECONOMY AND INNOVATION

The application of the principle of circular economy opens up an extremely broad horizon for innovation, related to product redesign, economic valorization of waste by a diversification of activity, or by the creation of partnerships, physically interconnected or not. The following sections and Chapter 5 illustrate this potential.

Circularity at the service of product innovation

The application of the principle of circular economy essentially means redesigning a product to allow the recovery of its components while maintaining the quality. The product can thus see its added-value reinforced, as exemplified by Steelcase. Nevertheless, such product modifications cannot generally be made without a relatively major reconfiguration of the company and its business model. In Chapter 5, we will see how Xerox organized a circular material flow of its photocopiers, allowing it to recover 70–90 percent of the components of old machines to reintroduce them into the new generations of photocopiers. The installation of these circular flows required a major reconfiguration of the company business model over and above simple product redesign. It is possible, however, to apply the circularity principle just to the perimeter of the product, without substantially impacting the company business model.

Application of the principle of circularity to the product perimeter

It can be judicious to (re)think about the functioning of a product by drawing an analogy with the functioning of natural ecosystems, regarding it as a system made up of subsystems able to interact by creating profitable flows with a broader system. This idea was applied to the braking system, for example, on the Toyota Prius. Basically, each time we apply brakes in a car, we are wasting energy because when the car slows down, the kinetic energy that was propelling it forward becomes useless.[29] On the Toyota Prius, a braking system was designed in order to capture this kinetic energy and convert it into electricity to recharge the car's batteries. This system of energy recuperation helps reduce fuel consumption and, by extension, the fuel bill for the customer. This principle of regenerative braking is also used in certain industrial machinery or certain elevators.

Another interesting example is the Aquaduct, a pedal-powered vehicle, similar to a bicycle, which transports, filters and stores water for poor countries.[30] As the rider pedals, a pump attached to the pedal crank draws water from a large holding tank, through a carbon filter, to a smaller clean tank. A clutch engages and disengages the drive belt from the pedal crank, enabling the rider to filter the water while traveling or while stationary. The clean tank is removable and closed for contamination-free home storage and use. The innovative combination of transportation and sanitation of water offers a possible way to provide clean, drinkable water for populations without access in poor countries.[31]

The case study next provides another illustration of this kind of development, this time applied to a domestic environment.

Whirlpool innovates with the Green Kitchen[32]

Whirlpool introduced its Green Kitchen as the kitchen of the future. It is an ecological avant-gardist kitchen, developed on eco-systemic grounds.

To reach its promised environmental benefits, all kitchen electric household appliances are conceived under the prism of eco-efficiency. The refrigerator, for example, is provided with a drawer that prevents cold air from escaping when the door is opened, which enables potential energy saving of 50 percent. The volume of the oven is flexible, adapting the heated zone surface to the dish size. The appliances are equipped with intelligent devices to self-regulate energy consumption resulting in substantial energy savings. The induction hob adapts the heating surface to the size of the pan; the oven adapts the cooking temperature to the type of dish it automatically detects; and the power of the hood is automatically adjusted to the quantity of vapor to extract.

But the Green Kitchen goes further. Taking inspiration from the natural circular cycles, its various appliances interact in order to reduce and recycle water, energy and heat. Consumers tend, for example, to waste liters of clean water "down the plughole" by carrying out simple gestures such as drinking, cleaning or rinsing. In order to limit this loss, clean water is collected in a tank and is subjected to an antibacterial treatment. It will be thus available to water plants or to wash floors or windows. And a part will be also filtered to be reused by the dishwasher, saving more than seven liters of water per cycle of washing. The preheating of the dishwasher water is done by exploiting some of the heat released by the refrigerator compressor. At a more anecdotic level, the residual heat of the oven and the moisture of the hood are reoriented toward a greenhouse integrated into the kitchen, which offers the ideal conditions to grow fresh aromatic herbs or other plants. On the whole, more than 60 percent of energies used are redirected toward other appliances in order to optimize their use.

All these innovations allow total savings of 70 percent in the energy bill. A strong argument for a kitchen planned to be launched by 2013. So far, Whirlpool has received several awards, like the coveted Product Design Award 2009 from the International Design Forum.

In such an innovation, the impact on the SBMC can be related to the redesign of a product by the prism of the eco-design detailed in Chapter 3. The marketing questions are nevertheless likely to vary. Thus a detailed marketing analysis of the Green Kitchen raises several specific questions concerning customer acceptability, which demand a rethink of the marketing strategy.

TARGETING AND POSITIONING

As a global kitchen concept, the Green Kitchen targets customers who are building a kitchen from scratch. The market is potentially vast, but the risk is to develop a premium positioning that is too specifically anchored on the environmental benefits of the kitchen, which could lead to a market segment that is too reduced to make the innovation profitable. A targeting aimed exclusively at "environmentally conscious" customers does not therefore seem very judicious. A detailed positioning study must be carried out to evaluate the value curve[33] of this kitchen and to be able to identify the most promising positioning on marketing and commercial grounds. This kitchen offers many unique benefits as regards the positioning, from functional to emotional benefits, and even of social distinction.

DEALING WITH ADOPTION BARRIERS

The significant functional and esthetic benefits that the kitchen offers do not detract from a number of consumer concerns or barriers that should be addressed. Certain questions are anecdotal, others more fundamental: for example, how do you clean an integrated cooker? How safe is an induction plate that turns on automatically when a container is posed upon? What if a child puts one of her toys there? How safe is dishwasher water that is recovered and filtered from the sink? Moreover, a purchaser of the Green Kitchen has no choice about the appliances. Questions regarding the modularity, adaptability and personalization of the kitchen can arise. Also, the purchaser must remain loyal to the brand for the kitchen's lifetime. The benefits of Whirlpool are obvious, but this may raise objections from customers who have become locked in to a single supplier. In addition, the systemic character of the kitchen is obviously tempting, but it can generate a risk perception from the customer. In the event of a refrigerator breakdown, does the dishwasher continue to function or is the kitchen paralyzed? The implementation of a particularly effective after-sales service seems essential, just like warranty conditions to deal with these concerns and barriers. All this obviously has a cost that is necessary to integrate in the price formation. Whirlpool seems to have identified some of these concerns: it has announced a 2.0 version of the Green Kitchen supporting product modularity and a gradual introduction of the eco-systemic kitchen.[34]

DEFINING AN ACCEPTABLE PRICE

With regards to the pricing strategy, the resulting energy savings can be used as a reason to justify the innovation premium price. But this criterion alone cannot be exaggerated; an energy saving of 70 percent represents an annual saving of approximately €100 to €150 (based on the average electricity consumption of household appliances in France).[35] This amount may vary in other countries where electricity is more expensive. However, an exaggeratedly elevated premium price would likely confine the kitchen to a small market niche, competing exclusively with top-of-the-range products. Whirlpool certainly has a brand capital to be credible for such a positioning, but would it not be more judicious to develop an offer allowing the creation of a new category within the accessible kitchens targeting the mass market, thus enabling the company to take advantage of first-home consumers? Those are difficult questions to arbitrate at both the strategic and operational levels. Marketing studies, initially qualitative then undoubtedly quantitative, would be necessary, in particular to refine the choice of the target, positioning and evaluate acceptability levels at various price points. Such a product innovation certainly requires strong marketing expertise, reinforced by the need to "educate" a market about its new characteristics, especially those potentially complex to understand because of their intangibility.

Circularity at the service of the economic valorization of waste

The principle of circularity gives an economic value to waste, or more broadly, to a by-product to be revalorized. This value can be considered from a number of angles, through indirect or a direct valorization.

Indirect valorization

Indirectly, any waste has a cost for the company. Reducing waste means working toward the reduction of these treatment costs. The impact on the *bottom line* will be positive if the cost associated with the reduction program is lower than the economic gain associated with reducing the cost of treatment. This profitability must be considered on the medium to long term, given that investment will always precede (possible) profitability. Evaluating the return on investment for the company, however, is not easy. The examples of Lush and Seacourt (see next) show how a company can benefit from a far broader financial return on its zero waste program than the suppression of its treatment costs alone.

Seacourt, the first zero waste printer[36]

Seacourt is a small family printing company based in Oxford, UK. For 15 years, the company has pursued a sustainable development strategy on all fronts to become one of the top three leading environmental printers in the world, according to the Waterless Printing Association.[37] It has received the coveted Queen's Award for Sustainable Development twice during the last five years. Its achievements are impressive: 100 percent of its printing is carried out via waterless printing technology (inducing a reduction of the water consumption from 120,000 liters a year to 420 liters); 100 percent of its inks are vegetable oil based; 100 percent of its energy is renewable; the company is carbon neutral; it reduced its VOC (volatile organic compounds) emissions by 98.5 percent; it is certified EMAS and ISO 14001; and so on.

Its latest achievement was to become the first closed-loop, zero waste company in their industry. On October 14, 2009 the company's last trash bin was thrown away. Throughout the whole printing process, all waste streams are being reused or recycled in some way; even the tea bags are composted. In other words, 100 percent of the company outputs are valorized inside or outside the company. This comes after 14 years of effort and was made possible by finally locating a company that would take on the silver foil-backed paper to burn (partly fuelled by the burning of the paper) to produce aluminum powder used in the metal castings industry.

The consequences of this radical commitment in favor of sustainable development are many, the most important being a capacity of unequalled market differentiation. In 2007, a third of the customers came to Seacourt because of its radical environmental policy, already far from being negligible. This increased to 98 percent by 2012. For Jim Dinnage, Seacourt's president, the development of the company is mainly explained by its environmental and social projects. And it is without hesitation that he affirms that the money invested in all these projects has had a positive return on investment.

Natural Systems Utilities (NSU) is a US-distributed infrastructure development and investment company specializing in sustainable water and energy solutions.[38] It uses natural systems, such as constructed wetlands, bio-swales and reed beds that mimic the conditions found in nature to provide the optimum environment to establish the microbial communities responsible for the removal of wastewater pollutants.

Its infrastructure systems use up to 50 percent less water and emit up to 2.5 times less carbon than conventional systems helping to optimize recovery and reuse water, nutrients and energy. In parallel it restores soil ecology and creates habitats for wetland wildlife. Circularity is thus at the core of the company business model, enabling the company to reduce its costs and increase its brand image by playing a restorative role in the local biosphere.[39]

Direct valorization

The application of a circular logic to waste can also confer a direct economic value to it, and help to build a value proposition for a new company activity. We already presented the example of Sadia in Chapter 1, but the following two examples, Waste Concern Group and Beijing Shengchang Bioenergy S&T Co., take this logic even further.

Waste is a Resource

Waste Concern Group is a Bangladeshi Social Business Enterprise (SBE) founded in 1995 comprising both "for-profit" and "not-for-profit" enterprises. Its motto is "Waste is a Resource" and it is active in the fields of solid waste management and resource recovery, clinical and hazardous waste management, wastewater treatment, community-based environmental improvement, urban environmental management, climate change and clean development mechanism, and organic farming, among others.

Its flagship activity is the development of waste management techniques that avoid methane emissions by composting organic waste with forced aeration. The flexibility of Waste Concern's composting model is adapted to urban, rural and slum areas with three sizes available:

– Small, to process up to 3 tons of organic waste per day

– Medium, to process between 3 and 10 tons of organic waste per day

– Large, to process more than 11 tons of organic waste daily.[40]

This system reduces GHG emissions and creates carbon offset credits that can be sold on voluntary carbon offset markets. It is participative by nature, involving the private, public and community spheres, and has been further developed and deployed in four management models for decentralized composting:

- Municipality owned – Municipality operated: Integrated into the existing municipal Solid Waste Management (SWM) system and focused on reducing waste which otherwise has to be transported and disposed of in landfills. Cost reduction through lower transport and disposal costs.

- Municipally owned – Community operated: The benefiting community is involved in the management of primary waste collection and composting. Non-profit seeking model. Cost reduction through lower transport and disposal costs.

- Municipally owned – Privately operated: The benefiting community is partly involved. Profit-seeking model if possible. Requires at least full cost recovery (from fees and compost sales as well as carbon credits). Cost reduction through lower transport and disposal costs.

- Privately owned – Privately operated (profitable with Carbon Credits): Profit-seeking enterprise based on ideal compost market conditions. Income is generated through compost sale, collection fees and carbon credits.[41]

This original waste management system has been replicated in Nepal, Pakistan, Sri Lanka and Vietnam, and has been receiving funding from the Bill and Melinda Gates Foundation to develop it in ten African cities in 2012. It is no surprise that the group collects awards for its social entrepreneurship initiative from, among others, Ashoka, Schwab Foundation and UNDP.[42]

Beijing Shengchang Bioenergy S&T Co. presents a similar case in China.[43] The company, founded in 2006, is a bioenergy manufacturer located in Lixian, Beijing. Operating two production and value chains,

> one collects and purchases bio wastes from farmers, then produces Biomass Pellet Fuel (BPF) and sells it to the users for cooking and heating; the other one develops and manufactures pellet boilers and stoves, then sells them to farmers and industrial users. Local farmers benefit by earning extra income selling agricultural waste to the company and also by reducing their fuel expenses if they switch from their traditional burners to biofuel burners.[44]
>
> Competition from coal is a burden for a private operator like BJ-SBST that had to clearly develop its business case to overcome this and other challenges like lack of funding, lack of senior professionals and the low density of energy in agricultural waste resulting in high transition costs.[45]

Similar initiatives have been taken by other companies, such as Greensulate in the US, which produces solar board insulation from agricultural waste, bonded by filamentous fungi;[46] Haathi Chaap in New Delhi, which creates paper from elephant dung; or Worn Again in the UK, which works with large companies to recover the value of their existing textiles waste – through upcycling, downcycling and reuse – while developing and integrating closed-loop textiles solutions for the future.[47] Worn Again has been working with companies like Marks & Spencer, Nationalgrid, McDonald's (that launched its new uniform for the UK during the London Olympics), and Eurostar (creating a bespoke bag for its train managers made from their disused uniforms).

Being in this case a diversification of activity, the SBMC is applied in an entrepreneurial logic, since an original business model must be built for this new activity. By following the method presented in Chapter 2, the reader has a particularly powerful tool of strategic design, while remaining simple to use, to help in the development of this new activity.

The opportunities to create new activities are numerous, and the most surprising creation projects are starting to appear. For example, if you pass by the French town of Nantes on the Atlantic coast, you will find at "40, rue des Collines," a house entirely built out of urban waste.[48]

Circularity at the service of local innovation systems

It is possible to implement circular economy even further by applying it to a specific geographical area. Eco-districts or eco-parks are largely inspired by the circularity of flows of materials and energy. There as well, a district or an industrial park is regarded as a system made up of interconnected subsystems. The examples of Kalundborg[49] in Denmark, Tianjin in China and Masdar City in the UAE illustrate this point.

Kalundborg in Denmark is internationally known for its industrial eco-park, a true pioneering example of industrial symbiosis among companies of various sectors. The founding principle of the park, created and developed spontaneously by the companies with the support of the city, is to favor exchanges of water, energy, flow of materials and activity by-products among the companies of the park. At the center lies a coal-fired power plant (Asnaes Power Station) that recovers its surplus heat to fuel 3500 local homes and a fish farm. Steam surplus from the power plant is sold to the pharmaceutical company, Novo Nordisk, and to a Statoil plant. Moreover, a by-product from the power plant's sulfur dioxide scrubber contains gypsum that is recovered by a wallboard manufacturer. The fish farm sells its sludge as a fertilizer, and fly ash and clinker from the power plant is used for road building and cement production.

Today, more than 30 flows established between 13 entities structure this industrial system. On average, the return on investment of the activities set in symbiosis is lower than five years. In comparison, in 2007, when 16 flows existed, the setting in symbiosis would have required a redeemable US$60 million investment with a 20-year return on investment.[50] Kalundborg has been visited by many foreign delegations, and has been taken by many as a model to develop experimental projects.

The Tianjin Economic Technological Development Area (TEDA) in China has worked with the European Union to create a network of industrial symbiosis and an environmental training program. TEDA is home to companies like Motorola, Toyota, Novozymes and Samsung, and aims to engage 800 firms in the network and become a role model in China. It has so far achieved ISO 14001 certification and passed the evaluation hosted by China Environmental Protection Administration. Much has to be done at TEDA to reach its ambitious goal, but given the major footprint of China in the world economy and environment, any advance counts.[51]

Another interesting development is Masdar City in Abu Dhabi. Built from scratch to be one of the most sustainable communities on the planet, it aims to become a cluster for clean-tech companies. Urban planning, engineering and architecture; energy management; water management; waste management; transportation and supply chain have all been developed under sustainability principles. For example, Hangzhou ISAW, a Chinese company developing technologies related to psychrometrics (engineering concerned with the determination of physical and thermodynamic properties of gas-vapor mixtures), has been working to develop a large-scale solar-powered liquid air-cooling system that saves energy and reduces CO_2 emissions.[52]

The main challenge is now to transform this impressive showroom into a real town with real companies facing real issues. Having a rich sponsor like the UAE can help to some extent, but one lesson from innovation is that it is first and foremost based on users' acceptance and capacity to integrate the new into their know-how, practices and identity. Top-down systems can work to a certain degree, but if there is no room for bottom-up appropriation, the system is doomed to fail. Nevertheless, it is an experiment to be watched closely.

Technology can be a major facilitator for developing these initiatives. International Synergies developed an industrial symbiosis web platform with this aim. SYNERGie™ is a bespoke resource management software platform that offers database, project management and reporting functionality to capture and store information about a company's resources and to easily identify commercial opportunities for reuse.[53] WWF-UK states that this platform is used by projects in China, Turkey, Brazil, South Africa, Hungary, Romania and Slovakia. In Brazil, 300 businesses in the state of Minas Gerais have used the tool and "this collaboration has prevented 94,500 tons of waste from going to landfill and reduced CO_2 emissions by 84,000 tons."[54]

LOCAL INNOVATION AS AN ENTREPRENEURIAL ENGINE

In contrast to the collective initiative at Kalundborg, a territorial project based on the circular economy can emerge or be supported by a single entrepreneurial initiative. We will illustrate this possibility with an example under analysis in a southern region of France: the implementation of a green waste valorization business at the scale of a geographical area. This mimics the projects developed, for example, by Waste Concern in Bangladesh or empowered by a platform like SYNERGie™. This is a considerable challenge given the amount of waste produced in most countries and the many possible applications to use this waste as an entrant.

Starting point: The missing link

In order to support the synchronization between available materials and their possible applications, it is first necessary to diagnose the types of materials available on the territory, their quantity and composition as well as their localization. In parallel, the needs in terms of materials should be identified.

The creation of a central resource office could be responsible for these tasks, which could eventually lead to the creation of a physical place centralizing all the available outputs. This would be improbable, however, due to the complexity, cost and logistic impact of a physical centralization of organic materials. A quick analysis of the SBMC would immediately highlight the quasi-incapacity to render such a project profitable. On the other hand, a "virtual" resource center (like the SYNERGie™ platform) could mitigate the disadvantages of a physical resource center while fulfilling the same functions. A web interface could thus be developed to offer a marketplace to material holders and the applications to recover these materials, to establish links and to implement direct logistic flows, consequently enabling the economic viability of the project. Besides its capacity to respond to already existing needs at a territory level, this platform could become a genuine local economic development tool. Indeed, by proposing a qualified and quantified cartography of available materials as well as a guarantee of minimum amount of inputs to scale the recovery activities, it would allow the identification of geographical spaces with stronger material concentration, thus being able to encourage the installation of new economic operators near them. The knowledge resulting from this entrepreneurial business may therefore be used to create positive externalities that could in turn be transformed into value capture. Such a project could be carried out completely by a single entrepreneur or by a cooperative initiative.

Design of a new economic activity

The SBMC would help to structure the development and the strategic design of such an activity. The value proposition would consist of an optimized provision of qualified and quantified organic materials on a given territory. This value proposition would be addressed to segments of customers recovering these materials and being based on a web platform and as distribution channel (business model of a virtual resource center). The management of customer relation/partner would be primarily automatic, with potentially a personalized direct relation for the establishment of the initial contacts.

The key resource would be obviously the organic material, which uncovers a second market: that of the material holders.

The business model is thus structured around a two-sided market. IT competences and equipment constitute another key resource for the development and the management of the web platform. Lastly, a sales force would be necessary to launch the project. This could be based on a network of partners to advertise the project, such as the Regional Agricultural Chambers, professional distribution or the restoration associations. Regarding key activities, the identification of the actors to build the cartography of available materials on the territory is a precondition to the project. The development of an ergonomic and easy-to-use platform is also essential, as well as the development of specific modules, such as, for example, a research function integrating logistic optimization algorithms. A partnership could again be established with a logistic operator taking charge of the physical transport of the materials and with whom negotiations would be established to pool transport, generate economies of scale and thus obtain optimized financial conditions for the whole of the participants. Lastly, the local Chambers of Commerce and Environmental Government Agencies could probably be financial and/or technical partners to the project.

The economic model

The economic model can be built around various scenarios that would have to be evaluated. If the costs can be estimated depending on the amount of resources to be deployed and the value chain configuration, there are various methods to generate revenue streams. The first option would consist of recovering economically the exchanged material, collecting the monetary flows and managing the remuneration of the actors, by taking a fee for the intermediation. An alternative formula could consist of a fixed monthly or annual subscription, plus a variable fee depending on the amount offered or demanded. In this case, the platform does not necessarily need to manage money transfers, which may create issues with large clients that could bypass the platform. The price fixing of the material itself can be established variously. Does the material as such have a fixed

Table 4.1 *Sustainable business model canvas of green waste valorization business*

Costs for Society and the Environment	Key Partners	Key Activities	Sustainable Value Proposition	Customer Relationship Management	Customers Segments	Benefits for Society and the Environment
• Downstream and upstream environmental externalities of the economic activities • Environmental negative externalities related to the operations (e.g. transport)	• Regional chambers of agriculture • Professional federations of the distribution or the hospitality industry • Logistic operators • Local or regional government • Environmental agency	• IT development, platform development, management and maintenance • Management of the system of actors and the partners • Establishment of a cartography of holders and needs for materials • Direct and indirect prospection (prescribers and partners) • Development of associated services (e.g. logistic optimization) **Key Resources** • Organic material • IT platform and the whole of human and physical resources associated • Sales force	Optimized provision of qualified and quantified organic material in a certain region	• Personalized management • Automatized relationships • Co-creation of value for the material qualification and quantification **Distribution** Web platform	• Holders of materials (by typology of materials) • Material users (by typology of usage and needs)	• Promotion of the local economic fabric • Creation of additional income to a large number of actors • Development of new economic activities by the valorization of waste • Effective management of this waste • Use of recycled material preventing fabrication of new materials (preservation of raw materials)

Shared Costs	Cost Structure		Revenue Streams		Shared Benefits
• Energy costs and entrants (raw materials) • Transport (externalized to the systems of actors) • Associated waste due to a volume strategy	• Costs of mobilization of the resources and configuration of the chain of value • Cost of development of the partnerships		• Option 1: Centralization and management of monetary flows with intermediation fee • Option 2: Subscription based on a dynamic tariffing related to exchanged tonnage + Remuneration related to the associated services		• Transforming waste into a productive resource

or variable price? Is the price progressive (or regressive) depending on the amount demanded or offered (in particular by the fall of the relative logistics cost in relation to the real flow)? Is the price related to the quality of the material and the applications it supports? Are we looking to define an auction process where prices are a function of offer and demand (which would require a larger number of actors taking part in the system)? As we observe, the options are multiple, and the development of *business cases* must be carried out to establish the economically viable and profitable scenarios, that will also maximize acceptability and motivation to take part in such a system.

From bottom line to triple bottom line

The profitability of such a project must obviously be measured by financial performance metrics, but not only. Thus, in the optics of the *triple bottom line* discussed in Chapter 2, the business model should also evaluate the project's environmental and social surpluses, based on relevant indicators. The environmental and social outcomes are numerous, like the promotion of the local economic fabric, the creation of additional income to a large number of actors, the development of new economic activities by the valorization of waste, and consequently an effective management of this waste, and so on.

This illustration, inevitably naive and incomplete here, allows showcasing the interest of the SBMC and the dynamic character of its construction.

This may sound hypothetical but it takes a real turn in places like Kalundborg in Denmark or in Sweden, which is currently importing waste. In fact, only one percent of domestic waste goes to garbage dumps compared to an average 38 percent in Europe: 36 percent is recycled, 14 percent composted and 49 percent incinerated. These energetic valorization centers provide 20 percent of the country house heating and electricity for 5 percent of domestic users. But Sweden is not currently producing enough waste to "nourish" these incinerators and started to import waste from Norway, bringing an extra proof to the fact that waste = resource.

Another country to be watched carefully is China that is taking bold actions to favor a circular economy. It voted in 2008 a particularly ambitious bill to promote circular economy at the country level, thus supporting the emergence of regional projects founded on industrial ecology, and in parallel stimulate companies to reconsider the use of materials.[55] By 2011, "27 provinces and municipalities, 29 recycling-oriented industrial parks and/or enterprises, 89 companies, four townships, and 44 industrial parks have become involved in these pilot activities under the supervision of the central government."[56] The main environmental economic instruments are natural resource prices and environmental fees; resources, energy and environmental taxation; green trade policy; emissions trading; green consumption; eco-compensation; green fiscal policy; and green finance.

HOW CIRCULAR ECONOMY MAY CHALLENGE MANY INDUSTRIES?

Remarkable work has been done by the Ellen MacArthur Foundation (EMF) since 2010 to give information about and promote circular economy. They are at the forefront in establishing a resource center to gain additional knowledge and access to business cases based on the circular economy principles.

The first main report on circular economy,[57] released in January 2012, invited readers to imagine an economy where today's products are the resources of tomorrow, creating a new operating system for a world of finite resources. The potential to transform several economic sectors like buildings, medium-life complex products, mobile and smartphones, light commercial vehicles and washing machines were explored and the associated gains clearly documented. The global impact that has been assessed is just tremendous. "Based on detailed product level modeling, the report estimates that the circular economy represents an annual material cost saving opportunity of USD 340 to 380 billion p.a. at EU level for a 'transition scenario' and USD 520 to 630 billion p.a. for an 'advanced scenario', all net of the materials used in the reverse-cycle processes."[58] And those figures are based only on a subset of EU manufacturing sectors. The report details the potential gains by industries, ranging from motor vehicles to machinery and equipment, furniture, radio, TV and communication. As an example the report highlights that the "cost of remanufacturing mobile phones could be reduced by 50 percent per device – if the industry made phones easier to take apart, improved the reverse cycle, and offered incentives to return phones." Associated environmental gains also show impressive figures on this sole mobile phone production case: eradication of at least 1.3 million tons of CO_2 annually in the transition scenario, net of the emissions produced during reverse-cycle processes; exclusion of energy and water-intensive production steps (like aluminum smelting); move toward less toxic materials (such as using more biological nutrients for consumables, for example, for food packaging); all contributing to reduce pressure on GHG emissions, water usage and biodiversity.[59] In February 2013, The EMF released its second report focusing on fast-moving consumer goods that have a lower unit cost, are bought more often and have a much shorter service life than durable goods. Knowing they represent up to 35 percent of material inputs into the economy, 75 percent of municipal waste and that they absorb 90 percent of the agricultural outputs, the Foundation has considered it important to test how circular economy may be applied to them.[60] A focus has been made on three industries: food and beverage, clothing, and packaging. Here are the main findings:

- Food and beverage: At global sales of US$ 8.3 trillion annually, this industry is the largest in the fast-moving consumer goods industry. "Processing the mixed food waste discarded by households and the hospitality sector in line with circular principles could generate an income stream of USD 1.5 billion annually in the UK alone."[61] It requires several triggers: collecting separate streams of food waste by improving current collection processes (experiments show it can be organized at no significant extra costs), increasing consumer participation in refuse-separation schemes, using regulations to channel food waste to the highest-value uses, being smart about synergies, location and optimal size of anaerobic digestion (AD), pursuing necessary technology innovation to make digestate a more versatile product, and investment requirements on AD plants.[62]

- Clothing and footwear are the second-largest category of spend within the consumer sector (US$ 1.8 trillion sales annually at a global scale).

  > There are profitable circular opportunities to reuse end-of-life clothing, which, in addition to being worn again, can also be cascaded down to other industries to make insulation or stuffing, or simply recycled into yarn to make fabrics that save virgin fibers. If sold at current prices in the U.K., a ton of collected and sorted clothing can generate a revenue of USD 1,975, or a gross profit of USD 1,295 after subtracting the USD 680 required to collect and sort each ton.[63]

  The report cites Worn Again – a zero waste textile company based in the UK – and Patagonia (see cases previously in this book) as role models.

- Packaging: Playing a crucial role in protecting and dispensing a product, they are generally discarded at the time of consumption, representing nearly 20 percent of household wastes. Single-used packaging may be redesigned as biodegradable packaging (that means designed for biological regeneration) to regenerate food/farming systems. Technical and/or durable packaging may be recovered for reuse. Keeping packaging in circulation longer will indeed deliver dramatically greater material savings and profit compared to the traditional linear one-way system, especially if collection rates are high. "Our modeling of beer containers shows that shifting to reusable glass bottles would lower the cost of packaging, processing, and distribution by approximately 20 per cent per hectoliter of beer consumed."[64]

According to the report,

> the full value of these circular opportunities for fast-moving consumer goods could be as much as USD 700 billion per annum in material savings or a recurring 1.1 per cent of 2010 GDP, all net of materials used in the reverse-cycle processes. Those materials savings would represent about 20 percent of the materials input costs incurred by the consumer goods industry.[65]

This would moreover result in innovation, land productivity and soil health, and job-creation potential.

Triggers for this transition emerge from the combination of (1) resource scarcity and tighter environmental standards; (2) information technology enabling traceability in the supply chain (e.g. RFID, connected devices); and (3) a shift in consumer behavior from ownership to access.

New circular business models in and for the consumer goods industry start to appear and the EMF report cites the following[66]:

- *Volume aggregators*: "Markets for residues and by-products are currently severely under-developed, creating arbitrage opportunities for volume aggregators who stand at the forefront of organizing these markets. Asos, an aspiring online 'fashion destination' that offers more than 850 brands of new clothes, has extended its scope to the reverse cycle by creating a parallel platform where consumers can resell end-of-life clothing, and small firms can market 'vintage' garments and accessories as well as new ones."

- *Technology pioneers*: "New technologies (such as PHA bioplastics production from industrial wastewater) offer technology leaders a vast array of opportunities. [...] Veolia has pioneered the production of bioplastics from sludge. Wastewater treatment systems today often use bacteria that eat sludge and neutralize it into carbon. Using proprietary technology, Veolia achieved a breakthrough in converting this 'wastewater carbon' into biomass rich in PHA, which has mechanical properties equivalent to polypropylene and is thus valuable in making consumer plastics and chemicals. Veolia produced the first biopolymers from municipal waste in 2011, and is now refining the process to meet end-customer specifications at full-scale wastewater treatment sites in Belgium and Sweden."

- *Micro-marketers*: "In the food and beverage industry, large retailers such as Woolworths in Australia, WholeFoods in the U.S., and Migros in Switzerland, as well as global food giants such as Unilever, Nestlé, Danone, and Kraft Foods, are preparing for markets with more local sourcing, distributed manufacturing, increased customer interaction, diversified customer demand, multi-channel purchasing (including home-delivery), and ultimately more intimate customer relationships."

- *Urban-loop providers*: "Urbanization in emerging economies will create urban and peri-urban systems where waste streams of nutrients, heat, partially treated wastewater, or CO_2 are converted back into high-value biological products using much shorter and more resilient supply chains than today. [...] An example of this is The Plant, Chicago, a vertical aquaponic farm growing tilapia and vegetables that also serves as an incubator for craft food businesses and operates an anaerobic digester and a combined heat and power plant. Discarded materials from one business are used as a resource for another in an explicitly circular system."

- *Product-to-service converters*: "In the textile industry, players like Patagonia – which pioneered the 'Common Threads Initiative' to reduce the environmental footprint of its garments – seek longer and more intimate customer relationships beyond the point of sale. Value-added offerings like repair, amendment, return and leasing offer much greater customer interaction at multiple touch points. Some players are beginning to redefine themselves as fashion or style partners with superior customer insights and value opportunities along the life cycle and across different categories."

CONCLUSION

Psychological and social representations distort the relation we have with waste. Waste, by definition, is deprived of any value. It is dirty, without interest, hidden or to hide. The associated activities are not noble, inevitably uninteresting and marginally creative or innovating.

How wrong could we be! We hope that this chapter has highlighted the notion that waste should be reconsidered as a resource, well beyond the prism of recycling alone. Thus the outputs of any activity, any production process or consumption should be observed with interest and curiosity to see if they are not masking a hidden value. We would even move from the concept of waste to that of by-product of an activity, useful for the same activity or a future activity.

Such a valorization sometimes presupposes radical changes, primarily in our cognitive mechanisms, and then in the way we design our products and more widely our industrial activities. An effective management of a product at the end of its lifetime must indeed be considered at the design phase. The change must also take place on the level of our production and consumption processes, by supporting circular flows of materials and energy.

Although certain economic actors have resolutely taken this track, several others remain skeptical, thinking that the circular economy is be a barrier to progress, and that to build a product that lasts is inevitably a heresy, since it deprives the company of its replacement market, or at least delays it. And then the difficulties are generally discussed even before the benefits. Therefore such a change imposes a bold move. It is necessary to buy new machines, to recondition existing ones, to train staff, to manage the change, to invent things a priori impossible (like getting 25 percent of building heating needs from the body temperature of commuters in a station). The financial gains can be very unequally distributed in the company, and may create problems involved in the allocation of budgets and P&L reporting. Thus the revalorization of a product at the end of its lifetime and the rehabilitation of part of its components in a new generation of products are likely to generate gains for the "procurement" department, but will probably degrade the "operations" results, which will have to deal with the operations of disassembling and remaking. Even if the total assessment is positive, this can induce resistance on behalf of the operations direction if new budgetary and reporting rules are not adopted. Still on the production side, building a reliable production plan on the basis of circular material flows, requires simultaneous control over the quantity of material and its return planning, which is not so simple given the product is sold and that its property is transferred to the customer.

As we see, such a move presupposes a total commitment at the top management level, since certain components of the business model can be particularly impacted. In certain cases, this stage can paradoxically be facilitated by a more radical evolution of the business model, making even the planned obsolescence principle void, while creating financially appealing incentives to support eco-efficiency and circularity. This is the subject of the last two chapters of this book.

5
From Products to Use-Oriented Services

As an introduction to this chapter, we will sum up some of the insights that have been presented so far:

- We have entered into a world of rare and expensive resources. Because these resources are already scarce in terms of quality and quantity, and will continue to be increasingly so, our relation with resources and with energy must change, moving toward more efficiency and a radical decoupling of the economic activity from the consumption of resources and energy. This is necessary for environmental and social reasons, and for the sake of competitiveness.

- The principles of eco-efficiency and a circular economy offer ways to redefine this relation. Although they may appear to be an inspiring option for managers, their implementation is not so straightforward.

- In a Western economy, largely saturated with consumer goods,[1] the principle of planned obsolescence is encouraged to instigate replacement by households and support economic activity. Would a product that lasts too long or that is easily reparable be in fact harmful for the economic activity?

- Another central argument constantly presented is that consumers are thirsty for innovation and change. Technical obsolescence is thus complemented by psychological obsolescence: a two-year-old telephone is obsolete, six-month-old clothing is out of fashion, a flat-screen television is already "has been" compared to a 3D television.

- And as soon as a manufacturer improves its devices – for example, the number of features of a smartphone or MP3 player increases on average by 28 percent in every new version – consumers want to benefit from these novelties even though, on average, they use only 10 to 12 percent of the features at their disposal.[2] How can we satisfy this appetite for novelty with products that last without end?

- The implementation of a circular economy on a large scale would mean that flows of material would have to be controlled more efficiently. However, when ownership of the product is transferred to the customer, it is the customer who becomes responsible for the management of the product at the end of its life. And despite public awareness campaigns, recycling behavior, for example, remains limited. For example, in 2010, less than 10 percent of cell phones were recycled.[3] Even if the quantities collected by waste treatment centers are increasing constantly (+15 percent between 2007 and 2009), less than 50 percent of packaging, glass and cardboards are deposited in selective waste treatment centers. At a global scale, we may estimate that 60 percent of total waste is not recycled, composted or reused.[4] At the micro level, a company eager to set up a circular material flow cannot count simply on the goodwill of the customers to bring the goods back at the end of the lifetime.

Given this context, how can a company be guaranteed that implementing these principles is a driver of value creation contributing to its economic performance and competitiveness? How can the concept of planned obsolescence become null and void? How can an individual's appetite for novelty be satisfied in a finite world and a new relation with goods be built? How can material flows be better controlled to allow circularity?

One answer consists in reconsidering the nature of transaction itself, substituting the sale of a good for its provision without transfer of ownership. This shift to a service model centered on use does not, however, automatically result in economic, environmental and social advantages. On the contrary, certain conditions are required to improve environmental and possibly social performance, conditions that we will now examine.

THE TRANSITION TO USE-ORIENTED SERVICES

Use-oriented services aim to redefine the relation with the tangible goods that surround us by making them available without transfer of ownership, and by invoicing their use. The examples of such services are numerous: hiring, leasing, pooling, shared consumption like car sharing or self-service bicycles, public transport, collaborative consumption and so on. As we will see, not every offer has the same sustainability potential.

Although these services may seem to have no particular interest at an individual level, the macro consequences of such a transition are potentially very important on economic, sociological, anthropological and even philosophical grounds.

Firstly, from an economic point of view, the provision of a good without transfer of ownership profoundly modifies the relation with the object and to time. In contrast to the sale of an asset, which produces a one-shot source of revenue, a good whose use is invoiced to the customer generates recurring revenue throughout its life. The profitability generated by a single good will thus be a function of the length of its use lifetime, rendering theoretically irrelevant the idea of planned obsolescence. Moreover, a good developed to be put at the disposal of a customer finds an economic interest in being robust and easy to maintain or repair, because any failure induces a rupture of service and a resulting loss of earnings, financial penalties or surcharges for the company. The passage to such a model thus encourages the company to develop the product within the perspective of eco-design, which specifies a greater longevity of the good through an increased robustness and a greater reparability.

The relation to the physical good is as such modified. A good that is shared among several users rather than one alone increases its intensity of use. While a personal vehicle remains more than 95 percent of its time in a car park, a shared car will be able to spend from 45 to 55 percent of its life in service, thus increasing the service rendered for the same amount of physical material in use. In the United States, each time the car-sharing leader Zipcar puts an additional car in circulation in an urban environment, it helps to remove 15 personal vehicles from circulation, considerably reducing the number of cars on the road and the associated congestion and pollution issues.[5] An increase in such services would reduce the demand for physical material while guaranteeing the access to the service offered by these goods.

The absence of transfer of ownership offers another significant benefit. The company keeps the control of the material and can thus organize a closed loop system according to an optimized scheme. The implementation of the principle of circularity is simplified, because the company knows exactly how much material is in use, can plan its return and can therefore control the production planning. The example of Xerox presents the scope and relevance of this model.

The first (r)evolution of Xerox: The leasing of machines[6]

When Xerox decided at the end of the 1980s to set up a policy for the provision of its photocopiers via a leasing system instead of selling machines, it did not expect to reap environmental benefits as well as important economic gains. It should be said that, initially, the motivation for such an evolution was more commercial than environmental. With the release of a large number of patents held by Xerox and the resulting intensification of competition, it became increasingly difficult to convince clients to pay a premium price to compensate for the (past) innovation and R & D investments made by the company. A new pricing model was thus necessary.

Thanks to this change in its business model, Xerox radically modified the trade relation it had with its clients by breaking down a single price over time. But the benefits far exceeded this commercial advantage alone. Despite this, the project was almost abandoned, because by preserving the ownership of the products used by its customers, Xerox had underestimated the importance of the re-internalization of a cost hitherto supported by the customer: the management of the product at the end of its lifetime. This cost was substantial at the beginning. It was by reconsidering this consequent and expensive flow of products at the end of their lifetime that Xerox kicked off a particularly innovative and visionary approach at the time.

Toward the revalorization of machines

In 1991, the company decided to launch a vast program of revalorization of machines and supplies at the end of their lifetime. Through an eco-design approach, the products and the supplies were redesigned around the principles of disassembly capacity, recycling and reuse for the next generation machines. A major reflection was carried out by design engineering teams in close cooperation with those responsible for product dismantling and remaking, environment and security experts, and commercial teams, in order to provide information about the quantities and types of machines arriving at the end of their lifetime in the client installed base.

This eco-design effort enabled impressive gains in effectiveness and considerable savings:

> [P]roducts now have ten times fewer components and variety of material than before; the fastening systems allow fast and easy disassembly; the components are interchangeable from one machine to another; the materials are selected based on their relevance with respect to the durability of the product, and not only on their cost: gold contactors can thus be preferred

to those made of aluminum or lead in the parts likely to endure several life cycles; the dangerous substances are clearly indexed and their localization well specified in order to facilitate their recovery; the materials which can be recycled – plastics in particular – are privileged; even inks are selected in order to be able to be easily washable with water and soap.[7]

What are the results?

Thanks to eco-design, 70 to 90 percent of the machine components at the end of their lifetime are currently recovered and reused in the manufacturing of new machines. This represents considerable financial profits, coupled with a considerable reduction of waste, use of raw materials and energy. Xerox thus estimates a gain of several hundred million dollars each year through its practice of reusing components and remanufacturing – US$2 billion is often quoted as the savings made by the group between 1992 and 2002 thanks to the redesign of its products and production processes.[8] Energy savings through this program in 2006 alone amounted to 175,000 MWh, that is, the energy necessary to light 136,000 American houses for one year.[9]

Extension toward other applications

Similar efforts were carried out for supplies. By encouraging the recovery of empty supplies or by managing it directly or through partners, in a single year, Xerox recovers and recycles 2.7 million cartridges, toner cartridges and toner bottles, and treats more than 480 tons of used toner powder for recycling. A new cartridge can thus contain up to 25 percent of this reprocessed toner powder.

All innovation projects of the company take into account eco-design specifications. Thus, the solid toner powder, a recent development, generates approximately 2.5 kg of waste over the average lifetime of a machine, compared to 70 kg for the use of a traditional (liquid) toner. This innovation has now been integrated into the entire Xerox product range. All these efforts have made it possible to reduce waste related to the cartridges, toner cartridges and toner powder by more than 40 percent, dropping from 6,830 tons in 2002 to 3,990 tons in 2006.

As this example suggests, the economic and environmental benefits of a transition to a use-oriented service are not automatic, and it would be false to think that service itself is virtuous. It is enough to remember that American and European economies have seen a continuous growth in the service sector during the 20th century, without any reduction in their environmental impact, on the contrary.[10]

To reap environmental benefits along with economic benefits, the substitution of sales of the product with the provision of these same products in a service system presupposes a reliance on certain principles; the better these principles are implemented, the higher the gains:

- The redesign of the product by the application of the principle of eco-efficiency, allowing better usability, greater resistance, increased facility for maintenance and repair, and an anticipated capacity for disassembly to allow the circularity of the components. Thus the transition from *ownership* to *usership*,[11] the latter qualifying the goods put at the disposal of their users and requiring a redesign to resist the intensification of their use.

- The redefinition of the production system by applying circularity of flows and implementing closed-loop systems.

An optimization of the use or an intensification of the use per unit of mobilized physical resources may deliver substantial environmental and social improvements while generating added-value to the offer and potentials for innovation. As an example, circling to find a parking space represents about 30 percent of driving in San Francisco,[12] generating many negative social and environmental spin-offs. The San Francisco Municipal Transportation Agency therefore decided to react by establishing SFpark, a new service that uses new technologies and policies to improve parking in San Francisco. Concretely,

> (SFpark works by collecting and distributing real-time information about where parking is available through a phone application so drivers can quickly find free spaces. To help achieve the right level of parking availability, SFpark periodically adjusts meter and car park pricing up and down to match demand. Demand-responsive pricing encourages drivers to park in underused areas and car parks, reducing demand in overused areas.)[13]

Thanks to this use-optimization service, there is a drastic reduction of time spent looking for a parking space. The associated benefits are numerous: less congestion, reduction of pollution, time saving, faster public transit, more safety for pedestrians and bicyclists (drivers looking for parking spaces are frequently distracted and fail to see bicyclists and pedestrians). All this contributes more generally to a better quality of life. As presented in detail later on, the consequences are numerous for traditional value chains. Indeed, manufacturers are the economic actors most likely to promote these transitions because they will potentially reap most of the associated economic gains. For instance, a car or tool hire company does not have the upward and downward control of the product, and can neither act on its redesign, nor benefit from the installation of circular flows.

IS THE CUSTOMER READY FOR THE TRANSITION?

To answer this question, we distinguish the business-to-business (B2B) market from the business-to-consumer (B2C) market.

The B2B market

In B2B, companies have a long tradition of outsourcing, going well beyond the simple question of "make or buy." They maintain many service relations with suppliers, whom they learned to control and evaluate. The relation to ownership is "colder," less emotional than its equivalent in B2C, and does not seem to constitute a real barrier here. Use-oriented services also offer many advantages appreciated by companies. They must by nature guarantee a quick management of any service disruption related to an equipment breakdown or failure, which is often sought by a company to guarantee continuity of operations. Suppliers are responsible for piloting and optimizing maintenance costs, as well as the management of the product at the end of its lifetime. Payment can be based on the equipment's effective use, potentially binding the cost of the service to the level of activity, and transforming a fixed cost or a capital expenditure into a variable cost or an operational expenditure. These services can as such reduce the need for immobilized capital, improving cash flow consequently. All these reasons confer a strong added-value to this kind of commercial offer if they answer real issues for the client, as in the case of the Michelin Fleet Solutions service described next.

Michelin goes farther with Michelin Fleet Solutions[14]

How to increase turnover by selling fewer tires and by increasing the added-value brought to professional customers? By finding an original answer to this question, Michelin got a considerable advance over its competitors.

The traditional business model of a tire manufacturer rests on the sale of a product. Not such a virtuous economic model when it comes to maximizing the lifetime of the tire. And not a particularly interesting model in the long term for the fleet operator, who must immobilize financial resources in a primarily fixed cost, and who must dedicate internal resources to manage the fleet's tires, even more in the case of an large fleet. Given that an under-inflated tire, for example, increases consumption and deteriorates more quickly, good tire management is an essential and expensive resource for the fleet operator.

An outsourced management of the fleet's tires

Conscious of these challenges, Michelin created a strategic rupture by developing a new business model for professional fleet operators. It offers them an outsourced management service of the fleet's tires, based on the provision of tires remaining the ownership of Michelin and invoiced on the basis of distance travelled.

This service comprises, in addition to the provision of tires, a maintenance service designed to optimize the fleet's uptime, regular checking of their pressure, retreading to optimize the road holding, and consequently fuel consumption and the safety of drivers and transported goods. Thanks to this system, the lifetime of the tire was multiplied by 2.5 and the tire casing, which constitutes 70 percent of the end product, is organized today in a circular flow.

The customer benefits

The advantages of such an evolution for the customer are numerous, which enhances its acceptance:

- It allows management processes to be streamlined by outsourcing an activity outside the fleet operator's core business, and thus eliminating hidden costs related to internal management (like the administrative costs of tire management, tire storage, breakdown service and immobilization in the event of a tire bursting and so on).

- It transforms a fixed cost (purchase of tires) into a variable cost (payment by distance traveled) thus binding this cost to the volume of activities (and thus to the turnover) of the fleet operator.

- It improves the productivity of the fleet by an optimized schedule of operations and by a reduction of incidents via the execution of preventive maintenance.

- Because it guarantees the best tire conditions and optimizes road holding, it improves safety for the drivers and goods.

- It enables fuel savings. Tires are responsible for up to 35 percent of fuel consumption. On average, the use of Michelin Fleet Solutions tires allows a reduction of 5 to 6 percent in fuel consumption (an amount equivalent to the budget necessary for the purchase of tires). Moreover, checking tire pressure and retreading enable this performance level to be maintained over time. Given current (expensive) fuel prices, these savings are particularly sought by fleet operators.

- Fuel savings contribute to reducing the fleet's CO_2 emissions and thus help operators respect their sustainability policies.

All these reasons contribute to the offer's acceptability and high perceived value. It has been a commercial success and more than 50 percent of large European truck fleets currently outsource the management of their tires. Michelin thus currently manages 260,000 vehicles in 20 European countries,[14] with a profitable offer generating considerable resource and energy savings.

Another example comes from the provision of office space. The economic crisis, mobile workers and widespread diffusion of wireless internet, among others, have resulted in more and more vacant office spaces. As a recent *Wired* article puts it: "that vast built environment now inhabits the American landscape like a massive untapped natural resource."[16] Liquidspace[17] is an American start-up addressing this potential with a business model of "office space as a service." It affirms that on average in North America, office space sits unused about two-thirds of the time, costing money without any productivity. Liquidspace aims to help "companies leverage unused office space, both their own and everyone else's. The more they can make use of unused space 'out there,' the less they have to spend leasing and maintaining their own."[18]

This model has several virtues: it prevents new buildings from being built, potentially reduces transportation and intensifies use of a resource that is already out there. This follows the example of companies like Deloitte who pioneered "hot desking," where employees do not have assigned desks and sit wherever available.

The B2C market

Evolution of the relation to ownership

If the acceptance of use-oriented services is generally positive in the B2B market, what about the end-consumers market? This kind of service presupposes first and foremost a renouncement of ownership, which can constitute a sacrifice that certain consumer segments are not ready to accept. It should be recalled that private ownership is a pillar of modernity in the West, and that, during the 20th century, it was praised and advertised as a central axis of distinction between capitalist and communist economic systems.

Moreover, much research carried out by psychologists, sociologists, anthropologists, social geographers or philosophers have highlighted the intrinsic value associated with ownership. Objects are seen as an extension of ourselves[19], the expression of the identity and the image customers want to convey.[20] Ownership has been shown to have an extrinsic value – as, for example, the expression of a status, a symbolic value, a social distinction, and a source of self-esteem – and an intrinsic value – linked to the pleasure, emotion or sacred character of the consumption. A famous experiment showed that the estimated value of a low involvement good, like a mug, varied in a significant way according to whether it was possessed or not. It was thus shown that the perception and the evaluation of a good are modified at the moment when there is physical possession, which has a value in itself.[21]

Nevertheless, in recent years, the relation to ownership has evolved in advanced economies, especially among younger generations privileging access and collaboration to ownership. In 2000 already, the American futurist Jeremy Rifkin caused a buzz with his book *The Age of Access*, where he voiced the entry into a new era based on concepts of access and networks, by affirming that "it is [...] access rather than mere ownership that increasingly determines one's status in the coming age[22]." A good example is the shift to mobility that is taking place in the car industry. The evolution is noteworthy, and innovative business models have switched from car ownership to car sharing, through ride sharing and now peer-to-peer car rentals.

Mobility as use-oriented service

What is the role of the individually owned car in the city of the future? This is a question under constant scrutiny by all carmakers and a common understanding emerges that we will no longer talk about transportation but about mobility.[23]

A first major evolution in the relation to cars was the emergence of the car-sharing system. Rather than buying a car, a driver may access a vehicle by being invoiced for its usage. The fast growth of the car-sharing service Zipcar in the US symbolizes this shift. Created in 2000, it promotes itself as the "world's leading car-sharing network with approximately 767,000 members and over 10,000 vehicles located in major metropolitan areas and college campuses throughout the US, Canada and UK."[24]

The operation principle is simple: a user first needs to create an account on the zipcar.com website. Rates and plans depend on occasional or regular use. The user will then receive an access card equipped with RFID technology that serves to unlock the car doors; the keys are located inside. Members can book Zipcars online at any time, by phone or via the iPhone or Android application, and have automated access to Zipcars using the access card. Gas, parking, insurance and maintenance are included in the price. Zipcar offers several models of vehicles, including petrol and low-emission vehicles. The company's IPO was in April 2011 and its stock was traded on NASDAQ. Proof of its success, it was bought up in 2012 by the rental car leader Avis Budget Group, Inc. for US$500 million in cash.

The car-sharing system can be implemented by a private operator such as Zipcar, but can equally be initiated by public institutions, as in the case of Autolib' in Paris.

A group of 46 municipal councils around Paris decided to set up an innovative car-sharing system based on electric cars in Paris and delegated the operation of the system to a private company, Bolloré. Interestingly, the core business of Bolloré was not initially in the mobility industry, the company being a lithium-ion battery maker. Classical mobility operators failed to convince the consortium of municipalities and the contract was finally awarded to a new entrant in the industry, demonstrating that innovation in sustainable development may break the rules of the game in a mature industry.

Bolloré has partnered with Pininfarina to develop an electric vehicle and plans to deploy 3,000 electric vehicles that can be picked up and dropped off at various locations around Paris. Cars will be available 24 hours a day to residents and tourists wishing to drive in the dense heart of the Paris region and surrounding areas.

Existing companies in this industry have started to react like rental car companies and manufacturers. For example, Hertz Corporation released Hertz on Demand in London, New York and Paris and has since expanded in these countries as well as in Canada, Germany and Spain. BMW, Mini and Sixt partnered to launch a premium car-sharing service called DriveNow,[25] a service currently deployed in Germany (Berlin, Cologne, Dusseldorf and Munich) and the United States (San Francisco). Other initiatives include Daimler AG car2go service[26] available in Europe and North America, Volkswagen with the Quicar in Germany, or Peugeot who launched Mu by Peugeot in France. The latter extends the mobility service a step further: it is based on the hire of petrol or electric cars, but also bicycles, scooters, commercial vehicles or additional accessories from the brand. The principle of operation is simple: the user must create an account on the Mu by Peugeot web site or smartphone application and credit it with an amount. The user can then book any vehicle of the Peugeot range at an advantageous rate. The vehicle will be made available in one of the Peugeot dealerships offering the service. In certain cases, a chauffeur service can also bring or take back the vehicle for an extra charge. The user is then able to use the vehicle for a maximum duration of 31 days. As this example shows, disintermediation within a value chain is a potential consequence of use-oriented services.

As the car-sharing system develops all over the world, alternative business models are emerging, such as the peer-to-peer car rental, highlighting the change in the status of the ownership car and the ability to share personal car with unknown persons.

Whipcar, for example, connected neighbors so that those with cars can cut their costs by hiring to those without. Based on collaborative consumption, it was launched in 2010 and by May 2012 had built up a database of 19,000 owners willing to rent out their car for around £8 an hour, or £30 a day, totaling 100,000 rental hours.[27] Its motto was "Love thy neighbor, drive their car" and for drivers it was organized in a clear-cut process from registration, search engine for cars, booking, car collection and return and feedback. A central component of Whipcar was its insurance model: "While the car is being hired out it is comprehensively covered by Whipcar's own insurance policy – so if the car is written of by a hirer, it will not affect the owner's insurance policy, and raise premiums as a result."[28] This shows the emergence of a true supportive environment to allow the development of peer-to-peer car rentals (the same occurs for home/rooms sharing with Airbnb, with peer-to-peer lending platform with Zilok, and others). For undisclosed reasons, Whipcar ended its operations on March 12, 2013.

What's next? With interoperability among different transportation modes, foldable cars like the Hiriko,[29] interactive cars like the Toyota Fun VII, or even driverless cars like the Google car,[30] it is certain that the car industry is going to be an exciting innovation field in the years to come.

A central assumption of these initiatives is that consumers are keen to try new mobility options based on access rather than ownership. Several studies have shown that behaviors are evolving in this direction. A TNS Sofres study on mobility insists on the evolution of the sector toward an intensification of the use and multimodality to the detriment of the traditional ownership of a vehicle.[31] Frost & Sullivan estimate that the car-sharing market in the United States would be worth US\$3.3 billion by 2016.[32] According to a study carried out by Research Latitude for the magazine *Shareable*, a publication of reference on the new collaborative economy, 75 percent of the 537 individuals in the sample thought they would intensify the sharing of physical goods and space in the five years to come.[33] Rachel Botsman[34] estimates that the private rental market will reach US\$26 billion in the next five years.

Initiatives empowered by the development of collaborative web technologies have created new relationships with objects and have furthermore installed a new culture of consumption. NeighborGoods, Ecomodo and Zilok are example of these web platforms.[35] US-based NeighborGoods enable participants to lend and borrow money and resources within a group where each group is charged a monthly fee and there are no transaction fees.[36] Ecomodo hosts hundreds of different circles and lending communities across the UK[37] and Zilok does the same in France.[38]

One impressive success story is Airbnb.[39] Created in 2008 in San Francisco, Airbnb is a trusted community marketplace for people to list, discover and book unusual accommodation around the world – online or from a mobile phone. In less than five years, it has over ten million nights booked, over 300,000 listings worldwide, over 33,000 cities in 192 countries, and over 600 million social connections. Not bad for a young start-up taking "bed and breakfast" to a new level.

These networks operating on a peer-to-peer basis have been joined by private operators offering shared consumption goods. Thus Hire Fitness addresses a situation experienced by many clients. The most popular New Year's resolution is to keep fit. Some people join a fitness center, while many others decide to invest in some fitness equipment like treadmills, exercise bikes, vibration plates and so on. After a few weeks of enthusiasm, the question soon changes from "How can I get into shape?" to "How can I get rid of this cumbersome equipment?"

Hire Fitness thus proposes to hire out fitness equipment (cross trainers, treadmills, exercise bikes, rowers and vibration plates), deliver to the client's home, install it and give basic instruction on how to use and maintain the equipment safely. A joining fee and a minimum commitment of four weeks are necessary. If the client perseveres in the fitness effort, he can sign up for a longer rental at significant discounts along with equipment swaps for variety of exercises.[40]

Similarly, in the US, the Home Depot proposes rental of cumbersome and scarcely used appliances like carpet cleaners, pressure washers and others.[41] In the UK, B&Q is exploring models of collaborative consumption using social networking sites. For example, "the firm's StreetClub initiative allows communities to form local community groups, while fellow Kingfisher brand Castorama has rolled out Les Troc'heures – a skills sharing website."[42]

These examples demonstrate that the relationship toward ownership is beginning to change, supporting the potential development of use-based services. Of course, the environmental gains of such offers based on collaborative consumption still have to be analyzed but they do point to the intensification of goods usage. This is taking place even in fashion, the epitome of planned obsolescence, as illustrated next. Moreover, these models generally create positive social spin-offs by promoting solidarity and enhancing the social fabric. In the long run, they could possibly impact the social representations and challenge individualistic behaviors.

Clothing as a use-oriented service

Buying second-hand clothes has been around for a long time, long before vintage became fashionable. But, as illustrated by eBay, technology has enabled physical barriers to be overcome to connect people and enact new offers. For example, Swapstyle.com is a dedicated web platform for women to exchange clothing, cosmetics, books and accessories.[43] By 2012, it had over 40,000 members according to the WWF-UK.[44] Thredup does the same for kids,[45] while Refashioner, Bag Borrow or Steal, and Tie Society[46] offer the same service for expensive garments. Although the second-hand market is interesting, it is still based on a linear flow of materials, even if the transformation of products into waste is delayed. Is it possible to go beyond this, to improve the use of resources radically and possibly to close the loop?

The recent report[47] of the Ellen MacArthur Foundation mentioned earlier, makes the case for radical new models for collaborative consumption in the clothing sector. It states that

> formal wear rentals, particularly men's wedding attire, have a long history and have been joined by other new-clothing rental models, mainly for one-off hire and expensive items. In the U.K., "Girl Meets Dress" provides one-off rental of formal wear and clothing for socializing; a counterpart in the U.S. is "Rent the Runway", which offers designer-label garments. The basic business model is also well established for other infrequently used items: ski hire has always been available at the slopes, skates at the ice or roller rink, bowling and golf shoes, and so on. Unsurprisingly, rental models for maternity wear have also joined this line-up, such as, "Love Your Bump".[48]

The EMF report then makes the case for a "Netflix for clothing" that could represent a substantial opportunity:

> If we assume six million subscribers in the U.K. (approximately equivalent to the share of the U.S. population that subscribes to Netflix), this adds up to a material savings of USD 236 million. Considering the full system, a scenario that includes rental and achieves 75 percent collection of all end-of-use clothing results in a material savings of USD 3.8 billion for the U.K. Projected to North America and Europe, the savings rise to USD 44 billion.

Some have already decided to implement innovative concepts that close the loop. Le Relais,[49] a French cooperative with the motto: valorizing clothes by valorizing people was created with a clear mission: to collect and recycle textile products and to create jobs. The initiative has clearly been a success. 1600 socially excluded people and longtime unemployed have been hired to collect and sort more than 85,000 tons of clothes annually. Without this initiative, these textiles would be simply incinerated or put in landfills and definitely lost. Of the collected clothes in good state, 7 percent are resold locally at a very low price, and 30 percent are exported to poor countries. The rest is valorized, for example, by transforming old jeans into cotton insulation products for building insulation.

Neal Gorenflo, founder and editor-in-chief of *Shareable* goes further, stating that something even more fundamental is happening:

We realize that this is not simply a fad. Publications are multiplying, consultants are becoming interested in the phenomenon, governments are considering laws to support the development of this collaborative economy, and start-ups are raising impressive seed capital: all which converge to suggest that a new economy is indeed emerging.[50]

As a whole, this provides proof that B2C customers are ready, under certain conditions, for the transition toward use-oriented services.

THE ACCEPTABILITY OF USE-ORIENTED SERVICES

Acceptability of use-oriented services is conditioned by certain factors.

First of all, it is important to remember that these services are an innovation and as such, their adoption depends on a certain variables. These variables, which were identified some time ago by Everett Rogers,[51] include: the services' relative advantage over competing solutions, their complexity, their compatibility with established or usual practices or possessed equipment, the observability of their benefits or characteristics, or the perceived risk associated with the innovation.

Moreover, an innovation always arrives in a certain user-specific context and users are able to make use of this context (assimilation to existing know-how, integration in daily practices, appropriation to the identity, and adaptation to the environment) to make sense of the innovation and build usage significations, that is, the place the innovation will occupy in the user's system of values. It is important therefore not to impose an innovation on a user, but rather to integrate it swiftly with the existing knowledge, practices, identity and environment in order to ensure the transition from use to usage.[52] The starting point is listening to the clients to detect signals of change. For example, B&Q exploration of nonownership models of leasing and collaborative consumption is based on the observation that

> Businesses like Zipcar and Zilok are causing people to ask whether they still need to own a car? Do they need to own specialist power tools? According to Mathew Sexton, CSR director at B&Q, people are no longer wedded to the idea of owning stuff.[53]

Similarly, certain authors[54] highlight that trends favoring hiring or shared use instead of purchase can be explained by an evolution of lifestyles privileging the here and now, as well as the freedom conferred by the use. The morose economic climate can also reinforce the interest for use-oriented services, either in a forced way (e.g. because a bad credit rating prevents obtaining credit necessary to the purchase of a capital equipment), or in a voluntary way, hiring being more flexible and less engaging than acquisition.

A key motivation for users of Hire Fitness or Lokeo in France lies in this point. Some of the additional motivations identified include psychological freedom, flexibility and variety of choice,

absence of financial and nonfinancial costs related to the possession (cleaning and maintenance, insurance and so on), gain of
space and access to material of a better quality for a specific use.

By revisiting Schrader's typology with the aforementioned elements,[55] factors conditioning the acceptability of such offers fall
in three categories:

- Characteristics specific to the product, such as price, intensity
  of use, need for storage space, involvement with the product
  and so on.

- Characteristics specific to the service offer, such as comparative advantages, redistribution of the rights and duties related
  to the offer,[56] overall costs of use, perception of risks related
  to the alternative, relative complexity, image of the service
  provider and the quality of its offer (good organization, reli-
  ability, availability) and so on.

- Characteristics specific to the consumer: age, sex, type and
  place of residence (urban versus rural, for example), lifestyle
  and associated values (materialism, need for independence,
  environmental sensitivity and so on).

These considerations help define the positioning of the offer
at its launch. For example, which customer benefits should be
emphasized in the launch of a car-sharing service: economic
savings, time savings in a congested urban environment with pool
car lanes, tranquility (no worries about insurance, maintenance,
breakdowns and so on), commitment to the reduction of pollution
or others? This is a fundamental choice that will strongly impact
the perception of the offer and the predisposition to test it.

Other elements not directly related to the acceptability of
such an evolution can favor the deployment of these offers,
support their diffusion and even facilitate their implementation. Pensioners and retired people constitute the main group of
Zilok[57] users, motivated by earnings but also by the socialization offered by opportunities to chat with occasional hirers who
come to pick up the material. Technological developments are

another example. As exemplified previously, the Internet offers today a means of connecting users at the local level, as Whipcar, Ecomodo, Zilok or Anyhire have done.[58]

The development of smart objects that can communicate information via the Internet may also contribute to the rise of these services. A few years ago, Electrolux developed a pilot project for a use-oriented service on the island of Gotland, in Sweden. The company had placed one of the most eco-powerful washing machines of its range at the disposal of the households taking part in the experiment. The household was no longer invoiced for the washing machine itself, but for its use, with a system of payment based on washing cycles. In order to measure the use of the service, a partnership was set up with the local energy supplier, and a smart metering system was installed in each service user's home. On usage grounds, the business model was sound; however, the project was abandoned, as the partnership with the energy supplier meant that Electrolux had lost control of its market. With today's technology of communicating objects that transfer information directly to the manufacturer via the Internet, Electrolux could have kept the control of its market. This is exemplified by the Internet of objects (as described further), an innovation supporting the deployment of use-oriented services. The Internet of objects, such as the development of innovative insurance policies that can support the development of use-oriented services, may indeed allow manufacturers to monitor and control the use of products and therefore control the market while optimizing the system.

The Internet of objects

Futurists have been announcing for the last decade that the next revolution would be in connected and smart devices. General Electric, a pioneer with its Ecomagination initiative in 2004, has just released a white paper titled "Industrial Internet,"[58] making the case for how these connected devices could improve productivity and energy efficiency, and reduce the use of resources.

This take place through "the convergence of the global industrial system with the power of advanced computing, analytics, low-cost sensing and new levels of connectivity permitted by the Internet," generating "better health outcomes at lower costs, substantial savings in fuel and energy, and more efficient and longer-lived physical assets"[58] thus delivering increased efficiency and productivity by cutting energy use and waste.

This is based on three key elements[59]:

- Intelligent machines: New ways of connecting the world's myriad machines, facilities, fleets and networks with advanced sensors, controls and software applications.

- Advanced analytics: Harnessing the power of physics-based analytics, predictive algorithms, automation and deep domain expertise in material science, electrical engineering and other key disciplines required to understand how machines and larger systems operate.

- People at work: Connecting people, whether they are at work in industrial facilities, offices, hospitals or on the move, at any time to support more intelligent design, operations, maintenance as well as higher quality service and safety.

IBM has been making the case for a smart planet for a while; what is interesting in GE Industrial Internet is the estimation of its impact. Taking five sectors where the company has extensive experience and assuming just 1 percent savings over 15 years, the figures are impressive:

- 1 percent fuel savings in commercial aviation: US$30 billion

- 1 percent fuel savings in gas-fired generation: US$66 billion

- 1 percent reduction in health-care system inefficiency: US$63 billion

- 1 percent reduction in rail freight system inefficiency: US$27 billion

- 1 percent reduction in capital expenditures in oil and gas exploration and development: US$90 billion

The company describes a scenario in which the Industrial Internet opportunity could represent as much as US$32.3 trillion (46 percent share of global economy today) and go hyperbolic, estimating that it would be the third wave of innovation after the industrial revolution and the Internet revolution.

As Joel Makower from greenbiz.com observed, it is fundamentally about how Big Data "transforms and even revitalizes the dirty work of manufacturing, transportation, and energy production."[60] One interesting point is that sustainability and the previous Ecomagination GE initiative are not mentioned at all. This is understandable in the United States given the political connotation of green and the lobbying of climate change skeptics.

It is also a sign that sustainability has become mainstream and today it is no longer a matter of ideology; it is just a business interest to use technology to reduce inefficiencies by saving energy and reducing waste to generate productivity, innovation and revenue growth.

NETWORK OF ACTORS AND PARTNERSHIPS

Deploying a use-oriented service may be managed by a single company, such as illustrated by the case studies of Xerox or

Electrolux described before. In this context, a company can manage the whole offering alone.

In some other cases, the ability to deploy such a service may not depend only on a single actor and calls for a network of actors that must cooperate to make the service available. We are talking here about system innovation. The example of the development of the Autolib' car-sharing system in Paris, already mentioned, highlights this need for partnership.

The development of Autolib'

The idea for the Autolib' system came from Betrand Delanoë, the Mayor of the city of Paris, a city with an estimated population of 2.2 million and a metropolitan area with a population of 11.8 million.

For the inhabitants of the city to benefit from a reliable system of self-service cars, the city of Paris invited 81 municipal councils in the dense heart of the city and in the neighborhood to participate in the project. Twenty-six councils initially decided to join the project on September 24, 2009. Together, they set up the "Syndicat mixte Autolib," which is the joint administrative association that launched and manages the Autolib' public service delegation. Twenty other municipal councils have since joined the association to form a group of 46 councils managed by different political parties.

The association decided to organize the Autolib' system through a public service delegation contract (DSP). In France, a DSP is a set of contracts under which a public authority (city, country, region or national government) delegates the management of a public service to a public, nonprofit or private organization whose remuneration is substantially related to the operating revenue of the service. The association is responsible for the whole project, including (a) the coordination and the management of the call for tender to select the partner that would operate the DSP contract, (b) the layout of the service, in particular the negotiation of dedicated public or private space for the stations and (c) the control of the operations achieved by the operator.

The call for tender was launched on December 21, 2009 and four candidates were preselected: Ada, Veolia Transport, the SNCF–RATP–Avis–Vinci[62] consortium and Bolloré Inc. It is worth mentioning that the first three candidates are involved in the transport of persons, while Bolloré is a diversified group involved in freight forwarding and international logistics, fuel distribution with dedicated terminals and systems, plastic films, batteries and super capacitors, communication and media. On December 16, 2010, Bolloré was chosen to operate the public service with a 12-year DSP contract. The choice was motivated by many factors, one being a financial guarantee of €60 million provided by Bolloré for the contract period. This means that Bolloré is committed to cover at least €60 million of the project cost even if operating results are poor. Above this amount, the financial loss will be shared by Bolloré and the Association. Another reason was the high numbers of employees present in the Bolloré solution – 800 employees were to be hired – to give customer support and to provide them with a high level of service.

As the operator, Bolloré has to bear all the costs of the project: investments in terms of infrastructure (note that a public subsidy was allocated to partially cover the infrastructure costs), development of the cars and their equipment, dedicated staff, management of the operations on a daily basis, financial risk due to potential vandalism and so on. Bolloré's revenue will be generated by the activities alone. But break-even conditions look especially hard to reach, as pricing policy has been predetermined by the association.

Bolloré is not a car manufacturer and was the only candidate not to rely on an existing car in its solution. Bolloré's logic was to equip a car with its new battery technology (battery design being a key strategic business unit of the group). It therefore signed an agreement with the Italian car manufacturer Pininfarina to produce 4,000 electric cars specifically for the Autolib' project. Under the terms of the contract, Pininfarina would lease a plant and provide staff from Cecomp Italian group specializing in the design of automobile prototypes to produce 4,000 electric cars for Bolloré. Pininfarina will receive €14 million for a three-year contract.

An important component of the system is the recharging station (described in more detail further). At an early stage of the project, the association collaborated with city planners, engineering consulting firms and mobility experts to define the number and the size of the stations needed on public and private spaces. For the public spaces, the participating municipal council commits to providing the predefined number of stations for its area A technical study was carried out in collaboration with municipal and regional councils to prospect the potential zones in the public space and to validate the technical feasibility of the implantation (in consultation with water companies to identify the location of sewers and water pipes, electrical and gas companies to locate the pipes and the cables, a geological study to check the quality of the ground and so on). The Prefecture of Police was consulted to assess the level of security of the zone, as were the emergency services to assess the accessibility in case of accidents. Specific authorization had to be obtained in the city of Paris, from, for example, architects from the Bâtiments de France.

In Paris, in addition to the 500 stations located in public areas, 200 stations are located on privately owned car parks. Negotiations were therefore necessary with existing car park operators to get access to parking spaces that could be converted into a station and could be equipped with the necessary infrastructure. Negotiations with SNCF, the RATP as well as the City of Paris and social housing operators were necessary to get access to dedicated spaces for the Autolib'.

Once the location was finally decided, the construction of the station was undertaken. Bolloré had concluded partnerships with industrial partners such as EDF – the leading French energy supplier – to install the recharging infrastructure and designers, R&D partners and architect to design and equip the stations.

A key risk facing Autolib' is that of vandalism. As well as special equipment installed on the cars, such as shock sensors or a GPS that allows for the car to be tracked, the charging station is equipped with a video surveillance system directly connected to the police. An insurance company insures every car up to €4,000 annually for potential damage from accident or vandalism). And users will be encouraged to take care of the cars through an evolving franchise policy paying €250 for the first incident, then €500, then €750 and so on. After one year without any incident, the franchise comes back to the initial €250 fee. Autolib' targets households already equipped with a car as well as those who are not. For households that already own a private vehicle, Autolib' would allow them to reduce its usage, or even to get rid of it. For households that have no vehicle, it allows them to benefit from the advantages without having the expense of buying.

WHAT IMPACT ON THE BUSINESS MODEL OF THE COMPANY?

The transition of the sale of a good to its provision via a use-oriented service is a truly strategic rupture demanding a complete reconfiguration of the business model.

We present the case of a manufacturer of baby prams to illustrate the suitability of switching to a use-oriented service offer.[62] We deliberately choose a B2C case because the implementation of this kind of offer is generally more complex than in a B2B setting. The lessons are, however, applicable to both market contexts.

First question: Why change?

With some exceptions, environmental considerations are rarely the reason for a company to break with a strategy: commercial or financial reasons, however, massively push companies toward making bold moves. In the present case, the company considering such a transition is confronted with a specific market problem. Leader of its market, it offers quality, robust baby prams with a use potential that far exceeds a single child use. It has difficulties keeping its activity profitable given a particularly active second-hand market. The new product is expensive, it has long-life quality, and the owner can thus obtain a good price of resale on the second-hand market, which is responsible for 65–75 percent of the sales. On sustainability grounds, lifetime extension through a second-hand market could be considered as positive given the successive uses of the product. The material flows, however, remain linear and the product will ultimately end up in a garbage dump.

The company thus aims to capture a share of the value being created in the second-hand market by creating a circular material flow (potentially more virtuous for the environment than in the case of the second-hand market) attractive to its client, and that would increase the odds of having a profitable activity. This is the context for this strategic evolution.

A new value proposition for a specific market

A new value proposition is at the core of the reconfigured business model. Instead of buying a baby pram, the customer is invited to rent an entirely refurbished one. The offer mainly targets customers considering a purchase in the second-hand market. The service added-value is clear: accessing an entirely refurbished baby pram with a guarantee of quality and robustness, without paying the price of a brand new baby pram. The value proposition could thus be formulated as follows: access to a fully refurbished baby pram with guaranteed quality and robustness for a price not exceeding that of a second-hand product in good state. Otherwise stated, it is a matter of obtaining guaranteed quality at lower price. The offer can also be attractive for customers looking for an entry-range new pram: for a similar amount, they could have a higher quality product.

To reach the target, it is important that the offer is less expensive than a similar quality product. The baby pram being designed to be rented more than once, it seems possible to build a profitable model.

A mandatory product redesign

As discussed beforehand, the installation of a use-oriented service presupposes the redesign of the baby pram:

- The baby pram must resist multiple, intense use because of the successive users. In this respect, the choice of more robust (and expensive) materials can be judicious since these materials have to turn in a circular way in several cycles of consumption.

- It must be able to be easily disassembled and refurbished. In this respect, the cradle-to-cradle[TM63] principles seem well adapted. Thus the redesign work should be able to differentiate the pram technical nutrients that will turn in successive cycles of product use (frame, wheels rims and so on), from biological nutrients that, once arrived at the end of the lifetime, could be easily biodegradable and compostable (fabric trimmings and protection foams, for example).

- In order to support redesign and adaptation to customer desires, modularity should be envisaged to enable customization of the refurbished product (in terms of color and style of trimming fabrics). Moreover, the baby pram must be simple to refurbish; the level of refurbishing will depend on the general state of the pram. Light reconditioning could thus be carried out by an actor external to the company, which opens possibilities regarding the configuration of the future value chain. Similarly, accessories (umbrella, rain cover, cup holder and so on) should also be standardized to be able to be easily adapted to the suggested models.

Changes in the business model associated with the eco-design approach described in Chapter 3 also apply here. For example, marketing must be closely associated to the redesign to ensure customer acceptability regarding the technical choices. One technique to be considered is to present use scenarios of the service enabling consumers to project themselves into the use context and express motivations and barriers for adoption.[64] Thus, should the fabrics be systematically changed or could they be washed? A study[65] shows indeed that regarding children articles, hygiene is a decisive choice criterion. Another example: do the customization possibilities add value given that the target clients were initially looking for products in the second-hand market?

An entirely revisited value chain

Impact on the supply chain and distribution

Implementing the principle of circularity is a considerable challenge with obvious implications on the supply chain. It is first of all important to identify the actors who will take part in the service value chain.

The strongly atomized nature of the market will condition logistic choices. Implementing circular flows indeed presupposes not only a one-directional flow of logistic organization toward the customer, but also a reverse logistic flow allowing the recovery of the baby pram for its refurbishment. Two options seem possible for the configuration of these flows:

- A direct relationship between the company and the final customer. Internet becomes the main channel of distribution and configuration of the baby pram, and an external logistics operator organizes logistic flows in the two directions, either via a direct delivery or recovery from the customer's home, or via a centralized relay point where the customer will receive and/or bring back the baby pram. Payment is made directly using an electronic format (credit card, debit card, PayPal, for example) during the contract. The obvious advantages are complete control of the value chain and the disintermediation – the margin no longer going to the distributor. The company controls all the refurbishing operations and guarantees the quality of the service offered. The disadvantage, however, is the substantial logistic and administrative burden of these operations, the associated logistic cost and the development of a new activity (with the associated resources) to organize these operations.

- The other option keeps the retailer in the value chain, but with a radical change of role. It will have to propose and manage the rental agreement, and to be able to manage a minimum part of the after-sales service. The question arises of who assumes the responsibility for refurbishment operations, with the basic operations ideally being entrusted to the distributor. Consequently, managing a simple and smooth interface for the execution of these enhanced operations is central to their success.

Selecting the best option requires developing a *business case* analyzing the organizational, technical and financial feasibility of each option. The kind of relations with retailers and their relative force will condition this choice. Thus, if the distribution channel is done primarily through hypermarkets or the like, the probability of a role redefinition is negligible as long as the power to negotiate is unbalanced and these distributors seek standardization. By contrast, a network of specialized distributors, composed in particular of independent stores, could more easily accept, and even help to develop such a transition, since it goes in the direction of a reinforcement of the partnership with the manufacturer.

In the *business case* presented by Mont et al. (2006), the analysis of the context and the financial costs associated with the two options led to the selection of the second scenario, for several reasons. Firstly, the financial costs of a direct logistic system were prohibitive given the structure of the market and the internal organization of the company. Moreover, it would have offset almost all the environmental benefits of the project because of the weight of transport. The company also depends strongly on the network of distributors for the sale of its other products, baby prams being only one of its divisions. Moreover, with this network the company maintains excellent relations that could be put at risk if these distributors were excluded from this new service.

The choice of maintenance by the distributors nevertheless has disadvantages. It means keeping stock at the distributors in order to make refurbishment simple and fast. This causes a reduction in the rate of components that turn in the circular flow. Also, as the distributor is not equipped to clean the fabric covers, they would simply be replaced at each refurbishing operation, which reinforces the interest to develop them following a logic of biological nutrients, since they will not be organized in circular flows in an industrial metabolic logic. Lastly, the choice of distributor raises questions relating to quality control by the manufacturer, even though, in this case, the interests between the distributor and the manufacturer converge, thus reducing this risk.

Redefinition of the role of the actors in the value chain

Given the choice to keep distributors in the value chain, it is necessary to redefine the role of this intermediary. Currently, the network of distributors manages the implementation of the two-year guarantee offered by the manufacturer. Distributors are, for example, brought in to carry out on-site minor repairs, and offer the customers a checkup service three months after the acquisition of the baby pram (which attracts the customers into the store once again so that they can potentially purchase extra items). The case study suggests specialized distributors would accept a change in their role, and to deal with the refurbishment. This is essential because the margin related to the sale of a service contract is smaller than that related to the sale of the product. The operations of refurbishing can thus, by the additional revenue streams they generate, compensate for any potential loss related to the smaller margin associated with the sale of a rental agreement compared to the sale of a new baby pram.

Impact on the other business blocks

The configuration of this value chain obviously has an impact on all the business blocks of the business model canvas. Thus the choice of the distribution system will strongly impact the nature of the relations with the customers. In any case, the customer relation will evolve from a transaction based on the sale of a product to a relational approach characterized by an offer of a service. If the direct distribution option had been chosen, the relation itself would have become direct, demanding the development of activities and resources dedicated to managing this relation previously undertaken by the distributor. By contrast, since the indirect option was preferred, the relation remains primarily managed by the distributors, requiring the manufacturer to maintain a qualitative relation with them to support its activities. The distributor becomes a sort of strategic partner since it will deal with the refurbishment of the baby pram in addition to the management of the traditional trade relation. Upstream, this choice impacts the specifications for product redesign, given that distributors are ready to accept a maximum of 30 minutes for the refurbishment work to take place and have limited equipment to complete this work. Downstream, a system of information exchange must be installed between the manufacturer and the distributors to organize and synchronize the operations of refurbishment, in particular via the sending of necessary parts and components. Networks of local distributors can be organized so that they exchange material flows in order to better synchronize the supply and demand of refurbished baby prams. The distributor must also fully understand what the benefits are of promoting this service, otherwise it will not choose this path. It must, for example, understand that this new service aims to attract customers who would otherwise have bought on the second-hand market and who would undoubtedly not have visited the distributor's store. This market expansion for the distributor can bring direct additional value, via the subscription of the rental agreement, and opportunities for cross-selling.

More classically, and like any new offer launch, the manufacturer's sales force must obviously be trained in this new offer and its benefits for the distributor and the end customer. This effort should not be minimized since such a change can generate resistance at many levels and change management is necessary to explain and train staff impacted by this evolution.

The deployment of the service can be made in a massive or progressive way. Navigo, the multimodal transport pass used in France's Ile-de-France region, took more than ten years to be deployed by RATP. Experimentation and progressive implementation allowed usage and practices to be well understood. In such scenario, distributors who have a privileged relation with the company can be used as pilots to evaluate the receptivity of the offer and any difficulties encountered to market it and thus collect invaluable information to improve the offer before its complete deployment. A massive deployment, on the other hand, would correspond to introducing the offer into the whole network at once. This is a risky option and may turn the whole operation sour. British Airways travelers who transited through the terminal 5 of London Heathrow Airport in the days following its opening in 2008 certainly remember what problems can be generated by an IT system that is not up to scratch in terms of delays and bags not travelling with its owners.

Lastly, this new service and its benefits compared to the purchase of a second-hand baby pram must be promoted. Like any innovation launch, considerable effort must be made to develop the service awareness both quantitatively and qualitatively and to build the perception of the offer's benefits. As previously explained, this change arrives in a specific use context and it is central to understand the usage significations associated with the new offer in order to choose the right benefit to be proposed to support its adoption. It goes without saying that this requires a substantial marketing involvement.

The economic model

The transition to a service model has a major impact on the economic model. The cost structure results from the whole of the activities to deploy and the resources to be mobilized.

The main difference between a sales model and a service or leasing scheme lies in the revenue streams and the level of the cash flow.

The manufacturer is no longer remunerated by asset sales, but by a monthly rental subscription. As mentioned previously, this price must be attractive to prospective clients and not exceed the price of a new, lower quality baby pram or a good quality second-hand pram. The Mont et al. (2006) *business case* was built with a subscription price range of between €17 and €32. The financial analysis showed that assuming eight cycles of use (determined by the lifetime of the main components of the baby pram), based on the lowest subscription price point, the new service model was more profitable than the traditional product sales model. However, there is a major implication for cash flow. In contrast to the sale of the product where the recovery of the cost is immediate, the leasing scheme would take ten months before the cash flow is positive. The implementation of this solution thus requires additional financial resources to cope with this shift. The system is overall more profitable but it does require increased capital availability.

The sustainability check

Despite their more virtuous nature, use-oriented services do have a certain number of costs for society and environment as well as shared costs.

Table 5.1 *The business model canvas for the baby pram leasing service*

Costs for Society and the Environment	Key Partners	Key Activities	Sustainable Value Proposition	Customer Relationship Management	Customers Segments	Benefits for Society and the Environment
• Upstream environmental spin-offs of the economic activities • Negative environmental spin-offs related to the operations (e.g. transport)	• Network of partners related to the product redesign (see Chapter 3) • Distributor becomes a key strategic partner for sales and refurbishment in case of indirect distribution channel • In the case of direct distribution channel, logistic operator is a key partner	• Redesign of baby pram following eco-design and C2C™ principles (and related activities => see Chapter 3) • Development of a reversed logistic flow by either deploying a direct distribution channel or redefining the role of the indirect circuit • Development of IT system to monitor material flows and the organization of the refurbishment operations • In the case of indirect distribution channel (via distributor), training of the sales force and development of a network of distributors • Considerable effort of consumer and distributor (if indirect channel) "training" about the service benefits **Key Resources** • Human resources • Financial resources, particularly an increased requirement in capital • Technical and technological skills and resources • Baby pram as a technical nutrient	Access to a quality refurbished baby pram with a warranty for a total price not exceeding that of the second-hand market for a product in good state	Impacted in every scenario due to the transition from transaction model (sale) to a relational model (service) Depends obviously on the choices regarding distribution **Distribution** Either development of a direct distribution system (disintermediation), or keep the distributors with an enhanced role	Main Target: customers currently buying a baby pram on the second-hand market Secondary Target: purchasers of new lower quality baby prams	• Development of local activities (e.g. refurbishment via distributors) • Use of recycled material preventing fabrication of new materials (preservation of raw materials) and reducing waste • Recyclability of materials • Enhancement of the use value of a product (that may generate social benefits)

Shared Costs	Cost Structure	Revenue Streams	Shared Benefits
• Energy costs and entrants (raw materials) • Transportation costs • Waste from components not entering the circular material flow (fabrics) • Waste at the product end of life	Associated costs to the development of the value chain, the deployment of the activities, the mobilization of the resources, and the management of the partnerships	Revenue streams generated by the monthly rental subscription of the baby pram	• Positive financial returns • Increased added-value of the value proposition and new spaces of differentiation/positive impact on the image • Better control of the quality/supply chain • Costs saving through an improved efficiency (in terms of raw materials and energy) • Cost reduction in terms of waste management • Production of new knowledge and fostering of innovation

The *costs for society and environment* include the upstream environmental spin-offs of the economic activities like sourcing raw materials (plastics, for example); and the negative environmental spin-offs related to the operations of the company, like manufacturing, distribution and transport.

The *shared costs* are energy costs and entrants (raw materials), transportation costs, waste from components not entering the circular matter flow (fabrics) and waste at the product end of life.

The *benefits for society and environment* include the development of local activities (such as refurbishment via distributors), use of recycled material preventing fabrication of new materials (preservation of raw materials) and reducing waste; recyclability of materials; and enhancement of the use value of a product (that may generate social benefits).

Finally, the *shared benefits* are positive financial returns, increased added value of the value proposition and new areas of differentiation; positive impact on the image, better control of the quality; supply chain, cost-saving through improved efficiency (in terms of raw materials and energy), cost reduction in terms of waste management and production of new knowledge and fostering of innovation.

To synthesis this, Table 5.1 presents the business model canvas of the new activity and highlights the major reconfiguration that such a transition imposes.

Although this reconfiguration may present common points to any evolution toward a service, it is neither generic nor a given; each case will present its own specificities.

HOW ABOUT DEVELOPING ECONOMIES?

This chapter has been developed so far under the perspective of mature economies where possession is a given for the majority of the population. Even if this assumption is less and less the case given the current impoverishment taking place in the United States[66] and Europe, this situation bears no resemblance to that of developing or underdeveloped economies.

In most parts of the world, access to basic needs such as a shelter, three meals a day, security and health is far from a reality. While progress in the achievement of the millennium goals shows an impressive number of people in countries like China, India and Brazil[67] rising out of abject poverty, much remains to be done. In this context, one could have the impression that discussing ownership is a rich world's occupation. This could not be farther from the truth, for several reasons.

First, the earth's finite resources mean that it is simply impossible for all the countries in the world to follow a development pattern similar to that of Europe or North America. The world's resources are just not enough. The Global Footprint Network is there to remind us about this reality every year.[68] This is both a constraint and an opportunity. Constraint, because the (false) abundance represented by the stereotype of the American way of life (suburban two story house, individual car possession and so on) is just not achievable for the whole of humanity. Opportunity, because it means leapfrogging this unsustainable mode of development is by creating a more virtuous one. As already mentioned, China is taking a leading role in promoting circular economy, certainly a need if the country is to fulfill its wish to become the world's biggest economy.

Second, given this impossibility to provide goods' ownership for all, use-based services are indeed a revolutionary way to provide access to individuals not able to afford the cost of ownership. Examples abound.

In Bangladesh, the Grameen Bank partnered with Telenor from Norway to create Grameen Phone. From the customer perspective, the value proposition changed from buying a monthly package (phone + air time) to borrowing a phone when needed and paying per minute. As presented by Nobel Peace Prize holder Muhammad Yunus,[69] "the success is based on the Grameen 'telephone ladies', who provide a phone service in their villages by lending users a phone for just a couple of minutes avoiding them having to make costly handset purchases." A key success factor is the design of a robust telephone device given the intensity of use and exposure to variable environmental conditions (such as high temperatures, humidity, rain and so on). And this same model has been replicated all over Africa. It has thus challenged the conventional wisdom that buying power was too low to build a profitable wireless network.

In Kenya, Ecotact, a social business, developed ikotoilet, a concept of shared use toilets for impoverished areas. It provides a sanitation service that serves an average of 1,000 persons per day through provision of quality WC and shower services in urban areas, markets, parks and others.[70] Use-oriented services seem a promising path to find "fortune at the bottom of the pyramid."[71]

These two cases exemplify the rise of social business models, a business model innovation itself. Indeed, as presented by Mohammed Yunus and colleagues,[72] social business models add a social profit equation (social and environmental profits in a triple-bottom line logic) to the three components of a conventional business model: economic profit equation, value proposition and value constellation.

The road is nevertheless long for the transition from ownership to usership in emerging countries, starting with cognitive barriers. For example, most inhabitants of Central and South America have been "brainwashed" for half a century on the primacy of the "American way of life" in such a way that individual car ownership is a strong identity issue for most of the population. It is enough to drive (or rather, get stuck in traffic) in São Paulo for a while to observe the number of new cars in circulation.

A striking example of this attachment to individual ownership is given by the boom of luxury goods consumption in emerging markets. In 2012, according to Bain & Co.,[73] Chinese clients bought the highest number personal luxury goods, and Asia's "love affair" with luxury is far from over. Even though some personal luxury goods are bought for their durability (like bags and watches, which can last for decades, resulting in stronger use intensity), reasons for these acquisitions are mainly for showing off, in order to demonstrate that a certain economic success has been achieved.

Chadha and Husband[74] present a five-stage luxury model that illustrates how and why the different Asian countries (Japan, China, India, Taiwan, South Korea, Hong Kong, Singapore) are at different stages of luxury consumption. These five stages are (1) subjugation, corresponding to deprivation where society as a whole experiences a lack of money, and authoritarian rule (e.g. Myanmar); (2) start of money, when an elite segment emerges and starts shopping by traveling abroad (e.g. Indonesia); (3) showing off, the stage where wealth comes to certain select segments of society that rush to acquire luxury brands as symbols of wealth to display money and status (e.g. China); (4) fitting in, when luxury goods are bought to fit in with the peers (e.g. Hong Kong); and (5) lifestyle, when luxury goods are bought for their intrinsic qualities as a way of life and expression of refined taste (e.g. Japan).

One key distinction between most emerging countries and Western developed countries is the role of the group versus the role of the individual.[75] Elites are seen as role models to mimic and, given their current emphasis in showing off their wealth, ownership is favored over other alternatives, as we can observe in China and Brazil regarding individual car ownership. The early 2013 pollution peak in China shows, nevertheless, the limits of the current development model and there is hope that initiatives toward circular economy taken by the Chinese government will be implemented.

Otherwise, collaborative web platforms and online social networks are powerful drivers of change and they have been massively adopted. Sina Weibo, a Chinese microblogging site, has more than 400 million users who react harshly to environmental issues in China. In Brazil, Engage is a company that designs, develops and incubates projects for people's empowerment. The platform "Materia Brasil," for example, assembles fabrics from responsible suppliers. As early 2013, 156 fabrics from 104 suppliers were collected on the platform to promote sustainable fabrics and production.[76]

To conclude this section, it is interesting to observe that emerging countries are starting to ask themselves which model of society they want, given that the United States and Europe are no longer perceived as role models for these countries. Increasing wealth is part of the answer to fight misery, hunger and unemployment, but how these emerging countries define well-being will have a great impact on how sustainability is tackled at the society and government level.

CONCLUSION

The transition from the sale of a good to its provision constitutes a real strategic rupture demanding a major reconfiguration of the company business model, when it aims to couple economic and environmental benefits. The implementation of the eco-efficiency principle, and those of circularity, demands a major redefinition of the value chain and the logistic flows, all the more complex if the market is atomized.

The consequences of such a transition are substantial at an economic level: it makes the principle of planned obsolescence null and void. It encourages robustness, durability and reparability. If circularity is well in place, and the industrial metabolism and supply chains are efficient, the consumer is able to satisfy his appetite for novelty by exchanging goods often, knowing that they will change hands and continue rendering the service for which they were conceived.

Indeed, certain services have already put this argument forward, like, for example, web sites offering the rental of luxury handbags or art pieces, giving access to variety where purchase limits you in quantity. The possibilities of deployment are infinite and new economic activities are waiting for some "animal spirits" to create them.

On economic and environmental grounds, a transition to these services is much more effective in terms of use of materials and energy resources. The *businesses cases* analyzed by studies financed by the European Union[77] estimate that, on average, it is possible to reach factor 2, that is, a reduction of 50 percent of the quantities in resources and energy necessary to produce the same quantity of wealth, if the system is well designed.

This transition potentially reconfigures entire value chains and opens up several disintermediation possibilities. It supports local production, because the development of circular matter flows requires short logistic flows, or rocketing cost risks.

But the consequences of such a transition are not only economical, they are also sociological, anthropological and even philosophical. Scarcity of resources means rethinking business and consumption 'as usual'. An infinite growth of material in a finite world is an illusion: trees do not grow up to the sky. This calls for change, but the timing, the pace and the distribution of effort requires debate. This transition is also that of mental and social representations related to a consumption of "possession" to one structured around "access." The status of the exchanged goods is thus deeply impacted. From private possession, we move to the concepts of shared goods, and potentially common goods. Thus a system of car sharing like Zipcar transforms the car into a quasi-common good, with new rules of governance to be developed.

A shared consumption is indeed one where the behavior of one individual can impact the quality of the experience of the others, and where the link and the interdependence between the individuals are much more tangible. If I return an Autolib' in a deplorable state, I affect the experience of the next client. If I degrade a collective laundry machine, I penalize the whole community of users. The emergence of collaborative consumption shows some triggers of these new agreements of governance for shared goods. Thus trust and reputation become a capital as essential as money to access or take part in exchanges. Reputation currencies start to appear to reward or penalize a user according to his past behavior, knowing that the lower his reputational capital the harder it is to access collaborative markets. If you already carried out transactions on eBay, you have, maybe without realizing it, performed a transaction in reputation currency, when you evaluated a seller or were evaluated by a buyer. As a buyer, would you trust a seller who has a disastrous score record with deeply dissatisfied comments from previous buyers?

So beyond a solitary act of consumption, the user of such a service can take part under certain conditions in the production of the social fabric, thus enriching the service. "Couchsurfing" – a more extreme form of collaborative consumption where an unknown agrees to lodge another unknown for free – allows people from different cities, countries or continents to meet and get to know each other for one evening or a short period. Humans become the center of the system on all its dimensions. This results in socialization and social capital, and not only economic capital.

Could the transition to this kind of service become an end in itself, a fully satisfactory alternative model with regard to sustainability? This is certainly not the case given that decoupling is, and can only be, partial at this stage. Use-oriented services remain a transitory step to truly disruptive models.

6

From Product- to Result-Based Integrated Solutions

We started this book explaining the difficulties facing a large number of business models to create value in a sustainable way. These models rely on a volume of goods or commodities, making it hard, or even impossible to decouple revenue generation from raw materials and energy consumption.

Although use-oriented services may provide a strategic answer enabling an evolution of the business model, they are not suited in call contexts. For fast-moving consumer goods, for example, this transition does not make much sense or, at least, it does not seem to be a natural one. The same holds true for commodities. A water supplier provides a volume of water associated with a certain consumption level. The invoicing unit is clearly the use of water, similar, for an energy company or the supplier of pesticides who delivers a volume of product depending on a farmer's needs. Consequently, any potential rationalization of the use would generate a destruction of value for these companies.

Consider the case of the energy sector. Because its revenue is tied to the volume of consumption of kW/h or m^3 of gas, an energy supplier does not have a true interest in encouraging consumption reduction other than in peak periods (i.e. when there is a consumption peak, especially during abnormally warm or cold temperatures). Because it relies on seldom-activated and in general less powerful generators, the cost of the energy at peak periods often exceeds its selling price, so it is economically profitable to eliminate these peaks by encouraging consumption reduction if a peak is anticipated. But beside these peaks, whenever the cost of energy produced is lower than its selling price, there is no economic incentive for encouraging a reduction in consumption.

However, in a context of scarce and expensive resources, and growing regulations, these models are coming under pressure. On December 12, 2008, the European Council ratified the energy and climate package with the 3×20 percent rule: by 2020, the European Union aims to reduce its GHG emissions by 20 percent, reduce its energy use by 20 percent and achieve 20 percent of renewable energy in its energy supply compared to its 1990 level.[1] The UK Climate Change Act 2008 set a goal of taking the net UK carbon account for all six Kyoto GHGs for the year 2050 at least 80 percent lower than the 1990 baseline.[2] Brazil has set ambitious carbon-reduction targets as well,[3] as has the American state of California that passed a bill aiming to reduce its CO_2 emissions by 25 percent by 2020 and to increase the amount of electricity generated from eligible renewable energy resources to 33 percent by 2020.[4] All these initiatives stress the importance of energy efficiency and ambitious plan to encourage consumption's reduction.

These regulations deeply impact energy suppliers' business models and are potentially a driver of value destruction. The same when industrial and tertiary companies invest massively in energy efficiency searching for cost savings. Admittedly, reduction of energy consumption on a worldwide base seems unrealistic given the strong demand from emerging economies. But on mature markets with low or zero growth, the question does make sense.

Another sector, another challenge: water. A growing number of local authorities are deploying their Agenda 21, an action plan concerning sustainable development at the scale of a territory. In Agenda 21, one chapter targets optimized management of water resources by a greater quality retreatment and a reduction of consumption. Consequently, the business model of water suppliers is under pressure.

How can these tensions be managed? How can value be created given these evolutions? Can this value creation be achieved within existing businesses models? Is it possible to configure new businesses models that are both profitable and promote a drastic reduction of raw materials and energy consumption? This chapter aims to answer these questions, by presenting paths of strategic rupture to prepare the businesses models of tomorrow.

FROM GOODS TO THEIR RENDERED SERVICE

Going beyond the physical good to grasp the service provided

A few years ago a passionate debate took place among services marketing scholars. For some, services marketing was inevitably a subdiscipline of marketing since services constitute a specific offer as a tangible good, and that services marketing differs, for example, from the marketing of the products. For others, on the other hand, services marketing was a lens through which the whole marketing field could be redesigned, physical goods being bought only for the service they provide.

Mentioning this debate has one interest: remember that a product is used to satisfy a customer's need or desire;[5] and it is perhaps possible to do it in a completely different way by reconsidering the role of the product itself and the service that it renders. The following example clarifies how this is possible.

When a farmer buys pesticides, he is looking in reality for an efficient way to protect his crops. But the practice is such that the means becomes an end in itself, the underlying need being hidden by the solutions that are available on the market. The farmer will thus generally seek the most efficient pesticide, without going back to the subjacent need for crop protection that could lead him to reconsider a broader spectrum of alternative solutions. Similarly, when a car breaks down, its owner will generally formulate his need around buying a new vehicle (my car is definitively out of use, I need a new car), without reconsidering in a broader way his need for mobility (my car is definitively out of use, it is necessary to reevaluate the best means for meeting my mobility needs). Sure, we all adopt cognitive frames in order to facilitate daily life and once a routine is in place, change is harder.[6]

Our point is that the product frames the formulation of the need and thus limits its resolution to its sole perimeter. But escaping from this framing may be a strong leverage for innovation, as illustrated by the Philips case described next.

Philips 'Pay per Lux' business model

The Dutch group Royal Philips Electronics, better known as Philips, is a world leader in health care, lifestyle and lighting, integrating technologies and design into solutions, based on customer insights and the brand promise of "sense and simplicity." It employs over 122,000 employees with sales and services of €22.6 billion in more than 100 countries worldwide in 2011. It is an innovative company holding 50,000 registered patents, 36,000 registered trademarks, 63,000 design rights and 3,900 domain names that recently adopted an Open Innovation strategy to leverage power of partnering companies and researchers to bring more innovations to the market effectively and faster.[7]

The company has a long-standing commitment to sustainability, channeling initiatives on eco-design, energy efficiency, recycling and eliminating and minimizing hazardous substances in its products. Its agenda 2010 resolved to fully leverage sustainability as an integral part of the company strategy and an additional driver of growth by committing to three key performance indicators under the company's ecovision:

– Bringing care to more than 500 million people

 o Target: 500 million lives touched by 2015

– Improving energy efficiency of Philips products

 o Target: 50 percent improvement by 2015 (for the average total product portfolio) compared to 2009

- Closing the materials loop

  o Target: Double global collection, recycling amounts and recycled materials in products by 2015 compared to 2009[8]

In 2010, it received an unusual demand from Thomas Rau, head of RAU Architects, a Dutch architectural agency:

> I told Philips, "Listen, I need so many hours of light in my premises every year. You figure out how to do it. If you think you need a lamp, or electricity, or whatever – that's fine. But I want nothing to do with it. I'm not interested in the product, just the performance. I want to buy light and nothing else."[9]

RAU is not a newcomer as regards to sustainability, on the contrary. It defines its architectural approach by the term "oneplanetarchitecture" where it designs buildings with a strong emphasis on sustainability. It is the first Dutch firm to have architects granted Cradle-to-Cradle™ certification, the company employing six certified architects. It aims to create buildings that can actually produce energy, and which consume and waste as few raw materials as possible. As a whole, it has adopted sustainability as a core value, and like Seacourt, the UK zero waste printer presented in Chapter 4, it has acquired a distinctive sustainable image. Recently, it launched turntoo®,[10] a platform that advocates performance-based consumption.

In order to meet RAU's demand, Philips had to get rid of thinking in terms of lamps, luminaires, cables or controls and move to providing "the exact amount of light for workspaces and rooms that his employees needed when using them for specific tasks."[11]

Eventually it came out with a new kind of light plan and solution together with its installation partner CasSombroek:

> [W]e took an existing LED recessed luminaire for ceiling systems and adapted it so it could be hung in RAU's high-roofed, industrial-type premises. This created individual, floating "ceilings" over workplaces, which could deliver effective, adjustable illumination directly on the areas where it was needed, while the rest of the office space remained relatively dim. A combined sensor and controller system further helped keep energy use to an absolute minimum, by dimming or brightening the artificial lighting in response to motion or the presence of daylight.[12]

Regarding environmental benefits, the project resulted in reduced ecological footprint due to closed material loops and energy efficient lighting solutions, including LED lighting.[13]

Rau got the job done: he acquired

> the exact amount of office illumination he needs at the price he wanted to pay. It's also very flexible lighting that can be personalized, changing in intensity – or from cool to warm white light – depending on the way the space is used and the preferences of the person using it. Nor was RAU burdened with the hassle of having to choose, decide or figure out how to achieve all this: Philips Lighting did it for him. Maintenance, of course, is included in the "Pay per Lux" concept. And whenever RAU's lighting needs change, we can either adapt the existing system further to his wishes, or simply reclaim our materials and recycle them via LightRec, our partner in responsible re-use of lighting components.[14]

Philips lighting had the opportunity to co-develop and experiment an innovative business model for delivering light in a new and sustainable way. It has advertised this use case getting many demands from other architectural agencies and clients, and it has also partnered with RAU on outside projects. In parallel, Philips lighting faced obstacles around insurance, legal ownership and accounting processes that it had to overcome with stakeholders in order to render the service viable. This highlights the shifts in the business model necessary for such a transition. All building blocks are impacted: from value proposition to key partners, not to mention the revised revenue model. For a client, the shift from a capital expenditure upfront on lighting equipment to operations expenditure adjusted to the volume of activity is great, but requires precise calculation from Philips to invoice its offer. Interestingly, in the corporate communication on this experience, no mention of an energy provider is made. This presents an example of disintermediation and reintermediation where the intermediary (i.e. Philips) becomes the client of the energy provider and no longer the architectural agency.

Back to the basic need or the job to be done

If a customer considers its basic need or the job he is looking to get done, other alternatives may exist to solve it besides the product currently in use. In our agriculture example, the farmer could enlarge his search from the best pesticide to a broader range of solutions enabling him to limit his crops loss rate to an acceptable level. A supplier who could sell him a service contract guaranteeing a maximum loss rate on his crops, at the very least on the controllable risk factors, would be able to develop a competitive advantage. The benefit would be mutual, both for the customer and the supplier. The first would have a guarantee of result instead of the provision of a means without a controllable result. Commercially, the difference is enormous. For the service provider, the complexity increases, but its capacity to deploy an integrated and optimized solution articulated around a service rate confers a decisive competitive advantage, when differentiation at the product level is increasingly difficult to reach. Moreover, by decoupling the revenue from a product volume, it is possible to create a true rupture as regards to the value curve, potentially characterizing a blue ocean (see hereafter for further details).[15]

Getting the job done at Rolls-Royce jet engines[16]

Rolls-Royce may at first glance conjure up the image of the gilded coach turned into a car. This is, indeed, the main brand association and refers to Rolls-Royce Motor Cars, a subsidiary of the German carmaker BMW.

But Rolls-Royce is not only a car manufacturer. It is also a provider of integrated power systems and services to the civil aerospace, defense aerospace, marine and energy markets. It had revenues of £12.2 billion in 2012 with pretax profits of £1.4 billion. More than half its revenue comes from its civil aerospace division (£6.4 billion), where its jet engines power 30 types of aircrafts, 300 airline and leasing customers, with 20 million flying hours in 2012. An interesting point is that 73 percent of its revenue is represented by long-term service agreements (LTSAs).

In fact, the company does not sell jet engines, but flying hours. The difference is not only semantic and has huge implications from a business model perspective. Rolls-Royce could have chosen a value proposition where it first sells jet engines and then spare parts and services. This would be possible but the company would probably face harsh competition on both fronts: jet engines are only one component in an airplane and unless the company keeps delivering superior technology time and time again (a very costly process), it would sooner or later be competing on costs; the same would happen in the service and spare parts, where other companies could sell spare parts more cheaply and provide service at competitive rates. Knowing that profits mainly come from servicing jet engines, not selling them, this is a situation where Rolls-Royce would be struggling to make decent profit margins.

Instead, it "has convinced its customers to pay a fee for every hour that an engine runs. Rolls-Royce in turn promises to maintain it and replace it if it breaks down." It is not about selling engines, but about selling "hot air out the back of an engine."[17] Airline companies get the job done: they do not need to care about the engine, a capital expenditure thus becomes an operational expenditure and they can focus on their core business.

Products remain at the core of the model (in this case, turning blades are the heart of the jet engine) and the company needs to keep its technology state-of-the-art in order to keep being chosen by Boeing and Airbus for its new projects; but it is servicing that gives it a competitive edge. Rolls-Royce hosts an operations room located in Derby, UK that continuously assesses the performance of more than 3,500 jet engines operating around the world. Each time a passenger jet is struck by lightning, the sensors placed at the engine collect data that is transferred in real time to Rolls-Royce, which check what is going on, its impact on the engine and decides if any inspection is needed when the plane lands in its next destination. This is critical for the safety of the airplane and because any maintenance work means delays for passenger and fees for the airline.[18]

Moreover, this data allows Rolls-Royce to continuously improve its products:

> [S]potting problems early helps it to design and build more reliable engines or to modify existing ones. The resulting evolution of its engines has steadily improved fuel efficiency and, over the past 30 years, has extended the operating life of engines tenfold (to about ten years between major rebuilds).

The transition toward result-based integrated solution calls for a shift of focus away from the product to think in terms of functional spheres. These are the generic needs that could be solved in an innovative approach thanks to an integrated solution. I need to move (mobility); I need to take care of myself (health and well-being); I want to learn (education); I want to be assisted or independent (dependency management); I want to have fun (entertainment); I need accommodation (habitat); I'm a citizen (citizenship) are examples of functional spheres that could help to design such innovative integrated solutions. As an example just imagine we want to innovate on new forms of education for emerging countries where the demand is enormous and difficult or expensive to meet with classical solutions (e.g. building new schools). Thinking in terms of existing products or services (such as selling books, access to public libraries or enrolling at a business school) clearly hinders innovation as it frames the potential answers to such a challenge. But by reconsidering the functional sphere, by de-compartmentalizing related activities (education, games, theaters, experimentation, participative media and open journalism and so on) and by deeply analyzing the context of the learners, it becomes possible to identify new ways of learning that could be encapsulated into an integrated solution based on the expected results.

An innovative approach favoring decoupling

This strategy creates the conditions of a possible decoupling between revenue growth, on the one hand, and consumption of resources and energy, on the other hand. The economic interest of a pesticide supplier is to sell the maximum possible volume. If a company no longer sells a pesticide, but a rate of maximum acceptable crop loss, the pesticide used to reach this service rate becomes a cost that is profitable to minimize. Better, alternative strategies can be developed in an integral crop protection approach, where several options are employed (new farming practices limiting risks, prophylactic measures,[19] biological fight and so on), chemical products being the last resort option. The difference is sizeable and enables offering a value proposition with a broader mix of benefits for the farmer, as in the example of Koppert.

Koppert partners with nature's ecological services

Koppert is a Dutch company created in 1967 offering systems of natural pollination and integrated pest management. In this highly competitive sector, the company provides a distinctive benefit: it offers customers a crop protection service invoiced by hectare, where, the farmer pays a fixed amount per hectare of crops to be protected.[20] And rather than using expensive chemical solutions that are potentially harmful for the environment, the health of the farmer and the consumers,[21] the company decided to build its offer based on nature intelligence and the free ecological services that it renders us.

A quick flashback is necessary. We are in 1960, and Jan Koppert is then the first farmer to create a biological farm in the Netherlands.[22] Allergic to chemical products and eager to find a simple, clean and reliable method to protect its crops, he identified predatory insects of the parasites that harmed its greenhouse vegetables.

Very quickly, he started breeding larvae that he shared with the neighboring farmers and then realized that there was a business to be developed. The company Koppert was then created and worked toward the identification, breeding and marketing of predatory insects of pests. Technical challenges abounded, in particular finding a predator for whiteflies, which were devastating the local tomato plantations at that time. It was the eventual discovery of a small wasp in Amazonia that provided a solution. Since the late 1960s, the range of solutions has continued to grow. Concretely, the company sells living organisms in the form of larvae, pupae, eggs or microorganisms (mushrooms, for example).[23] The company also released a range of pollinating insects to replace or improve manual pollination. In 1987, for example, the company identified and promoted the role of the bumblebee in the pollination of tomato seedlings, which gives farmers substantial labor economies, an improvement in the quality of the fruit, and even an increase in production.[24] Furthermore, the company has developed an entirely natural product range to fight against diseases for which the solutions of predatory insects are not possible. Beyond farmers, the company extended to other markets, by offering solutions to fight nuisances for local authorities, helping protect their green spaces in a clean and natural way.

Advantages for Koppert customers are numerous: implementation of a natural system of disease prevention, enabling to stop or to reduce use of pesticides that cost time, money and demand handling hazardous substances; improvement of biological quality of the grounds, positive impact on the outputs, possibilities of qualifying for organic farming certification and so on.

In nearly 40 years, Koppert became the world leader in the biological integrated pest management and natural pollination market, being present in 57 countries.

A TRUE STRATEGIC RUPTURE

If use-oriented services constitute an important strategic rupture, they do not impose a complete redefinition of the company scope of activities. Admittedly, the company switches from a product sales model to a service model, which is in itself more than an evolution, but the industrial base can remain identical, even if new activities are added (product remaking or redesign operations, for example). Xerox thus continues to manufacture photocopiers; Michelin still produces tires.

A change in the scope of activities

With result-oriented services, the rupture is still more fundamental, because it is the scope of activities that is likely to
change. By passing from a model of pesticide sales to a model
of an integrated solution offering a maximum acceptable crop
loss rate, a company operates a true diversification, requiring not only chemical and agronomic competences, but also
biological, entomological and hydrological, among others.
Continuously monitoring and servicing jet engines requires
deploying a company's operations around the world to be
where the airline companies takeoff and land. It would not be
easy for an existing company to imagine undertaking such a
rupture by evolving an existing business model but rather by
creating a new operation based on a new business model that
can coexist with the old one. Difficult to imagine that a water
or energy supplier would embrace such a strategic change by
purely and simply discarding a confirmed and competitive
business model.

The project needs to take a truly entrepreneurial shape, carried
either by a new entrant or by an incumbent or existing actor.
Paradoxically, the latter is rarely the case, because, as explained
a while ago by Clayton Christensen, disruptive innovation is
often carried by new entrants, *incumbents* (actors in place)
developing mainly incremental innovations to sustain its industry
(*sustaining innovation*).[25]

Disruptive innovations do, often, emerge through new actors.
Large groups of course keep a close eye on these new entrants
and often acquire innovative start-ups (as Avis's acquisition
of Zipcar). Given the associated difficulties to integrate these
new activities to the older perimeter and to protect the innovation, these acquisitions are generally localized in new, relatively
autonomous *business units*. Another path for large groups consists in setting up an internal incubation structure where promising projects can spin off quickly, with the company retaining
a share of new venture. In every case, this journey is often
experimental.

Safechem gets it cleaner[26]

SAFECHEM is a subsidiary of The Dow Chemical Company, a corporation with a portfolio of products and solutions on specialty chemicals, advanced materials, agrosciences and plastics businesses, operating in approximately 160 countries and in high-growth sectors such as electronics, water, energy, coatings and agriculture. In 2011, it had sales of US$60 billion and EBITDA of approximately US$8.4 billion.[27]

SAFECHEM specializes in the safe and sustainable use of solvents for high-precision cleaning. In a volume business model, the company would have sold solvents for its clients, aiming to maximize volume sold. But this would have transferred to clients the problem of dealing and disposing these solvents. Several years ago, the company innovated with its COMPLEASE™ chemical leasing offer that leases the complete cleaning process including the equipment, solvents, services and expert know-how.[28] Among its clients are companies in the automotive sector like Volkswagen, Daimler, Chrysler, Ford, Toyota, Volvo and GM; in the semiconductor industry like STMicroelectronics and Motorola; and in the pulp and paper industry.[29]

This offer enables a drastic reduction in the use of solvents and offers a safer solution to its clients. Under the original product sales model, the company used to sell an average of 754 kg of product to its customers for 100 kg of grease to treat. The use of these products generated 233 kg of waste and 520 kg of particularly harmful emissions for the environment. Today, after the implementation of the principle of circularity and the passage to result-oriented services, the quantities used on average by customer to reach the same result fell to 4 kg, generating 1 kg of emissions and 3 kg of waste.[30]

Solvents become an input in a process, a cost that the company has an economic interest in minimizing to provide a certain service level. This offer thus enables revenue generation to be decoupled from resource use (i.e. solvents).

A similar solution is available in dry cleaning with the use of the cleaning agent perchloroethylene (tetrachloroethylene, PER or PCE) in a closed-loop system. This new standard is supported by leading cleaning machine manufacturers like Böwe, Firbimatic, Ilsa spa, Multimatic, Renzacci and Union.[31]

A catalyst for blue ocean strategies[32]

In 2005, W. C. Kim and R. Mauborgne published the best seller *Blue Ocean Strategy*. They distinguished two strategic spaces, red oceans and blue oceans:

- Red oceans refer to the current strategic space, with clearly defined boundaries where companies fight among themselves in a bloody way to gain market shares. As this space is densely occupied, growth and profit prospects are limited and innovation is primarily incremental, inducing a commoditization of offers.

- Blue oceans, by contrast, refer to new strategic spaces not exploited and as such free from competition, where demand is created and the company that crafted a particularly original value proposition is alone in the market. Emerging in a radically innovative way, blue oceans are generally created out of red oceans when an actor stretches the strategic boundaries previously drawn.

This distinction leads the authors to break a strategy dogma, and even if they have not been the first to do so, they managed to popularize the concept that a company does not necessarily need to choose between a generic strategy of cost domination or differentiation. Kim and Mauborgne show with the blue ocean strategy, on the contrary, that it is desirable to simultaneously pursue differentiation and low cost. *Value innovation* is the cornerstone of this strategy. The idea is simple: it is a matter of creating a leap of value for buyers and for the company, rendering competition irrelevant by opening up new and uncontested market space:

> Because value to buyers comes from the offering's utility minus its price, and because value to the company is generated from the offering's price minus its cost, value innovation is achieved only when the whole system of utility, price and cost is aligned.[33]

Blue ocean creators thus simultaneously pursue value increase while minimizing the cost structure associated with the new value curve.

Kim and Mauborgne present evidence that blue oceans are profitable. They analyzed 108 cases of new activity launches: 86 percent were characterized as red oceans consisting of incremental innovations (extensions of line or range) representing 62 percent of turnover and 39 percent of profits; the remaining 14 percent characterized blue oceans capturing 38 percent of the turnover and 61 percent of the profits.

Despite this persuasive rationale, few companies actually put it into practice. Reasons are numerous. Companies are generally more inclined to add functionalities than to remove low perceived valued features. Such a strategy, although potentially profitable, is also riskier, and large groups are more reticent to take risks compared to apparently less risky continuous and incremental innovation. The time span is certainly different, blue ocean strategies taking longer to be developed, far exceeding the quarterly time frame of some CEOs looking to maximize shareholder value in the short term. Inertia to change is also a major challenge: financial markets actors are rather resistant to strategic ruptures and organizations themselves have embedded knowledge and practices that are not easily modifiable.[34] Even if Michael Dell's reasons to make a bid to take Dell private can be debatable, he is right to argue that major strategic shifts are often punished by stock markets.[35]

Moreover, barriers can be cognitive: it is not that easy to represent what could be a value leap in its economic sector. It is precisely on this point that the transition to a result-based integrated solutions can provide a frame to conceive this leap. Certainly, this transition contains all the ingredients to favor blue ocean strategies.

DESIGNING THE NEW BUSINESS MODEL

Defining a new value curve

The strategy canvas is a particularly interesting tool to represent the current strategic space and to structure the value-innovation approach to identify a value leap. It will be particularly relevant here to conceive the new value proposition.

The strategy canvas consists of a visual method to depict the market space in two dimensions[36]:

- On the x-axis, the competing factors, that is, the characteristics of the offer, like advantages, functional or symbolic benefits expected by the customer to solve one of his needs.

- On the y-axis, the offering level that customers receive across these competing factors.

The value curve is the central component of the strategy canvas with a graphic depiction of a company's relative performance across its industry's factors of competition.

Figure 6.1 presents the strategy canvas for two competing pesticides, evaluated on four criteria expected by a farmer: price, product effectiveness, ease of use and impact on the ground and its biodiversity. It is essential for this information to reflect the offering level in the customer's eyes, not the company's perception of its market. This is to prevent analysis based on a partial representation of customer expectations, a form of myopia systematically favoring the company offer benefits compared with those of competitors. This could be obtained through the purchase of syndicated market research or by conducting a study

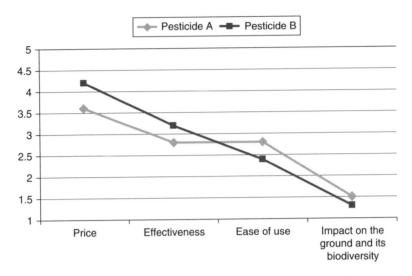

Figure 6.1 *Strategy canvas for two competing pesticides*

with customers to evaluate the expected characteristics of the offer.

As a preparatory step, the company can draw the strategy canvas to kick off the initiative and later input market information. In this case, a focus group can be organized within the company with key account managers, after-sales service personnel and marketing to identify the relevant characteristics. The offers' comparative performance evaluation can take place in a similar way, by exploiting firstly all observable quantitative information (prices, for example).

Examination of these curves shows a slight difference between the two offers: product B proves more effective in protecting crops from the nuisances they are exposed to, this additional effectiveness being rewarded by a higher selling price; on the down side, the product is more difficult to use and has a more aggressive impact on the soil and its biodiversity.

Even if these offers are somehow different, there is no major competitive advantage for one player, and companies certainly fight vigorously to frame customer's perceptions in favor of their superior attributes. This is characteristic of a red ocean where actors fight for market share on somehow commoditized offers.

The blue ocean strategy aims to configure a new value curve by breaking with the current logic of industries and business model by posing four questions:

- Which of the factors that the industry takes for granted should be *eliminated*?

- Which factors should be *reduced well below* the industry's standard?

- Which factors should be *raised well above* the industry's standard?

- Which factors should be *created* that the industry has never offered?[37]

The transition from the sale of a product to its result allows the value curve to be radically redefined by applying one or several of these actions. New factors can be developed and the existing ones can potentially be eliminated, raised or reduced. By doing this, a new value proposition can emerge. Continuing with our pesticide example, and by reasoning this time on a comprehensive solution guaranteeing a maximum rate of acceptable loss, we can indeed proceed to a much more radical reconfiguration of the value curve compared to the concurrent offers (see Figure 6.2).

A value proposition addressing the same basic need for crop protection but structured as a result-oriented service introduces characteristics that were not previously presented in the strategic space. It is thus possible to enact a radically new value curve, radically different from existing offers, creating a new strategic space without real competition. This offer guarantees, by principle, a certain service rate based on a predefined target. Constructed on a set of diversified protection methods and not exclusively on a chemical pesticide, it has a higher expected effectiveness. And because it develops natural ecological services and eliminates or reduces low value-added attributes, its price could be equivalent, if not lower than the chemical solution. It

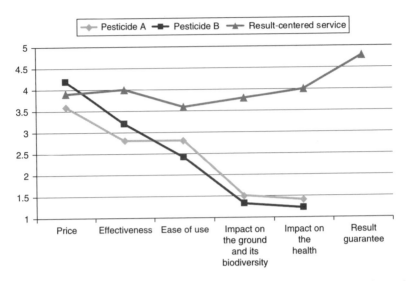

Figure 6.2 *Reconfiguration of the value curve by a result-based integrated solution*

thus increases the level of certain competing factors and creates a new one: a result guarantee.

This gives us the possibility of a strategy of simultaneous differentiation and low cost. Moreover, this new solution integrates or improves underlying needs of farmers, distributors or final clients (food-processing companies or end consumers, for example), currently not addressed. As discussed before, Koppert's solution facilitates application by the farmer, enriches the biodiversity of crops and contributes to a less risky agriculture (e.g. dependent on the risk of handling of chemical pesticides[38]). At the end, the reduction of phytosanitary inputs helps to improve the sanitary quality of the products, by proposing an alternative to fight potentially dangerous pests for vegetables and health (see Table 6.1).

The contractual innovation based on a new invoicing unit

If the strategy canvas helps to configure the new value proposition, writing the commercial contract will take a central part in its development. Since the service rate will be the base for the evaluation

Table 6.1 *Sustainable business model canvas for an agricultural result-based integrated solution*

Key Partners	Key Activities	Sustainable Value Proposition	Customer Relationship Management	Customers Segments	Benefits for Society and the Environment
• Chambers of agriculture/farming associations supporting the evolution of agricultural practices • NGOs • Distributors • Ministry of agriculture • Agricultural/ entomological research centers • Educational institutions • Agro-food industry	• R & D/life forms inventory and ancestral practices analysis • Risk assessment (periodic monitoring, observation networks, agricultural warnings) • Education and assistance in the development of practices (genetics prevention, agro-technical and cultural practices • Organization of co-creation • Breeding of insects/production/supply chain • Marketing and sales	Provision of an integrated and effective sustainable crop protection by giving priority to (1) biotechnical, (2) organic (insects), (3) bacteriological, (4) chemical aspects, offering increased yields, reduced environmental and social risks, time savings and financial gains (in the long run)	• Dedicated personal assistance • Co-creation with the farmers • Automated relationship (e.g. in terms of monitoring)	Main target: Farmers Secondary target: Local authorities	• A drastic reduction in major environmental and health impacts for both farmers and consumers (social benefits) • Regeneration of biodiversity and soil • Increased resilience of farming systems through diversification of approaches (=> food safety) • Support the development of a competitive extensive agriculture
	Key Resources • Intangible: Trust, listening capabilities, being able to understand the intelligence and interdependence of nature => expertise (agronomic, entomology, green chemistry, legal and lawful – for example, for the contract – etc.), organizational capabilities, cooperation between parties • Human: Staff, external researchers • Physical: Monitoring tools in fields, greenhouses, factories, customers interfaces • Financial: Capital and cash		**Distribution Channels** Direct distribution or exclusive short channel (fragile living organisms)		

Costs for Society and the Environment					
• Choice not completely free of phytosanitary inputs but last resort					

Shared Costs	Cost Structure	Revenue Streams	Shared Benefits
• Energy costs and entrants (raw materials) • Transportation costs	• Fixed costs: Payroll, production facilities and equipment depreciation, overheads, etc. • Variable costs: Production costs, budget for educating the market, management of partnerships, monitoring costs, etc.	• Revenue (fee) based on the surface (acres) that need to be protected • Ability to monetize free ecological services	• Positive impact in terms of crop performance • Better risk management • Guarantee of result • Facilitate the acquisition of quality/environmental labels • Increased added-value of the value proposition and new spaces of differentiation/positive impact on the image • Production of new knowledge and fostering of innovation

and the remuneration of the service, it is thus necessary to parameter in a legally sound contract not only the true nature of this service rate, but also the methods for follow-up and measurement, like all the provisions accompanying the service, and the rights and duties of both parties. As such, we can truly speak here about contractual innovation. The new contractual base will be the *service level agreement*. The service level agreement is a part of a service contract where the level of a service in terms of nature, quality, duration, performance, length and so on is formally defined.[39]

The example of Suez Environnement exemplifies how the transition to a result-oriented service can give birth to a radical new value proposition based on a service rate.

Suez Environnement experiments with a bold business move

Suez Environnement is a global player in the water and waste sector. It was created 120 years ago and operates all around the world, from Australia to Africa, including the United States and several European countries. Through its subsidiaries, it supplies 91 million people with drinking water, 63 million with sanitation services, and provides 57 million people worldwide with waste collection services, and currently employs 80,410 employees.[40] In 2011, the company had revenues of €14,830 million and EBITDA of €2,513 million.

The group launched its EDELWAY initiative in 2008, aiming to become a long-term partner to its customers by offering contractual commitment to environmental performance in three areas: curbing GHG emissions, conserving natural resources, and protecting biodiversity.

The offers must follow three criteria: "time lined and quantified performance guarantees that attract financial compensation, measurement tools approved by an independent third party and/or mutually agreed with the customer in advance, a clearly displayed and legible commitment."[41]

Some examples of innovations developed are

- Biocontrol + technology developed by Ondeo Industrial Solutions allowing industrial customers to reduce sludge production by up to 90 percent

- "Degrés Bleus" system developed by Lyonnaise des Eaux for producing heat from wastewater pipelines, thereby reducing its customers' carbon footprint

Suez Environnement's French subsidiary, Lyonnaise des Eaux, has indeed been a pioneer in exploring new paths to conciliate economic and sustainable performance.

The company is testing a business model innovation in the French town of Dijon: instead of invoicing a volume of water consumed, it has fixed its remuneration based on attaining the environmental objectives of the city. It aims to improve the output of the 525 km network of the city (150,000 inhabitants) and to maintain it on a desired optimum level higher than 80 percent. Lyonnaise des Eaux is remunerated via a compensation system on the degree of attainment of this service rate. To do so, the company has deployed a permanent diagnosis of the level of leakages on the network, through the installation of 180 sensors. Results outperformed initial expectations: in a year more than 50 percent more leakages were detected and repaired, allowing the safeguarding of 1.2 million m^3 of water, creating value for the company and the city. As a result, the Dijon authorities have confirmed water and wastewater services contracts until 2021 for Lyonnaise des Eaux.

According to Helene Valade, sustainable development director,

> This kind of project is very strategic because it questions the company's economic model. It is coherent with the Suez principles demanding an evolution from remuneration on a quantitative logic, that is,

volume of water, to a model which will make it possible to be remunerated on the service that we provided to the environment [...] The first stage of this evolution is to make commitments to reduce the environmental footprint of local authorities, with a certain number of indicators. It is then necessary to set-up a no-claims bonus system (bonus/penalty) to be remunerated on the achievement of these environmental objectives. This obviously has a very strong impact on the contract of public service delegation which is defined by law. The contract is no longer founded on a quantitative logic, but on the environmental performance of our solutions.[42]

Similarly, the company recently won a contract in Fontainebleau, close to Paris, for the management of the sewage treatment plant of the city, with a precise target to reduce energy consumption of the stations by 21 percent and GHG emissions by 9 percent.

These new contracts based on environmental service rates illustrate the transition to result-oriented services. They bind the remuneration of Lyonnaise des Eaux to its capacity to deliver the contractually defined service rate, any additional performance being shared between both parties.

Defining the target service level and the appropriate invoicing unit

In order to conceive the value proposition and the adequate contractual base, several parameters must guide the specification of the service level; these are presented next.

A reliable indicator of the service level

The service level can be defined in terms of availability, performance, operation or any other relevant attribute. It can define a target or a minimum service to be delivered. These indicators are sometimes directly accessible, sometimes more complex to define. As an illustration, what is the adequate indicator for a supply of electricity given its multiple uses? The example of RAU and Philips covered only lighting. If we focus on heating, it could be defined that instead of selling a volume of kW/h, the offer would be a service of thermal comfort. More generally, it could be determined as selling the customer an Energy Performance Contract, defined by a European directive like "a contractual arrangement between the beneficiary and the provider of an energy efficiency improvement measure, where investments in that measure are paid for in relation to a contractually agreed level of energy efficiency improvement."[43]

Feasibility assessment and installation

The target objectives must be specified, with a precise description of the methods and schedule of measurement. In our example, thermal comfort could be measured by a certain temperature. This temperature could be stable through day and night, or variable according to the occupation. This supposes a shift in the status of the delivered kW/h. In a sale of volume logic, kW/h is the unit of invoicing. In the present case, it becomes a cost that the service provider aims to minimize in order to reach the service level. Moreover, the capacity to deliver this level and the quantity of energy to mobilize to reach this target temperature will depend on the building's energy efficiency.

This demands a feasibility study. Although it may be inexpensive to provide a comfort temperature of 20 °C to a *passive building*,[44] the situation is quite different for an *energy voracious building*. The service must thus be calibrated by a preliminary diagnosis of the building energy class. This diagnosis will enable to assign an economically realistic price for the service level. It will also suggest additional measures enabling price reductions in the contract. Thus a work of insulation of the building could be suggested to improve its energy class and to decrease the contract price. In such a case, the service provider could develop an integrated solution where activities would be entrusted to partners or subsidiaries of the group, allowing additional value capture, in the best interest of the customer. In certain cases, financial innovations can be proposed based, for example, on the principle of the third investor, at the example of ESCO (Energy Saving Economy)[45] mentioned in Chapter 1. As such, the service calibration can lead to complementary needs that can enrich the solution and its value for the customer, enabling a win–win situation for capturing additional value.

This is how an energy services company like Anesco in the UK operates: it defines an Energy Saving Performance Contract (ESPC), where it examines current energy usage and all aspects of a building's performance, before calculating the financial savings that could be made through the implementation of a range of key energy-efficiency measures. These measures cover all aspects of a building's performance, including voltage optimization, lighting, insulation and wastewater heat recovery. Anesco makes the investment to fund the ESPC and recoups investment made over an agreed payback period, based on energy savings generated.[46]

Ongoing monitoring and reporting to control compliance with the contract terms

Piloting the service level supposes identifying and potentially sanctioning any noncompliant behavior in the execution of the contract. Thus, if a comfort temperature of 20 °C or a 20 percent energy savings is agreed and fixed by contract, but on a cold winter's day, the client opens the windows, the amount of energy needed to reach the target would consequently increase. It is necessary therefore to set up methods and tools for monitoring the service level, validating compliance with the agreed contract terms and the flexibility authorized in the execution of the service. In the current case, a device should measure the internal and external temperature, and to react in the event of a window being opened, for example, by ordering the heating to be cut in the specified zone.[47] The development of communicating objects and intelligent networks makes these possibilities of measurement and remote piloting economically and technically feasible and desirable, as demonstrated by the section in the previous chapter on the Internet of objects. *Smart grids* have indeed the potential for generating substantial energy savings.

Key parameters of the contract

In addition to the specification of the service level, its indicators, its methods and its schedule of measurement, the service-level agreement must anticipate possible issues and the way they will be treated. A key point relates to the penalties incurred or the bonus granted in the event of nonobservance or exceeding the service level. It is necessary to specify any penalties and conditions for application and exclusion of these penalties.

Thus a customer subscribing to an offer of integrated crop protection will have to insure against risks not related to pests, such as bad weather or drought. Expiry of guarantee terms must be based in factual indicators, or they risk opening the door to interminable court battles in the event of a problem. In the same away, any performance beyond the service rate must entail a shared division of benefits.

The contract must also clearly define the rights and duties of each party by specifying the penalties in the event of noncompliance of these terms. In certain cases, the correct execution of the contract requires the access for both sides to potentially sensitive, even confidential, information, so confidentiality and data access terms must be clearly specified. In addition to these terms, usual contractual conditions must obviously be integrated (such as, for example, the conditions for contract cancellation or the competent jurisdiction in the event of litigation).

As we can see, the contract is closely related to the value proposition and becomes a central element in the customer relationship. Its development calls for strategic new resources, like legal experts, or partnerships with insurance companies or legal firms.

HOW TO BUILD THE MARKET?

While identifying target customers for the reconfigured offer may be straightforward, converting them into clients is more challenging. The change associated with this value proposition is likely to generate resistance, even rejection from some customers. This is the typical situation of a rupture: a vast majority of customers prefer to "wait and see" the results of the adoption by some pioneers before taking the plunge to try the new solution themselves. This situation is obviously uncomfortable and risky for the service provider and thus requires adequate innovation management.

Co-creation with early adopters

How to obtain the first contracts that will make it possible to develop the market? David Midgley[48] explores this question in the blue ocean strategy value innovation frame. He recommends firstly identifying the innovating customers' potentially sensitive to such an offer. These early adopters indeed have a particular reference frame that makes them perceive the specific characteristics of the novel offer as a source of advantages. Simple novelty can be enough, as being a pioneering user confers a value in itself. Potentially, these innovative customers (e.g. a farmer for the integrated crop protection service) can take part as a partner in the offer development process, becoming *co-creators* of the solution and providing invaluable feedback for the service improvement. This is characteristic of a co-creation process where a customer-partner helps to co-develop the value proposition. Thus, the idea is to develop a first version of the service for customers to try, collect their suggestions for improvements, adjust the offer, test again and so on.[49] This enables a quicker development process and generates knowledge and feedback from service use, which is difficult to capture otherwise.

For example, Suez Environnement gives co-creation a special role:

> This approach, built on several levels, entails dialogue with economic partners, customers, employees, civil

society and ordinary citizens, producing new responses and solutions by working together. In research and innovation, the approach means forging partnerships with public and industrial bodies or seeking out innovative players and providing them with financial support. In operational terms, co-construction involves setting up new governance mechanisms and creating new models for water and waste management.[50]

Building the perception for the differentiating attributes

Then, it is necessary to develop a positioning to emphasize the differentiating attributes of the offer compared to the classically considered alternatives (here, product sales). This is fundamental. Many marketing and economic studies show that the evaluation of an offer primarily depends on the selected points of comparison. Emphasis should therefore be placed on those product attributes that are linked to the service offer. In this respect, the strategy canvas competing factors (see Figure 6.2) are potential candidates to define comparison points, the guarantee of result being undoubtedly the most persuasive element versus a product offering with only a guarantee of means. This positioning aims to persuade early followers, who, if they are not ready to take a bet as early adopters, do not wish to lag behind if the offer results among the first customers are convincing. This enables clients to be added successively to the firm's portfolio to develop the market. It also makes it possible to prepare the third stage: management of criticisms. No doubt that established competitors will do all they can to discredit the new offer wherever they can.

Management of criticism

The management of detractors is a substantial task in the market construction process. Opposing forces can be strong and may ruin innovation. Competitors will obviously fully exploit the risky character of any disruptive innovation (too young, technologies not completely stabilized, dubious return on experiments, lack of financial means of the service provider if it is a start-up, maybe leaving a messy situation in the event of bankruptcy and so on). Jack Trout[51] reminds us of this immutable marketing principle: it is all about customer perception! And the market will be built (or not) on a favorable customer perception. The capacity to attract clients to a co-creation process or to convince a reference client in the market to be an early follower will strengthen arguments against any detractors. Consequently, a co-creation process is often an investment that should be taken. The early adopter willing to play the role of a 'beta tester' could thus be offered particularly advantageous conditions.

A BUSINESS MODEL TO BE CONFIGURED

On operational grounds, while the definition of the value proposition and the unit to be invoiced provide the starting point in an evolution toward a result-oriented service, this must be followed up with an analysis of their impact on the remaining components of the business model: their impact on the remaining components of the business model.

The implementation of a new value proposition will thus demand the definition of a new value chain, sustained by new resources. For start-ups, this is the classical entrepreneurial path. For large groups with product offerings, this new value chain construction is not simple, because the transition from goods to services is much more than a semantic jump. A service is managed very differently than a tangible good, a fortiori when it requires high labor intensity. The appreciation of the service, and the resulting satisfaction will be largely guided by the experience of the service. It should be possible to develop a true customer-oriented service culture, with processes sustaining the qualitative management of this experience. Moreover, the customer relations will generally become direct where it was previously managed by distributers or sales reps. Developing a frontline that can manage this customer relation becomes essential, demanding specific resources and competences. All these elements show the impossibility for a large group to carry out such an evolution in its core business, because current processes and practices would de facto destroy any attempt of evolution and innovation.[52]

The capacity to guarantee a result instead of the sale of the means to reach that result will often require the development of partnerships, a potential source of innovation and value. As we mentioned earlier, selling comfort temperature or quantified energy saving requires an initial audit, as well as energy efficiency improvements. The service-level agreement seller will seldom execute all the activities to be deployed. Often, part of these activities will be entrusted to external partners. The construction of these partnerships must take place once again under the prism of value capture. Thus an energy supplier, having developed a subsidiary controlling these new agreements, may want to participate financially in the companies, constituting a true business support system for the activities of this subsidiary, so that cross-selling among the partners can potentially generate direct incomes (commissioning, for example) and/or indirect incomes (such as through financial participation). In addition to commercial partnerships, expert partnerships play a particular role, because the field of competences and expertise held can vary largely. The company must thus consider operating in an *open* model, where the permeability with a partners' network replaces the perspective of a closed and secretive company. We observe as such the transition from a value chain to a value constellation.[53] If this open-networked company model appears natural for some actors – in particular certain Internet actors for whom the distributed and interconnected model is the expression itself of their business model and organizational model[54] – it is much less the case for industrial companies that are used to developing their products in-house.

Obviously, the nature of customer relations is strongly impacted by such an evolution because, essentially, it becomes a personalized direct relation. Instead of a mass market, there is a mass of niches to be satisfied according to particular needs, not excluding, however, standardization and automation, necessary, for example, for piloting contracts. Indeed, value innovation seeks simultaneously to increase the perceived value for the customer while minimizing the cost structure to reach that point.

LEGAL FRAME SUPPORTING
RESULT-ORIENTED SERVICES

We mentioned some cases where companies are developing offers to comply with regulations, like the Agenda 21, or under some legal frames, like Energy Performance Contracting. In the coming years increased regulations are expected to put a "price on the planet"[55] accounting for all the services that nature renders for "free" for companies.

Examples can be found around the globe. The WWF-UK cites the example of California, where the Californian Power Utilities Commission "applies a complex body of legislation comprising regulation of utilities and financial incentives" and has recently started a program aiming

> to decouple energy sales from profit by fixing the revenues that utilities can collect from customers in advance. Utilities under this system are not incentivized to sell more energy to customers, and instead pursue rewards offered by regulators for creating customer energy efficiency savings, and the reduction of their own fixed or variable costs.[56]

Another example brought by the WWF is that of the 'benefit corporation' laws enacted by the American states of Maryland, New Jersey, Vermont and Virginia to "create a new legal status for organizations that wish to pursue environmental or social goals in tandem with the pursuit of shareholder returns." The directors and officers have legal protection

> to consider the environment, the interests of employees, customers, and the communities where the firm operates, in addition to the interest of shareholders. The benefit corporation's legal framework locks the environmental

and social goals of a firm into its governing documents, enabling these goals to survive regardless of the intentions of new investors, management or company ownership.[57]

Companies are also pushing government to take action, as in the example of Virgin.

Virgin's corporate activism

We could think of Virgin first and foremost as an impressive public relations war machine at the service of its various businesses, wisely orchestrated by Sir Richard Branson's communications acumen. So, when a few years ago the Virgin Group committed to sustainability, there was some reasonable suspicion about the depth of the initiative. It turns out, as demonstrated by the Group's Corporate Responsibility and Sustainable Development Report, that companies like Virgin Atlantic are making a serious effort in that direction, like being the first carrier to call for global legislation on airline CO_2 emissions, the first to fly on renewable fuels, being a founding member of the Aviation Global Deal Group and the Sustainable Aviation Fuel Users Group,[58] and having committed to a 30 percent reduction in the carbon intensity of each passenger and cargo kilometer flown between 2007 and 2030.

Similar actions are being taken in other companies in the Group like Virgin Holidays, Virgin Trains, Virgin Media, Virgin Mobile and so on. Even if the reach of these initiatives is limited, it is mainly the Group's high profile that helps to shape the public debate on sustainability. Indeed, through Virgin Unite, the group's charitable branch, some high-profile initiatives of "cause marketing" have been launched, such as the Elders (a group of veteran statesmen that helps mediate conflicts like that taking place in Syria) or the Carbon War Room (an attempt to bring business leaders together to find profitable ways to reduce fossil-fuel use in the most carbon-intensive industries). The most recent initiative of Sir Richard Branson, the B Team, aims to do no less than change the way business is done. Its objective is to

> form a small group of business leaders who will campaign for reforms to make capitalism more oriented to the long term and socially more responsible [...] The idea is that each member will champion a particular reform and work with the others to get all the reforms adopted. A consultation exercise is already under way to find which reforms are ripe to be pushed through. Proper accounting for environmental impact, an end to quarterly reporting of results and the phasing-out of fossil-fuel subsidies are likely to be near the top of the list.[59]

The team will support ideas that have both a big potential impact and a good chance of being achieved. Some skepticism is also necessary for this kind of initiative, but it is good news that business leaders are engaging their efforts to make business synonymous with sustainable development.

Given scarce and expensive resources, companies will eventually find it in their best interest to reduce the volume of inputs per offer as much as they can.

Financial markets can help up to a certain extent by offering opportunities for a player like Sun Edison (see Chapter 2) to develop innovative finance schemes to enact a new business model. On a broader level, regulations can help accelerate this process and favor the emergence of result-oriented services in the best interest of companies' competitiveness and the common good.

EMERGING MARKETS

Given "emerging" economies' fast-growing environmental foot-print, the development of result-oriented services would certainly be good news for everybody. The potential certainly exists, but some considerations should be taken into account. The first is that these services demand a solid institutional frame and the respect of the rule of law. This is unfortunately not the case everywhere. In some countries, private interests prevail over justice; in others, courts can be sometimes biased to favor local actors compared to foreign companies. Due diligence is fundamental before deploying these services abroad to validate their feasibility and opportunity.

Tarun Khanna and Krishna Palepu identify emerging markets as characterized by "institutional voids," the fact that the institutions (like labor markets, product markets and capital markets) that make up a market ecosystem are either missing or not functioning as expected in emerging economies.[60]

A central challenge lies in the existing infrastructures: most emerging economies are at the stage of providing basic infrastructure to their population; putting sensors in the water network as Lyonnaise des Eaux has done in France seems a bit unreal in countries where pure water is simply nonexistent, not to mention waste treatment.

One of the book's co-authors recently stayed at a well-known Shanghai five-star hotel. Considerable funds were invested to build a hallmark for the city skyline, but apparently there was no money left to install double glazing. This is maybe a cultural left over from Mao's decision that only Chinese houses above the Yangtze River would get heating. Shanghai is not as cold as Beijing in wintertime, but the amount of supplementary energy necessary to heat houses and building without proper insulation is huge. When it is known that coal plays an important role in China's energy mix, it is not hard to imagine ways of reducing the country's carbon footprint. This is set to evolve, as the Chinese government has been announcing bold moves regarding sustainability, but the path is long.

Brazil and India provides a similar example regarding air conditioning. Indeed, all over Brazil, it is a *must have* to face the hot and humid summers (and in some regions to face wintertime). Given again the poor building insulation, energy waste is phenomenal.

Opportunities thus abound in these countries. Can result-oriented services be an answer to them? Rolls-Royce is offering its services for airline companies from all over the world. Sun Edison operates in China, Brazil, Korea, India, Thailand and Chile, besides Europe, North America and Japan. Veolia and Suez Environnement have just signed important contracts in India.[61]

Interestingly, the financial crisis favors lean management (i.e. increasing productivity by using less resources and energy) and an alignment of ecological and financial incentives. Given scarcity in society, companies in emerging markets have long been favoring a lean mentality. *Reverse Innovation* is the latest book urging Western companies to learn from these markets to bring forward innovations back home or be disrupted by new global champions.[62]

It is important nevertheless to highlight that the challenges faced by different countries vary according to their development situation and their own natural resources.

Brazil provides an interesting case. The country is home to an exceptional biodiversity comprising the Amazon forest, the Pantanal, the Cerrado and so on; it has one of the world cleanest energy matrices with 46.8 percent coming from renewables: hydroelectric, ethanol, biomass, wind;[63] it hosted the Rio-92 United Nations Conference where the Agenda 21 and the Rio+20 were designed, and has been experiencing growing public awareness about the issues of sustainability.[64]

Brazil is also a world champion of food export, resulting sometimes in the deforestation of virgin forests. To get its clean energy matrix, it needs to displace local populations, and this is a country that first and foremost wished to eliminate abject misery before the end of 2014.

Its main environmental concern is to preserve its rich biodiversity by protecting forest, fauna and water ecosystems. One pioneer action is the "ICMS-E (*Imposto sobre Circulação de Mercadorias e Serviços*, with environmental revenue-sharing criteria, ICMS-E),"[65] an ecological value-added tax for the services rendered by nature. The ICMS is a state levy on the circulation of goods, services, energy and communications, being the largest source of state revenues in Brazil. The ICMS-E is an alternative to ICMS that rewards local governments for their commitment to protecting forest and biological resources and mainly aims to pay for services provided by standing forests. Instead of deforesting to create space for economic activities, they have an incentive to keep forests standing. This measure has been adopted in several states (but not in Para and Amazonas, home to the biggest part of the Amazon forest) and is showing promising results.[66]

Is there a place for result-oriented services in Brazil? They could certainly find fertile ground for development, but it is just one measure-taking place in the broader sustainability context of the country, where companies like Natura are pushing carbon neutral initiatives[67] or Brasken are developing products like green polyethylene.[68]

CONCLUSION

The 2010s are a decade of paradoxes. The triad – United States, Europe and Japan – is facing the most critical economic crisis since the Second World War. Employment and growth are the expressions that dictate the political agenda and few political leaders are able to assume that sustainability is a driver and not a barrier to growth and employment. *Business as usual* remains largely dominant in many parts of the world, especially in the United States. And unconventional energy sources like shale oil and gas and oil sands are not priced at their environmental cost[69] thus hindering the development of clean sources of energy. Some even promise a future of abundance.[70]

Price volatility thus remains a reality favored by speculative movements in a depressed economic context where not that many investment options remain attractive. G20 has announced its will to control this volatility in raw materials' prices, but seems impotent to take effective measures. All the indicators seem to point in the direction of a major need for rationalization on the use of the resources and energy. But factual results are not very convincing.

Tim Jackson made a serious call in 2010 for "prosperity without growth," indicating that

> a massive technological shift; a significant policy effort; wholesale changes in patterns of consumer demand; a huge international drive for technological transfer to bring about substantial reductions in resource intensity right across the world: these changes are the least that will be needed to have a chance of remaining within environmental limits and avoiding an inevitable collapse in the resource base at some point in the (not too distant) future.[71]

In this chapter, we presented a credible economic alternative to businesses models built on logics of volume that are increasingly under pressure. According to several studies, this transition toward result-oriented services would make it possible to reach factor 4, that is, a reduction of 80 percent of resources and energy consumption for the creation of identical wealth.[72]

Result-oriented services are certainly not an easy, risk-free path. Disruptive innovation comes at a price. But where disruption usually generates maximum uncertainty, result-oriented services have the advantage of offering a frame and tools to elaborate this transition. Admittedly, uncertainty remains high, and many will prefer to affirm that an obligation of result is a utopia and represents an unacceptable risk for a company. But is business as usual an alternative?

Strategy is a reframing process.[73] Leaders should keep a close eye on the changing business landscape and reframe its mental models to develop capabilities for purposeful emergence.

Which forces are shaping the business landscape for the years to come? Emerging markets growth is the first. This means resource scarcity is here to stay and tackling it is a basic competitive issue. Technological developments (Internet, digitization, smart grids) will help to a certain extent, but fully addressing this issue requires a leap in the management "software." We presented examples of prime movers that are reconfiguring entire value constellations and shaping the business landscape. They are both small and big companies, incumbents and new entrants.

Xerox launched its second revolution. With Xerox Global Service, the company no longer sells machines, nor does it rent them. Instead, it offers a total document management service for its customers on the basis of the context of the customer and of its true needs to render document management more effectively and definitely less expensive. It is today the only one to commit itself contractually to the savings made by the customer. Service sales are going well according to Xerox. Safechem, a subsidiary of Dow Chemical, decided to stop sales of a highly toxic chlorinated solvent, which is under threat of being prohibited by regulators, to offer instead a machine degreasing service, in other words, the result sought by the use of solvents. It thus shows that it is possible to drastically reduce the volume of products used when the business model is grounded in an alternative logic; and this massive decoupling was accompanied by an increase of the turnover and profitability of the company. Nordaq was interested in the result sought by high-end hotels and restaurants when they buy bottled water. It is obviously a question of offering their customers pure water of great quality. It then endeavored to offer hotels and restaurants a tap water microfiltration solution, allowing their clients to get the same results without the need to buy an expensive and cumbersome number of bottles. Water is of an exceptional purity and contains all the minerals and trace elements, positively influencing taste. No more need for these customers to buy bottles, which have a considerable environmental impact in terms of packaging and transport.

These examples, albeit limited, show that while many businesses remain reticent, some are taking the plunge, in truly innovative spirit or because their competitiveness, even their existence, is threatened. Clearly, they are ahead of their competitors, and are developing, sometimes in an experimental trial-and-error approach, the drivers of a revisited competitive advantage for what will come next.

What's next regarding sustainability? Some companies are engaged in restorative activities and positive economy where a company has a net positive environmental impact. Decarbonating the economy through, among others, renewable energies will also be a major challenge of the 21st century.[74] Additionally, the sharing economy empowered by Internet platforms is a major societal change favored by a context of economic crisis and awareness of environmental issues.[75]

Our central contribution in this book is to challenge established management "mental models."[76] Decoupling value creation from energy and raw materials consumption is a major cognitive leap. We presented four steps supporting this change: eco-design, circular economy, use-oriented services and result-oriented services; and one tool to support this process and constructing scenarios[77] of different business model choices: the sustainable business model canvas. This tool should really be considered as a prototyping tool to support business model innovation. Its practical value has been largely demonstrated and

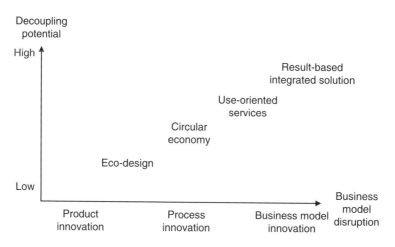

Figure 6.3 *Business model disruption and decoupling potential*

its effectiveness to support the transition toward use- or result-based service is strong.

These changes are gradually moving from product and process innovation to business model innovation. This requires reframing the company activity at the functional unit level and considering the stakeholders in the value constellation instead of the value chain alone. It thus addresses people and the planet as a means of support to increase a company's competitive situation (see Figure 6.3).

Sure, execution and leadership are central for this transition to take place, but cognitive change is often the major challenge and its absence the source of many myopic decisions that eventually lead industry leaders into a dismal situation.[78] It was our goal to provide food for thought and action for leaders aiming to build tomorrow's business models.

Conclusion

This book comes to an end. A large number of ideas were developed, illustrated by many examples. As a conclusion, we wish to share ten lessons that express the core of our message:

First lesson: Strategy is the correct level to integrate sustainable development in the value creation process of a company.

Second lesson: Sustainable development (or sustainability, or doing more with less, or any other term that better suits your company vocabulary) offers an opportunity to reconsider the nature of the competitive advantage itself and to redesign it. If we fully understand its consequences, sustainability impacts the strategy pillars and consequently the company's competitiveness.

Third lesson: The business model and the sustainable business model canvas are powerful tools to conceive scenarios for the strategic evolution of a company. Genuine, systemic tools highlighting the interdependence of its building blocks, they offer a suitable framework to analyze and instigate competitiveness.

Fourth lesson: If companies invest massively to improve work productivity, sometimes at the expense of their human wealth, it is time to find new resorts of productivity. Productivity of the resources is such a resort and concerns every single economic actor.

Fifth lesson: The eco-efficiency principle enacts to take the first step toward a greater productivity of resources. In substance, the governing idea is to make the same thing with less, and to replace as far as possible what is toxic and pathogenic for humans and the environment by what is less. It is a matter of profoundly reconsidering products, services or process. Potential benefits are immense.

Sixth lesson: Enough with the linearity of processes and flows! Waste is an unvalorized resource. Closing the loop generates savings, reduces requirements in raw materials and energy, and stimulates innovation. The principle of circularity is the second step toward greater productivity of the resources.

Seventh lesson: In many cases, traditional business models do not encourage eco-efficiency or circularity. Should a company thus ignore these two principles? If a business model is not appropriate, this is an opportunity to innovate it. We do not minimize the reach of this statement; the business model is the gravity center of a company. But if the very existence of a company is threatened, this is an invitation to take action. We presented a form of business model innovation consisting in substituting the sale of a good by the provision of a service centered on use- or result-based integrated solution. It is here the third and last step of our staircase.

Eighth lesson: When a good is sold, there is no incentive for it to be reparable and to last a long time. How to implement circularity of flows in a linear model, which, once the property is transferred to the customer, does not enable the company to preserve the control of the materials? If planned obsolescence had its raison d'être in a past era, it is no longer a realistic option. Regulators are taking a closer scrutiny and the Internet has given voice to consumers to revolt and to fight this principle. To render null and void planned obsolescence demands the shift toward an economy of access. The opportunities lying ahead, especially for durable or semi-durable capital equipment, are considerable.

Ninth lesson: As long as companies build their revenue model on a volume to be sold, there will be issues regarding resource management. It is necessary to add value to volumes or, better still, to switch to business models that reward to the detriment of volume. Result-based integrated solutions open up avenues for thinking and developing this transition.

Tenth lesson: Innovation is the engine of this change. Incremental innovation has its role to play, but disruptive innovation is nowadays clearly needed. It is not the easiest way, but it is the one that changes rules of the game and will give birth to the leaders of tomorrow.

If the paths presented here are potentially rich and promising, they interact with the broader economic, regulatory and technological context. Systemic innovation, for example, carried not by a single actor but by a true network of actors coordinated around a common objective, seems a more radical and promising way ahead in terms of decoupling. It leads to systemic changes in soft issues (attitudes and values of people, regulations, relations between actors and so on) and hard issues (infrastructure, technology, modes of production and so on). Moreover, it interconnects these levels, analyzes the mechanisms of interdependence and combines innovation at a number of levels: product, service, process, organizational, social and so on. Also, collaborative and collective intelligence constitutes a promising field to support bottom-up innovation, empowered by the Internet and social networks.

There is more to come and we invite you to continue the conversation by sharing your feedback, ideas, projects or achievements regarding the topic developed in this book. You can contact us at: christophe.sempels@skema.edu or jonas.hoff mann@skema.edu.

Notes

INTRODUCTION

1. Conference of Philippe Maystadt, "Europe, the lost continent?" Verviers, Belgium February 21, 2013.

1 TACKLING SUSTAINABLE DEVELOPMENT AT THE CORPORATE STRATEGIC LEVEL TO CREATE VALUE

1. See P. Van Beurden and T. Gössling (2008), "The Worth of Values – A Literature Review on the Relation between Corporate Social and Financial Performance," *Journal of Business Ethics*, vol. 82, pp. 407–424, for a meta-analysis on this topic.
2. See, for example, the excellent book of H. Mintzberg, B. Ahlstrand and J. Lampel (2008), *Strategy Safari: The Complete Guide through the Wilds of Strategic Management*, 2nd edn, Toronto: Pearson Canada, on different schools of thought on strategy, and W. Kiechel III (2010), *The Lords of Strategy*, Boston: Harvard Business Press.
3. See, for example, G. Johnson, R. Whittington and K. Scholes (2009), *Exploring Strategy: Text & Cases*, 9th edn, New York: Prentice-Hall.
4. D.J. Teece, G. Pisano and A. Shuen (1997), "Dynamic Capabilities and Strategic Management," *Strategic Management Journal*, vol. 18, p. 516.
5. Source: personal interview with Ms. Férone and http://www.veolia.com/en/group/strategy/, accessed on September 16, 2012.

6. See http://www.ibm.com/smarterplanet/us/en/smarter_cities/ overview/index.html?re=spf, accessed on September 16, 2012.

7. Report of the Interministerial Pole of Prospective and Anticipation of the Economic Mutations in the Car Industry (April 2010), available at http://www.industrie.gouv.fr/p3e/ etudes/automobile/automobile3.pdf, accessed on September 16, 2012.

8. *The Economist* (2012), "Special Report: Natural Gas," July 12.

9. See http://www.iea.org/weo/docs/weo2010/weo2010_es_ french.pdf, accessed on September 16, 2012.

10. See D. Briaumont (ed.) (2011), "Évaluer et rendre compte de sa stratégie développement durable," rapport du réseau Comité 21 des acteurs du développement durable, available at http://www.comite21.org/docs/economie/rse/notes-21-reporting-2010-2011.pdf and http://www.areva.com/EN/ operations-404/renewable-energies-wind-solar-biomass-hydrogen-and-energy-storage.html, both accessed on September 16, 2012.

11. While for others, it is an illusion, the dematerialization requiring IT hardware that consumes energy and resources to be built and maintained in operation.

12. See http://www.amazon.com/gp/seller-account/mm-summary-page.html?topic=200260520, accessed on October 7, 2012.

13. See R. Karayan (2011), "Les chiffres qui font la magie d'Apple," *Trends-Tendance*, Avril 27, available at http:// trends.levif.be/economie/actualite/high-tech/les-chiffres-qui-font-la-magie-d-apple/article-1194997038322.htm, accessed on October 7, 2012.

14. See "With Google, Apple and Facebook, the Music Industry Rebuilds a New Oligopoly via Internet" at http://www. atlantico.fr/decryptage/google-music-itunes-apple-face book-nouvel-oligopole-internet-industrie-musicale-virginie-berger-212449.html, accessed on September 17, 2012.

15. See M. Porter (1985), *Competitive Advantage: Creating and Sustaining Superior Performance*, New York: Free Press.

16. See, for example, Johnson, Whittington and Scholes, *Exploring Strategy* or Porter, *Competitive Advantage*.

17. Readers interested in the impacts of sustainable development on the functions or sectors of activities can find a well-documented work in the book PwC (2010), *Développement durable: Aspects stratégiques et opérationnels*, Editions Francis Lefebvre, Levallois. This section is partly inspired by this book.
18. See http://www.pwc.lu/en/sustainability/docs/pwc-pe.pdf, accessed on October 6, 2012.
19. See Briaumont, "Évaluer et rendre compte de sa stratégie développement durable."
20. Based on C. Boechat, N. Werneck and L. Miraglia (2007), "Sadia Program for Sustainable Swine Production (3S Program): Bringing Sustainability to the Supply Chain," *United Nations Development Program Growing Inclusive Markets Case Study*; and http://www.sadia.com.br/sobre-a-sadia/, http://www.sadia.com/, http://www.abipecs.com.br/, all accessed on September 14, 2012.
21. Boechat, Werneck and Miraglia, "Sadia Program for Sustainable Swine Production (3S Program)," p. 6.
22. See http://www.goesco.com/financing.html; in France, Akol Energie operates under a similar principle: http://www.akol.fr/index.html, both accessed on October 6, 2012. Thanks to Bernard Alfandari, CEO of Resistex, for these examples.
23. See N. Klein (1999), *No logo*, London: Picador.
24. Agenda 21: Action plan released and the Rio 1992 Conference aiming at "Development that Meets the Needs of the Present without Compromising the Ability of Future Generations to Meet Their Own Needs;" see more at http://www.un.org/esa/sustdev/documents/agenda21/french/action0.htm, accessed on October 7, 2012.
25. See http://ec.europa.eu/internal_market/smact/docs/brochure-web_fr.pdf, accessed on October 7, 2012.
26. See C. Sempels and M. Vandercammen (2009), *Oser le marketing durable: Concilier marketing et développement durable*, Paris: Pearson, for an in-depth discussion on the opportunity for companies represented by sustainability grounded call for tenders.

27. See the extended value concept of G. Bascoul and J-M. Moutot (2009), *Marketing et développement durable*, Paris: Dunod.

28. All the congress speeches are available on video and podcast on the web site of Centifolia: see http://centifolia-grasse.net/wp/, accessed on September 17, 2012.

29. O. Dubigeon (2009), *Piloter un développement responsable*, 3rd édn. Paris: Pearson-Village Mondial.

30. General information on Patagonia comes from Patagonia's web site: http://www.patagonia.com/us/environmentalism; and the Wikipedia page on Patagonia: http://en.wikipedia.org/wiki/Patagonia_(clothing); both accessed on September 17, 2012.

31. See http://www.patagonia.com/us/patagonia.go?assetid=2047& ln=24, accessed on September 17, 2012.

32. Y. Chouinard, J. Ellison and R. Ridgeway (2011), "The Big Idea: The Sustainable Economy," *Harvard Business Review*, October.

33. Source: Annual Report 2010–2011; available at http://www. aravind.org/downloads/reports/AnnualReport2010_2011. pdf, accessed on October 5, 2012.

34. See V. Govindarajan and C. Trimble (2012), *Reverse Innovation: Create Far from Home, Win Everywhere*, Boston: Harvard Business Press.

35. Available at http://www.uncsd2012.org/resources_publica tions.html, accessed on September 14, 2012.

36. Available at http://ec.europa.eu/enterprise/policies/raw-materi als/files/docs/report-b_en.pdf, accessed on September 15, 2012.

37. Source: http://www.periodni.com/rare_earth_elements.html, accessed on October 6, 2012.

38. Source: http://www.reuters.com/article/2009/08/31/us-mining-toyota-idUSTRE57U02B20090831, accessed on September 17, 2012.

39. Source: FIEEC report: "Une stratégie efficace sur les matières premières, enjeu de compétitivité de notre industrie," May 2011.

40. E. Ries (2011), *The Lean Startup: How Today's Entrepreneurs Use Continuous Innovation to Create Radically Successful Businesses*, New York: Crown Business.

41. J. Barrand (2006), *Le Manager agile. Vers un nouveau management pour affronter la turbulence*, Paris: Dunod.
42. L. Dibiaggio and P-X. Meschi (2012), *Management in the Knowledge Economy*, Paris: Pearson.
43. *The Economist* (2012), "Good Business; Nice Beaches, in Schumpeter," May 19.
44. Case study based on the article of C. Guélaud (2011), "À l'usine Bosch de Vénissieux, une leçon de réindustrialisation," *Le Monde*, Décembre 20.

2 THE BUSINESS MODEL – A POWERFUL TOOL TO DRIVE A STRATEGIC SHIFT

1. See J. Santos, B. Spector and L. Van der Heyden (2009), "Toward a Theory of Business Model Innovation within Incumbent Firms," *Working Paper*, Insead.
2. See the example of Aravind Eye Care.
3. A. Osterwalder and Y. Pigneur (2010), *Business Model Generation: A Handbook for Visionaries, Game Changers and Challengers*, Hoboken: John Wiley & Sons.
4. M. Yunus, B. Moingeon and L. Lehmann-Ortega (2010), "Building Social Business Models: Lessons from the Grameen Experience," *Long Range Planning*, vol. 43, no. 2–3, pp. 308–325.
5. Sources: http://www.quirky.com and www.bulletins-electroniques.com/actualites/68400.htm, accessed on February 7, 2013.
6. Source: http://www.vcgate.com/2012/09/10/quirky-gets-68-million-of-funding/, accessed on February 7, 2013.
7. J. Elkington (1998), *Cannibals with Forks: The Triple Bottom Line of 21st Century Business*, Gabriola Island, BC: New Society Publishers.
8. The authors thank Wiley for granting us permission for using the picture of the 'Business Model Canvas' originally published in A. Osterwalder and Y. Pigneur (2010), *Business Model Generation: A Handbook for Visionaries, Game Changers and Challengers*, Hoboken: John Wiley &

Sons. Source of the evolution of the BMC into the SBMC: C. Sempels and T. Lesueur (ENEA).

9. S.L. Vargo and R.F. Lusch (2004), "Evolving to a New Dominant Logic for Marketing," *Journal of Marketing*, vol. 68, pp. 1–17.

10. For a review, see J. Hoffmann (2007), "Développement et test d'un modèle des déterminants individuels de l'adoption des innovations technologiques dans l'industrie des TIC," Thèse de Doctorat, Université Pierre-Mendès France, Grenoble, Juin 11.

11. C. Sempels and J. Hoffmann (2011), "The Role of Value Constellation Innovation to Develop Sustainable Service Systems," SD Logic Forum, Capri, June.

12. C. Zook and J. Allen (2011), "The Great Repeatable Business Model," *Harvard Business Review*, November, pp. 107–114.

13. J-J. Lambin and C. de Moerloose (2012), *Marketing Stratégique et Opérationnel: Du marketing à l'orientation marché*, 8th edn, Paris: Dunod.

14. Source: http://www.internetworldstats.com/stats.htm, accessed on October 6, 2012.

15. Source: http://forwardthinking.pcmag.com/internet/282251-skype-aiming-for-1-billion-users, accessed on October 6, 2012.

16. *The Economist* (25 February 2012), "Making it Click," available at http://www.economist.com/node/21548236, accessed on February 5, 2012.

17. Source: http://www.psfk.com/2012/07/audi-opens-first-interactive-digital-car-showroom-for-urban-shoppers-video.html, accessed on February 5, 2012.

18. Source: http://www.youtube.com/watch?v=CokbQWI_15U, accessed on February 5, 2012.

19. This is certainly not the reason for the issues experimented by the airplane with its lithium-ion batteries, due to outsourcing and design issues.

20. J. Hoffmann, C. Sempels and M. Felix (2012), "Integrating Knowledge from the Customers through Co-creation at Pas de Calais Habitat," in L. Dibiaggio and P-X. Meschi (eds) *Managing in the Knowledge Economy*, Paris: Pearson, 207–230.

21. Source: http://www.forbes.com/sites/work-in-progress/2012/ 12/18/10-brand-marketing-trends-that-should-dominate- 2013/, accessed on February 5, 2012.

22. Sources: http://atwonline.com/airline-financedata/news/ brussels-airlines-falls-loss-fuel-hedges-0309; http://www. reuters.com/article/2010/05/29/belgium-brussels-airlines- idUSLDE64S04D20100529; both accessed on February 5, 2012.

23. Source: https://www.globalreporting.org/Pages/default.aspx, accessed on February 7, 2013.

24. Case study based on "Diversity of the Human Capital and Economic Performance of the Company," available at http://www.goodwill-management.com/images/stories/pdf/ mission-diversite-et-performance-ims-goodwill-manage ment-11-2010.pdf, accessed on February 7, 2013.

25. Report of the Arpejeh about employment and the qualification of handicapped individuals in different European countries, available at http://www.arpejeh. com/documents/Emploi_et_formation.pdf, accessed on February 7, 2013.

26. See, for example, L. Dibiaggio and P-X. Meschi (eds) (2012) *Managing in the Knowledge Economy*, Paris: Pearson.

27. Source: http://www.economist.com/blogs/schumpeter/2013/ 01/special-report-outsourcing-and-offshoring, accessed on February 5, 2012.

28. Source: http://www.sunedison.com/wps/portal/memc/aboutus/ corporatecitizenship/, accessed on February 5, 2012.

29. WWF-UK (2012), *Green Game-Changers: Insights for Mainstreaming Business Innovation*, Verdantix, p. 36.

30. www.sadia.com.br, accessed on February 7, 2013.

31. WWF-UK, *Green Game-Changers*, p. 34.

32. Source: http://www.psa-peugeot-citroen.com/fr/psa_espace/ communiques_presse_details_d1.php?id=1343, accessed on February 5, 2012.

33. This example adapts information presented on the UNDP Case Study from C. Boechat and R.M. Paro (2007), "Natura's Ekos: Perfume Essences Produce Sustainable Development in Brazil,"

United Nations Development Program Growing Inclusive Markets Case Study.

34. Natura Investor Report, 10 September 2012, available at http://natura.infoinvest.com.br/enu/s-17-enu.html, accessed on September 21, 2012.

35. Idem.

36. The Natura policy for the sustainable use of biodiversity and associated traditional knowledge, available at http://natura.infoinvest.com.br/static/enu/abordagem.asp?language=enu, accessed on September 21, 2012.

37. See Boechat and Paro, "Natura's Ekos."

38. Boechat and Paro, "Natura's Ekos," p. 13.

39. Idem.

40. Source: http://www.naturabrasil.fr/Products/Collections.aspx?tcid=969&bg=default&m=2&ctid=Default, accessed on February 7, 2013.

41. Source: http://scf.natura.net/Conteudo/Default.aspx?MenuStructure=5&MenuItem=10, accessed on February 7, 2013.

42. This example is developed in length at Chapter 5.

43. Osterwalder and Pigneur, *Business Model Generation*.

44. Source: http://www.airbnb.com/home/about, accessed on February 7, 2013.

45. Source: http://forwardthinking.pcmag.com/internet/282251-skype-aiming-for-1-billion-users, accessed on February 5, 2012.

46. Source: http://thenextweb.com/us/2010/08/09/skype-800-million-revenue-02-at-a-time/, accessed on February 5, 2012.

47. Source: http://www.silicon.fr/rachat-de-skype-officialise-a-85-mrds-microsoft-en-fera-quoi-51366.html, accessed on February 5, 2012.

48. See Y. Chouinard, J. Ellison and R. Ridgeway (2011), "The Big Idea: The Sustainable Economy," *Harvard Business Review*, October.

49. Sources: http://www.danone.com/en/what-s-new/focus-4.html; http://www.youtube.com/watch?v=4pUd7eCf7Sg; both accessed on February 5, 2012.

3 ECO-EFFICIENCY AND ECO-DESIGN – A FIRST STEP TOWARD SUSTAINABLE PERFORMANCE

1. A.Y. Hoekstra and A.K. Chapagain (2007), "Water Footprints of Nations: Water Use by People as a Function of their Consumption Pattern," *Water Resources Management*, 21(1): 35–48.
2. See http://www.wbcsd.org/home.aspx, accessed on February 7, 2013.
3. Sources: Levi's web sites: http://www.levistrauss.com/sustainability/planet/water, http://store.levi.com/waterless, http://www.levistrauss.com/sites/default/files/library document/2010/12/lsco-ceo-water-mandate-cop-2010.pdf, all accessed on October 10, 2012.
4. Source: LVMH Sustainable Development 2009 Report.
5. Source: WWF-UK (2006), "Deeper Luxury," available at http://www.wwf.org.uk/deeperluxury/, accessed on February 7, 2013.
6. Source: http://www.institutoe.org.br/, accessed on February 7, 2013.
7. Source: http://www.mobigreen.fr/ecoconduite_laposte.htm, accessed on February 7, 2013.
8. See C. Sempels and M. Vandercammen (2009), *Oser le marketing durable: Concilier marketing et développement durable*, Paris: Pearson, and the World Business Council for Sustainable Development.
9. Source: Unilever Sustainable Living Plan Progress Report 2011, p. 27.
10. Source: LVMH Sustainable Development 2009 Report.
11. Source: https://www.lush.co.uk/content/view/783, accessed on October 30, 2012.
12. Source: http://www.plasticdisclosure.org/, accessed on February 7, 2013.
13. Idem.
14. Source: https://www.lush.co.uk/content/view/4092, accessed on October 31, 2012.
15. Source: https://www.lush.co.uk/content/view/783, accessed on February 7, 2013.

16. Source: https://www.lush.co.uk/content/view/5432, accessed on October 30, 2012.

17. Source: http://www.worksmart.org.uk/company/company.php?id=04162033&showShareholders, accessed on October 30, 2012.

18. Source: http://www.lighting.philips.com/main/lightcommunity/trends/led/, accessed on February 7, 2013.

19. Zero Discharge of Hazardous Chemicals.

20. The initiative defines hazardous chemicals as follows: "Hazardous chemicals are those that show intrinsically hazardous properties (persistent, bio-accumulative and toxic (PBT); very persistent and very bio-accumulative (vPvB); carcinogenic, mutagenic and toxic for reproduction (CMR); endocrine disruptors (ED); or equivalent concern), not just those that have been regulated or restricted in other regions." Source: Joint Roadmap: Toward Zero Discharge of Hazardous Chemicals, Draft for Consultation, November 15, 2011, available at http://www.roadmaptozero.com/, accessed October 6, 2012.

21. The interested reader on planned obsolescence is invited to watch the documentary "Ready to Discard" produced by the German-French television Arte.

22. Source: http://en.wikipedia.org/wiki/Planned_obsolescence for a precise explanation, accessed on February 7, 2013.

23. Based on a case proposed by the eco-calculator developed by the Bio Intelligence Service and Ademe, available at http://www.ecocalculateur.com/guide-eco-conception/fondamentaux-eco-conception/cycle-de-vie-du-produit, accessed on October 10, 2012.

24. This example is written based on the Ben & Jerry's Social & Environment Assessment Report 2010, http://www.benjerry.com/company/sear-reports, accessed on July 11, 2013.

25. The FSC certification stands for paperboards that comes from forest that are managed for the protection of wildlife habitat, maintenance of biodiversity, avoidance of genetically modified tree species, protection of traditional and civil rights, among other criteria. See http://www.fsc.org/, accessed on February 7, 2013.

26. Source: Ben & Jerry's Social & Environment Assessment Report 2010.
27. HIER is a consortium of 40 NGOs, see http://www.hier.nu/, accessed on February 7, 2013.
28. This section is structured on several sources the most important being M.R.M Crul and J.C. Diehl (2006), "Design for Sustainability: A Practical Approach for Developing Economies," report published by the UNEP and Delft University of Technology; and J.E.M. Klostermann and A. Tukker (eds) (2010), *Product Innovation and Eco-Efficiency: Twenty-Three Industry Efforts to Reach the Factor 4*, Dordrecht: Kluwer Academic.
29. See also WWF-UK (2012), *Green Game-Changers*, available at http://www.wwf.org.uk/what_we_do/working_with_business/green_game_changers/, accessed on February 7, 2013.
30. See http://www.epa.gov/nrmrl/std/lca/lca.html, accessed on February 7, 2013.
31. See http://www.environment-agency.gov.uk/, accessed on February 7, 2013.
32. Sources: http://www.ademe.fr/internet/video/jt_tf1/streaming 2.asp; http://archives.lesechos.fr/archives/2005/LesEchos/19409-85-ECH.htm; both accessed on 10 October 2012.
33. Source: PUMA's Environmental Profit and Loss Account for the year ended December 31, 2010.
34. Idem.
35. http://www.puma.com/news/introducing-the-puma-re-suede-pumas-most-sustainable-shoe retrieved 11 July 2013.
36. See P. Pizelle, J. Hoffmann, M. Aubouy and C. Verchere (2013), *L'Innovation par les usages*, lulu.com.
37. Source: Adapted from G. Bascoul and J-M. Moutot (2009), *Marketing et développement durable*, Paris: Dunod.
38. See C. Sempels and M. Vandercammen (2009), *Oser le marketing durable: Concilier marketing et développement durable*, Paris: Pearson. The reader will find a thorough discussion in the first part on motivational factors structured on egocentric, pro-social and biospheric values (see p. 23) and strategies for perceived-risk reduction related to eco-design (p. 33 and on).

39. Sources: http://guayaki.com, accessed on October 10, 2012, and B. Boyd, N. Henning, E. Reyna, D.E. Wang and M.D. Welch (2009), *Hybrid Organizations: New Business Models for Environmental Leadership*, Sheffield: Greenleaf Publishing.

40. The Atlantic Forest had originally covered a large surface in Brazil, Paraguay, Argentina and Uruguay around the Capricornia Tropic. Less than 10 percent of the original surface remains nowadays (see http://fr.wikipedia.org/wiki/For%C3%AAt_atlantique). Not to be confused with the Amazon Forest, accessed on February 10, 2013.

41. Around 81,000 hectares.

42. C. Berneman, P. Lanoie, S. Plouffe and M-F. Vernier (2011), "Les retombées intangibles de l'éco-conception pour l'entreprise," Actes du colloque "Réseau entreprise et développement durable," Montréal, Octobre 20–22, 2011.

43. See, for example, D.L. Rainey (2006), *Sustainable Business Development: Inventing the Future through Strategy, Innovation and Leadership*, Cambridge: Cambridge University Press; E.U. Von Weizsäcker, A.B. Hunter and L.H. Lovins (1997), *Factor Four: Doubling Wealth, Halving Resource Use – A Report to the Club of Rome*, London: Earthscan Publications; and Berneman et al., "Les retombées intangibles de l'éco-conception pour l'entreprise."

44. Source: http://www.asknature.org/article/view/what_is_bio mimicry, accessed on February 7, 2013.

45. Source: http://biomimicry.net/about/biomimicry/case-exam ples/, accessed on February 7, 2013.

46. Source: http://biomimicry.net/about/biomimicry/case-exam ples/transportation/, accessed on February 7, 2013.

47. Sources: http://www.ted.com/talks/michael_pawlyn_using_ nature_s_genius_in_architecture.html; http://www.wired. co.uk/news/archive/2012-02/22/biomimicry-in-architecture; both accessed on February 7, 2013.

48. Source: http://biomimicry.net/about/biomimicry/case-exam ples/architecture/, accessed on February 7, 2013.

49. WWF-UK (2011) *Green Game-Changers: 50 Innovations to Inspire Business Transformation*, p. 88, available at http://

www.wwf.org.uk/what_we_do/working_with_business/
green_game_changers/, accessed on February 6, 2013.

50. Idem.

51. See http://www.dyesol.com/, accessed on February 10, 2013.

4   CIRCULAR ECONOMY: TRANSFORMING A "WASTE" INTO A PRODUCTIVE RESOURCE

1. Leaves of a tree drop and become nutrients for the ground that will nurture the roots of this same tree.

2. As an illustration, "some 65 billion tons of raw materials entered the global economic system in 2010 – a figure expected to grow to about 82 billion tons in 2020" (Ellen MacArthur Foundation, 2012, *Towards the Circular Economy: Economic and Business Rationale for an Accelerated Transition*, p. 15, available at http://www.thecir culareconomy.org/, accessed on October 31, 2012).

3. See D. Bourg and N. Buclet (2005), "L'économie de fonctionnalité: Changer la consommation dans le sens du développement durable," *Futuribles*, no. 313, Novembre, pp. 27–37.

4. See W.R. Stahel (2000), "From Products to Services: Selling Performance instead of Goods", *Working Paper*, available at http///www.greeneconomics.net/Stahel%20Essay1.doc, accessed on February 17, 2010.

5. Source: http://www.planetoscope.com/recyclage-dechets/ dechets, accessed on October 30, 2012.

6. Source: http://www.defra.gov.uk/statistics/environment/ waste/wrfg01-annsector/, accessed on February 7, 2013.

7. Source: http://www.preciousmetals.umicore.com/PMR/ News/show_20120201_Capital_eScrap.pdf, accessed on October 30, 2012.

8. Sources: http://www.new-ventures.org/company/a7-brasil; http://www.wwf.org.uk/what_we_do/working_with_busi ness/green_game_changers/reduce__reuse__recycle.cfm; both accessed on October 30, 2012.

9. UNEP (2011), *Towards a Green Economy: Pathways to Sustainable Development and Poverty Eradication – A*

Synthesis for Policy Makers, p. 18, available at www.unep. org/greeneconomy, accessed on February 10, 2013.

10. Concept developed by W. McDonough and M. Braungart (2002), *Cradle to Cradle: Remaking the Way We Make Things*, New York: North Point Press.

11. As an illustration, consider the enormous public health problems generated in some African countries by the massive reception of electronic waste that is burned, sometimes by children, to recover some materials without any protection (see, for example, http://www.cipaco.org/spip. php?article1815, accessed on October 30, 2012).

12. Source: Interview with the CEO Christophe Aldunate.

13. Source: http://www.lasuededurable.com/gare-de-stockholm-gare-au-chaud-et-froid-ecolo.html, accessed on October 30, 2012.

14. WWF-UK (2011) *Green Game-Changers: 50 Innovations to Inspire Business Transformation*, p. 88, available at http:// www.wwf.org.uk/what_we_do/working_with_business/ green_game_changers/, accessed on February 7, 2013.

15. Source: http://www.triogen.nl/what-is-an-orc, accessed on February 10, 2013.

16. Source: http://www.triogen.nl/home, accessed on February 10, 2013.

17. See M. Rouer and A. Gouyon (2007), *Réparer la planète, la révolution de l'économie positive*, Paris: J-C. Lattès.

18. Ellen MacArthur Foundation, *Towards the Circular Economy*.

19. Source: http://www.mbdc.com/, accessed on February 10, 2013.

20. Source: http://www2.warwick.ac.uk/newsandevents/pressreleases/NE1000000097300, accessed on October 30, 2012.

21. Source: http://www.designtex.com/climatex_Environments. aspx?f=36310, accessed on October 30, 2012.

22. Source: http://www.appropedia.org/Cloth_versus_disposable_ diapers, accessed on October 30, 2012.

23. Source: http://www.realdiaperassociation.org/diaperfacts. php, accessed on October 30, 2012.

24. For a list of all the products certified C2C, see http://c2c.mbdc. com/c2c/list.php?order=type, accessed on February 10, 2013.

25. Case developed based on information from Steelcase and documents of the C2C certification. The interested reader can find the LCA report of the Think Chair and C2C report at http://www.steelcase.com/en/products/Category/Seating/task/think/Documents/Environmental%20Product%20Declaration_04-0012421.pdf, accessed on October 30, 2012.

26. Source: http://www.globenewswire.com/news-release/2012/03/02/469722/247939/en/Steelcase-Inc-Named-One-of-Fortune-s-Most-Admired-Companies-in-the-Home-Equipment-Furnishings-Category.html, accessed on October 30, 2012.

27. Source: http://www.treehugger.com/sustainable-product-design/mcdonough-braungart-product-certification.html, accessed on October 30, 2012.

28. Ellen MacArthur Foundation, *Towards the Circular Economy,* p. 30ff.

29. Source: http://auto.howstuffworks.com/auto-parts/brakes/brake-types/regenerative-braking.htm, accessed on October 30, 2012.

30. See http://www.youtube.com/watch?v=-U-mvfjyiao for a presentation of this innovative bicycle, accessed on February 10, 2013.

31. Source: http://theaquaduct.blogspot.fr/, accessed on February 10, 2013.

32. See http://www.youtube.com/watch?v=mEwG0nJpz2g (accessed on October 30, 2012) for a video presentation of the Green Kitchen.

33. W.C. Kim and R. Mauborgne (2005), *Blue Ocean Strategy,* Boston, MA: Harvard Business Press.

34. Source: http://www.whirlpool.fr/decouvrez-whirlpool/developpement-durable/green-kitchen.content.html, accessed on October 30, 2012.

35. See, for example, http://www.eco-sapiens.com/dossier-35-La-consommation-des-appareils-electriques.html, accessed on October 30, 2012.

36. Sources: http://www.seacourt.net; http://www.ellenmacarthurfoundation.org/fr/francais/entreprise/syckmergekey0x

00000004897980-nous-navons-plus-de-poubelles-une-entre
prise-doxford-atteint-lobjectif-zero-dechets; http://www.
sustainablebusinessonline.com/news/news.asp?id=265, all
accessed on October 30, 2012.

37. Source: http://www.waterless.org/Default.aspx?pageId=112
2845&mode=PostView&bmi=952953, accessed on October
30, 2012.

38. Source: http://www.naturalsystemsutilities.com/about-us-2/,
accessed on February 10, 2013.

39. WWF-UK, *Green Game*-Changers, p. 34.

40. Source: http://www.wasteconcern.org/model.html, accessed
on October 31, 2012.

41. Source: http://www.wasteconcern.org/documents/Models.
pdf, accessed on October 31, 2012.

42. Source: http://www.wasteconcern.org/awards.html, accessed
on October 31, 2012.

43. C. Dou (2011), "Beijing Shengchang Bioenergy S&T Co:
A Leading Bioenergy Benefits both Business and Local
Farmers," *UNDP Growing Inclusive Markets Case Study*,
available at http://cases.growinginclusivemarkets.org/
documents/12, accessed on October 31, 2012.

44. Dou, "Beijing Shengchang Bioenergy S&T Co," p. 2.

45. Dou, "Beijing Shengchang Bioenergy S&T Co," pp. 18–19.

46. Source: http://www.greensulate.com/ and WWF-UK, *Green
Game*-Changers, p. 21.

47. Source: http://www.wornagain.co.uk/pages/our-story-2,
accessed on February 10, 2013.

48. See https://www.facebook.com/villadechets for some pic-
tures, accessed on July 11, 2013.

49. Source: http://www.symbiosis.dk, accessed on October 30,
2012.

50. See C. Drapeau (2007), "L'industrie à l'heure du développement durable: Les stratégies de développement
éco-industriel," document de veille de l'Observatoire du
ministère des Affaires municipales, des Régions et de l'Occupation du Territoire, Québec, Canada.

51. See http://en.investteda.org/whyteda/ecologicalenvironment/
default.htm, accessed on February 10, 2013.

52. WWF-UK, *Green Game*-Changers, p. 79.

53. Source: http://www.international-synergies.com/capabilities/
synergie-essential-resource-management-platform, accessed
on February 10, 2013.

54. WWF-UK, *Green Game*-Changers, p. 48.

55. See http://www.smh.com.au/business/world-business/china-
aims-for-sustainable-development-20120712-21yg0.html;
http://www.guardian.co.uk/sustainable-business/china-devel
opment-renewables-sustainability; both accessed on October
30, 2012.

56. UNEP (2011), Decoupling Natural Resource use and
Environmental Impacts from Economic Growth, available at
http://www.unep.org/resourcepanel/publications/decoupling
tabid/56048/default.aspx, accessed on July 11, 2013.

57. Ellen MacArthur Foundation, *Towards the Circular Economy*,
p. 8.

58. Ellen MacArthur Foundation, *Towards the Circular Economy*,
p. 66.

59. Ellen MacArthur Foundation, *Towards the Circular
Economy*, pp. 68 and 75.

60. Ellen MacArthur Foundation (2012), *Towards the Circular
Economy: Opportunities for the Consumer Goods Sector*,
available at http://www.thecirculareconomy.org/, accessed on
February 8, 2013.

61. Idem, p. 8.

62. Idem, pp. 48–49.

63. Idem, p. 8.

64. Idem, p. 8.

65. Idem, p. 9.

66. Idem, pp. 10–11.

5 FROM PRODUCTS TO USE-ORIENTED SERVICES

P. Pizelle, J. Hoffmann, M. Aubouy and C. Verchere (2013),
L'Innovation par les usages, lulu.com.

1. The rate of possession of refrigerators in France was, for
example, 99.8 percent in 2007; that of televisions rose to 97.3
percent, while video tape recorders or DVD players equipped

83.3 percent of the households according to M. Fabre and W. Winkler (2010), "L'obsolescence programmée, symbole de la société du gaspillage: Le cas des produits électriques et électroniques," report of the National Centre of Independent Information on Waste and the NGO "Amis de la Terre."

2. Source: MauroNewMedia (2008), "What New Trends in Product Complexity for Marketing Success," available at http://www.mauronewmedia.com/, accessed on February 16, 2013.

3. Source: http://www.brighthand.com/default.asp?newsID=16 664&news=Cell+Phone+Recycling, accessed on November 10, 2012.

4. Ellen MacArthur Foundation (2013), *Towards the Circular Economy: Opportunities for the Consumer Goods Sector*, available at http://www.thecirculareconomy.org/, accessed on February 8, 2013.

5. Source: http://org.elon.edu/Sustainability/documents/Zipcar% 20FAQs.pdf, accessed on November 11, 2012.

6. Case originally presented in C. Sempels and M. Vandercammen (2009), *Oser le marketing durable: Concilier marketing et développement durable*, Paris: Pearson; additional source: A. King, J. Miemczyk and D. Bufton (2006), "Photocopier Remanufacturing at Xerox UK: A Description of the Process and Consideration of Future Policy Issues," in D. Brissaud, S. Tichkiewitch, P. Zwolinski, (eds), *Innovation in Life Cycle Engineering and Sustainable Development*, Springer, Dordrecht: The Netherlands, Part 2, pp. 173–186, 448.

7. J. Van Niel (2007), "L'économie de la fonctionnalité: Définition et état de l'art," available at http://www.inspire-institut.org/leconomie-de-fonctionnalite-definition-et-etat-de-lart.html, accessed on November 11, 2012.

8. E. Laville (2009), *L'Entreprise verte*, 3rd edn, Paris: Village Mondial.

9. Internal source at Xerox and http://www.xerox.com/Static_HTML/citizenshipreport/2007/nurturing-page9-3.html, accessed on November 11, 2012.

10. The interested reader can find an excellent discussion on the environmental impact of the service sector in J. Gadrey

(2008), "La crise écologique exige une révolution de l'économie des services," Actes du troisième congrès international sur les services, l'innovation et le développement durable, Poitiers, pp. 1–21.

11. See, for example, R.W. Obenberger and S.W. Brown (1976), "A Marketing Alternative: Consumer Leasing and Renting," *Business Horizons*, October.

12. Source: http://www.spur.org/blog/2010-07-30/sfpark_re_imagining_how_we_park_sf, accessed on March 6, 2013.

13. Source: http:sfpark.org/about-the-project/.

14. See http://www.michelintransport.com/ple/front/affich.jsp?codeRubrique=20051018154228&lang=FR. This case has been extensively presented in reports linked to Functional Economy and more formally by F. Dalsace, W. Ulaga and C. Renault (2003), "MICHELIN FLEET SOLUTIONS: From Selling Tires to Selling Kilometers, CCMP Case Study," available at http://www.ccmp.fr/collection-hec-paris/cas-michelin-fleet-solutions-from-selling-tires-to-selling-kilometers, accessed on February 15, 2013.

15. Source: http://www.michelintransport.com/ple/front/affich.jsp?codeRubrique=20051018154228&lang=EN, accessed on February 15, 2013.

16. M. Wohlsen (2013), "Unused Office Space is like a Massive Untapped Natural Resource," *Wired*, available at http://www.wired.com/business/2013/02/office-space-as-a-service/, accessed on February 15, 2013.

17. Source: https://liquidspace.com/, accessed on February 15, 2013.

18. Wohlsen, "Unused Office Space."

19. R.W. Belk (1988), "Possessions and the Extended Self," *Journal of Consumer Research*, vol. 15, September, pp. 139–168.

20. M.B. Holbrook (1996), "Customer Value – A Framework for Analysis and Research", *Advances in Consumer Research*, vol. 23, pp. 138–142; M.B. Holbrook (1999), *Consumer Value: A Framework for Analysis and Research*, London: Routledge.

21. D. Kahneman, J.L. Knetsch and R.H. Thaler (2009), "Experimental Tests of the Endowment Effect and the

Coase Theorem," in E.L. Khalil (ed.), *The New Behavioral Economics*, vol. 3, *Tastes for Endowment, Identity and the Emotions*, Cheltenham: Elgar, pp. 119–142.

22. J. Rifkin (2000), *The Age of Access: The New Culture of Hypercapitalism where all of Life is a Paid-For Experience*, New York: J.P. Tarcher, p. 111.

23. B. Adler (2012), "Vers une voiture 2.0 et servicielle," *Influencia*, 1 (L'innovation), pp. 36–41.

24. Source: http://www.zipcar.com/, accessed on February 15, 2013.

25. Source: https://us.drive-now.com/?language=en_US&L=2, accessed on February 14, 2013.

26. Source: https://www.car2go.com/en/austin/, accessed on February 14, 2013.

27. M. Brignall (2012), "Need to Hire a Car? Rent Your Neighbour's," *The Guardian,* available at http://www.guardian.co.uk/money/2012/may/04/hire-a-car-use-neighbours, accessed on February 16, 2013.

28. Source: https://www.whipcar.com/how-it-works/#how-drivers, accessed on February 10, 2013.

29. Source: http://www.hiriko.com/, accessed on February 16, 2013.

30. Source: http://www.ted.com/talks/sebastian_thrun_google_s_driverless_car.html, accessed on February 16, 2013.

31. Source: http://www.groupechronos.org/projets/etudes/l-etude-auto-mobilites-tns-sofres-chronos-objectifs-et-methodologie, accessed on November 11, 2012.

32. Source: http://www.fastcompany.com/magazine/155/the-sharing-economy.html, accessed on November 11, 2012.

33. K. Gaskins (2010), "Shareable/Latitude: The New Sharing Economy Study," available at http://latd.com/2010/06/01/shareable-latitude-42-the-new-sharing-economy/, accessed on March 6, 2013.

34. R. Botsman and R. Rogers (2010), *What's Mine is Yours: The Rise of Collaborative Consumption*, New York: HarperCollins.

35. WWF-UK (2012), *Green Game-Changers*, p. 16, available at http://www.wwf.org.uk/what_we_do/working_with_business/green_game_changers/, accessed February 7, 2013.

36. Source: http://neighborgoods.net/, accessed on February 16, 2013.
37. Source: http://ecomodo.com/, accessed on February 16, 2013.
38. Source: http://fr.zilok.com/, accessed on February 16, 2013.
39. Source: https://www.airbnb.com/about?locale=en, accessed on February 16, 2013.
40. Source: See http://www.hirefitness.co.uk/about.php, accessed on February 16, 2013.
41. See http://www.homedepot.com/webapp/catalog/servlet/Content View?pn=Tool_Truck_Rental&storeId=10051&langId=-1&catalogId=10053, accessed on February 16, 2013.
42. WWF-UK, *Green Game-Changers*, p. 18.
43. Source: http://www.swapstyle.com/, accessed on February 16, 2013.
44. WWF-UK, *Green Game-Changers*, p. 24.
45. Source: http://www.thredup.com/, accessed on February 16, 2013.
46. L. Kaye (2013), "Sharing Economy Increases Access to Luxury Goods," available at http://www.triplepundit.com/2013/02/luxury-goods-rise-of-the-sharing-economy/, accessed on February 16, 2013.
47. Ellen MacArthur Foundation, *Towards the Circular Economy*.
48. Idem, p. 59.
49. Source: http://www.lerelais.org/decouvrir.php?page=ebs, accessed on February 20, 2013.
50. Source: http://consocollaborative.com/983-economie-du-partage-consommation-collaborative.html, accessed on March 6, 2013.
51. E. Rogers (2003), *Diffusion of Innovations*, 5th edn, New York: Free Press.
52. The interested reader will find in P. Pizelle et al., *L'innovation par les Usages*, several methods and tools to facilitate this transition, like the CAUTIC Method®; see also www.ixiade.com, accessed on February 20, 2013.
53. WWF-UK, *Green Game-Changers*, p. 10.
54. R. Meijkamp (2000), "Changing Consumer Behaviour through Eco-Efficient Services: An Empirical Study

of Car Sharing in The Netherlands," Thèse de doctorat, Delft University of Technology, Delft; U. Schrader
(1999), "Consumer Acceptance of Eco-Efficient Services: A
German Perspective," *Greener Management International*,
vol. 25, pp. 105–121; J.F. Durgee and G.C. O'Connor
(1995), "An Exploration into Renting as Consumption
Behavior," *Psychology and Marketing*, vol. 12, no. 2, pp.
89–104.

55. For example, O. Rexfelt and V. Hiort af Ornäs (2009),
"Consumer Acceptance of Product-Service Systems: Designing
for Relative Advantages and Uncertainty Reductions," *Journal
of Manufacturing Technology Management*, vol. 20, no. 5,
pp. 674–699.

56. The transition to a car-sharing service open rights (adaptability of the vehicle to the usage, access to a dedicated
parking, etc.) and frees from some duties (insurance, taxes,
maintenance, etc.).

57. Source: Interview of Marion Carrette, founder of Zilok on
BFM ("Green Business" talk show, February 2, 2012).

58. Source: http://anyhire.com/, accessed on February 20, 2013.

59. P.C. Evans and M. Annunziata (2012), "Industrial Internet:
Pushing the Boundaries of Minds and Machines," available at www.ge.com/docs/chapters/Industrial_Internet.pdf,
accessed on February 7, 2013.

60. Evans and Annunziata, "Industrial Internet," p. 3.

61. Idem.

62. Source: http://www.greenbiz.com/blog/2012/12/03/ge-indus
trial-internet-and-radical-efficiency, accessed on February 7,
2013.

63. SNCF is the French public train operator (and related
service); RATP is the bus, metro and RER operator; Avis
and ADA are car rental companies; Vinci is a big private
parking/infrastructure operator.

64. Data for this case comes mainly from O. Mont, C.
Dalhammar and N. Jacobsson (2006), "A New Business
Model for Baby Prams based on Leasing and Product
Remanufacturing," *Journal of Cleaner Production*, vol. 14,

pp. 1509–1518, with a necessary adaptation to our goals and the methods discussed in this chapter.

65. See Chapter 4 – the C2C acronym will be used in the remaining of this chapter to refer to cradle-to-cradle™.

66. See Pizelle et al., *L'innovation par les Usages*.

67. CRIOC (2007), "La dématérialisation, attitudes et comportements des consommateurs," study for the Eco-Consumption convention of the Wallone Region, available at http://www.crioc.be, accessed on February 20, 2013.

68. *The Economist* (November 10, 2012), "The Poor in America: In Need of Help," available at http://www.economist.com/news/briefing/21565956-americas-poor-were-little-mentioned-barack-obamas-re-election-campaign-they-deserve, accessed on November 11, 2012.

69. See http://www.brasil.gov.br/sobre/cidadania/brasil-sem-miseria, accessed on February 16, 2013.

70. See http://www.footprintnetwork.org/fr/index.php/gfn/page/earth_overshoot_day/, accessed on February 20, 2013.

71. M. Yunus, B. Moingeon and L. Lehmann-Ortega (2010), "Building Social Business Models: Lessons from the Grameen Experience," *Long Range Planning*, vol. 43, no. 2–3, p. 309.

72. See http://www.ecotact.org/index.php/articles/ikotoilet.html, accessed on February 20, 2013.

73. C. K. Prahalad (2004), *The Fortune at the Base of the Pyramid: Eradicating Poverty through Profit*, Upper Saddle River, NJ: Wharton School Publishing.

74. Yunus, Moingeon and Lehmann-Ortega, "Building Social Business Models."

75. Bain & Co (2012), *Altagamma Worldwide Markets Monitor 2012*, available at http://www.bain.com/offices/italy/en_us/publications/altagamma.aspx, accessed on July 22, 2013.

76. R. Chadha and P. Husband (2007), *The Cult of the Luxury Brand: Inside Asia's Love Affair with Luxury*, London: Nicholas Brealey Publishing.

77. G. Hofstede (2013), "National Culture Dimensions," available at http://geert-hofstede.com/national-culture.html accessed on February 16, 2013.

78. Source: http://materiabrasil.com/sobre#/i/sobre, accessed on February 16, 2013.
79. See the conclusions of A. Tukker and U. Tischner (2004), "New Business for Old Europe: Product-Service Development as a Mean to Enhance Competitiveness and Eco-Efficiency," final report of the European Project Suspronet, available at http://www.suspronet.org/fs_reports.htm in 2008 and now available at Greenleaf Publishing; also the Work Group 38 of the "Grenelle de l'Environnement" in France. Both accessed on February 20, 2013.

6 FROM PRODUCT- TO RESULT-BASED INTEGRATED SOLUTIONS

1. Source: http://www.assemblee-nationale.fr/12/controle/delat/dates_cles/paquet_energie-climat.asp, accessed on February 25, 2013.
2. Source: http://www.legislation.gov.uk/ukpga/2008/27/contents, accessed on February 25, 2013.
3. Source: http://www.wri.org/stories/2009/11/brazil-pledges-ambitious-emissions-reductions, accessed on February 25, 2013.
4. Source: http://www.climatechange.ca.gov/state/legislation.html and http://www.worldwatch.org/node/4499, both accessed on February 25, 2013.
5. Or an expectation or a "job to be done;" cf. C. Christensen and M. Raynor (2003), *The Innovator's Solution*, Boston: Harvard Business School Press. We conceive need in a broad sense.
6. Humans are also wired to adopt cognitive frames in order to facilitate daily life, and once a routine is in place, change is harder. See D. Kahnemann (2012), *Thinking Fast and Slow*, New York: Penguin.
7. Source: http://www.philips.com/about/company/company profile.page, accessed on February 28, 2013.
8. Source: http://www.philips.com/about/sustainability/ourfocus/ecovision5.page, accessed on February 28, 2013.

9. Philips (2012), *Case Study: RAU Architects*, available at http://www.lighting.philips.com/pwc_li/main/shared/assets/downloads/casestudy-rau-int.pdf, accessed on February 28, 2013.

10. Source: www.turntoo.com/en/, accessed on February 28, 2013.

11. Idem, p. 3.

12. Idem, p. 3.

13. WWF-UK (2012) *Green Game-Changers: Insights for Mainstreaming Business Innovation*, p. 16, available at http://www.wwf.org.uk/what_we_do/working_with_business/green_game_changers/, accessed on February 16, 2013.

14. Philips, *Case study: RAU Architects*, p. 4.

15. W.C. Kim and R. Mauborgne (2005), *Blue Ocean Strategy*, Boston: Harvard Business Press.

16. This case has been explored in previous publications in sustainability like C. Holliday, C. Hollidsy and S. Schmidheiny (2002), *Walking the Talk: The Business Case for Sustainable Development*, London: Berrett-Koehler Publishers; it is just presented briefly here.

17. Source: *The Economist* (January 8, 2009), "Rolls-Royce: Britain's Lonely High-Flier."

18. Idem.

19. "A preventive measure. The word comes from the Greek for 'an advance guard,' an apt term for a measure taken to fend off a disease or another unwanted consequence. A prophylactic is a medication or a treatment designed and used to prevent a disease from occurring." Source: http://www.medterms.com/script/main/art.asp?articlekey=11902, accessed on December 5, 2012.

20. See M.R.M. Crul and J.C. Diehl (2006), "Design for Sustainability: A Practical Approach for Developing Economies," report published by the UNEP and Delft University of Technology.

21. See, for example, F. Nicolino and F. Veillerette (2007), *Pesticides: Révélations sur un scandale français*, Paris: Fayard.

22. See S. Darnil and M. Le Roux (2006), *80 hommes pour changer le monde*, Paris: J-C. Lattès.

23. Source: http://www.trianum.com, accessed on February 20, 2013.

24. Source: http://www.koppert.com, accessed on February 20, 2013.

25. See C. Christensen (1997), *The Innovator's Dilemma*, Boston: Harvard Business School Press.

26. This case has been explored in previous publications in sustainability like Holliday, Hollidsy and Schmidheiny, *Walking the Talk*; therefore we just present it briefly here.

27. Source: http://www.dow.com/investors/dow-at-a-glance/index.htm, accessed on February 25, 2013.

28. Source: http://www.dow.com/safechem/solutions_na/complease.htm, accessed on February 26, 2013.

29. WWF-UK (2011) *Green Game-Changers: 50 Innovations to Inspire Business Transformation*, p. 23, available at http://www.wwf.org.uk/what_we_do/working_with_business/green_game_changers/, accessed on February 7, 2013.

30. Source: Conference of Steffen Saecker (Safechem) at the World Forum Lille (November 15, 2011). The interested reader can find further information in the report "Chemical Product Services in the European Union," which is available online, http://bookshop.europa.eu/en/chemical-product-services-in-the-european-union-pbLFNA22213/, accessed on July 11, 2013.

31. Source: http://www.dow.com/safechem/eu/en/solutions/dry cleaning.htm, accessed on February 26, 2013.

32. Kim and Mauborgne, *Blue Ocean Strategy*.

33. Source: http://www.blueoceanstrategy.com/about/concepts/value-innovation/, accessed on February 28, 2013.

34. G. Gavetti (2011), "The New Psychology of Strategic Leadership," *Harvard Business Review*, July.

35. Source: *The Economist* (February 5, 2013), "Dell's Buy-Out: Heading for the Exit," Schumpeter.

36. Source: http://www.blueoceanstrategy.com/about/concepts/strategy-canvas/, accessed on February 28, 2013.

37. Source: http://www.blueoceanstrategy.com/about/concepts/4-actions-framework/, accessed on February 28, 2013.

38. On February 13, 2012, a French farmer from Bernac (Charente) won a legal case against Monsanto for intoxication due to the use of phytosanitary products sold by the American company.

39. Source: http://en.wikipedia.org/wiki/Service-level_agreement, accessed on February 28, 2013.

40. Suez Environnement 2011 annual report available at http://www.suez-environnement.com/, accessed on December 5, 2012.

41. Source: http://www.suez-environnement.com/sustainable-development/edelway-label-environmental-performance/, accessed on December 5, 2012.

42. Interview at BFM Radio France, Green Business radio program, April 25, 2009.

43. European Energy Service Initiative – EESI – IEE/08/581/ SI2.528408 – December 2010 available at http://eaci-proj ects.eu/iee/page/Page.jsp?op=project_detail&prid=1862, accessed on February 20, 2013.

44. Source: http://www.passivhaustagung.de/Passive_House_E/ passivehouse_definition.html, accessed on February 28, 2013.

45. See http://www.goesco.com/financing.html, accessed on February 28, 2013.

46. Source: http://anesco.co.uk/site/en/content-folder/our-solu tions/the-esco-model, accessed on February 28, 2013.

47. As it is already the case in some hotels, where opening a window automatically cuts the supply of air conditioning.

48. D. Midgley (2009), *The Innovation Manual*, Hoboken: Wiley.

49. This Lean Startup method is suggested by E. Ries (2011), *The Lean Startup: How Today's Entrepreneurs Use Continuous Innovation to Create Radically Successful Businesses*, New York: Crown Business, for entrepreneurial projects.

50. Source: Suez Environnement 2011 annual report, p. 38.

51. J. Trout (2008), *In Search of the Obvious*, Hoboken: Wiley.

52. Source: Christensen, *The Innovator's Dilemma*.

53. R. Normann and R. Ramirez (1994), *Designing Interactive Strategy: From Value Chain to Value Constellation*, London: John Wiley & Sons.

54. Like Google that renders its resources available for other users enabling them to build new services, generating traffic and potential advertising revenues for themselves and for Google as well.

55. Source: McKinsey (2010), "Five Forces Reshaping the Global Economy: McKinsey Global Survey Results," *McKinsey Quarterly Review*, available at http://www.mckinseyquarterly. com/Five_forces_reshaping_the_global_economy_McKinsey_Global_Survey_results_2581, accessed on February 28, 2013.

56. WWF-UK, *Green Game-Changers: 50 Innovations to Inspire Business Transformation*, p. 77.

57. WWF-UK, *Green Game-Changers: 50 Innovations to Inspire Business Transformation*, p. 29.

58. Source: Virgin Group's Corporate Responsibility and Sustainable Development Report 2010. Available at http:// www.virgin.com/people-and-planet/blog/virgin-group-s-corporate-responsibility-and-sustainable-development-report-2010, accessed on July 11, 2013.

59. *The Economist* (October 6, 2012), "Call in the B Team: Richard Branson's Big Idea for Building a Better Version of Capitalism," available at http://www.economist.com/node/21564197, accessed on October 30, 2012.

60. T. Khanna and K. Palepu (2011), *Winning in Emerging Markets*, Boston: Harvard Business School Business Press.

61. Source: http://bourse.latribune.fr.latribune-agbourse.latribune. lbn.fr/actualites/toutes-les-actualites/0/veolia-environnement-contrat-pour-de-leau-potable-en-inde-3a6a05c061960e04. html; http://www.boursorama.com/actualites/suez-environ nement-remporte-un-contrat-en-inde-3332d6aee35313d7c 76cee4ae33f04cf; both accessed on February 28, 2013.

62. Source: http://www.radarrio20.org.br/index.php?r=conteudo/ view&id=14&idmenu=17, accessed on February 28, 2013.

63. V. Govindarajan and C. Trimble (2012), *Reverse Innovation: Create Far from Home, Win Everywhere*, Boston: Harvard Business Press.

64. A non-exhaustive list related to business initiatives includes the work by Instituto Ethos (http://www3.ethos.org.br/), CEBDS (Brazilian Business Council for Sustainable Development – www.cebds.org), IBGC (http://www.ibgc.org.br/English.aspx), the FGV Center for Sustainability Studies (http://www.gvces.com.br/) and the Petrobras Center for Sustainability at FDC (http://www.fdc.org.br/en/research/Pages/center_sustainability.aspx), accessed on February 20, 2013.

65. Source: http://www.icmsecologico.org.br/, accessed on February 28, 2013.

66. P. May, F. Veiga Neto, V. Denardin and W. Loureir (2012), "The Ecological Value-Added Tax: Municipal Responses in Paraná and Minas Gerais, Brazil," in S. Pagiola, J. Bishop and N. Landell-Mills (eds), *Selling Forest Environmental Services: Market-based Mechanisms for Conservation*.

67. Source: http://www2.natura.net/Web/Br/Inst/CarbonoNeutro2009/src/default.asp, accessed on February 20, 2013.

68. Source: http://www.braskem.com.br/site.aspx/green-products-USA, accessed on February 28, 2013.

69. See *The Economist* (November 17, 2012) "Oil in America: Energy to Spare."

70. P. H. Diamandis and S. Kotler (2012), *Abundance: The Future is Better than you Think*, New York: Free Press.

71. T. Jackson (2010), *Prosperity without Growth*, London: Routledge, p. 75.

72. A. Tukker and U. Tischner (2004), "New Business for Old Europe: Product-Service Development as a Mean to Enhance Competitiveness and Eco-Efficiency," final report of the Suspronet European Project, available at http://www.suspronet.org/fs_reports.htm in 2008 that is current available for purchase at Greenleaf Publishing, accessed on February 20, 2013.

73. R. Normann (2001), *Reframing Business*, London: John Wiley & Sons.

74. WWF-UK, *Green Game-Changers: Insights for Mainstreaming Business Innovation*.

75. J. Dangerman and H.J Schellnhuber (2013), "Energy systems transformation", *Proceedings of the National Academy of Sciences of the United States of America (PNAS)*, available at http://www.pnas.org/content/early/2013/01/02/1219791110, accessed July 11, 2013.

76. Norman, *Reframing Business*; A. Wooldridge (2011), *Masters of Management: How the Business Gurus and Their Ideas Have Changed the World – for Better and for Worse*, New York: HarperBusiness.

77. R. Ramirez, J. Selsky and K. Heijden (2010), *Business Planning for Turbulent Times*, 2nd edn, Oxfordshire: Earthscan.

78. G. Gavetti (2012) "Towards a Behavioral Theory of Strategy", *Organization Science*, vol. 23, no. 1, pp. 267–285.

Index

Printed and bound by CPI Group (UK) Ltd, Croydon, CR0 4YY